T0182566

Also by Barrett Rollins

In Sickness: A Memoir

FIRST THE PATIENT

THE LIFE & TIMES OF
DAVID G. NATHAN, MD

BARRETT ROLLINS

A POST HILL PRESS BOOK
ISBN: 979-8-88845-392-6
ISBN (eBook): 979-8-88845-393-3

First the Patient:
The Life and Times of David G. Nathan, MD

Cover design by Cody Corcoran
Cover photo by Mark Ostow

This is a work of nonfiction. All people, locations, events, and situations are portrayed to the best of the author's memory.

Post Hill Press
New York • Nashville
posthillpress.com

Published in the United States of America
1 2 3 4 5 6 7 8 9 10

For Lynn

❦

It is important that we first do everything for the patient; science can wait, research can wait. First the patient, second the patient, third the patient, fourth the patient, fifth the patient then maybe comes science.

—Béla Schick, pediatrician and immunologist

TABLE OF CONTENTS

INTRODUCTION

One of America's signal accomplishments during the twentieth century was achieving international preeminence in biomedical research. Scientists elsewhere were, of course, doing important work of their own, but by the 1950s, American researchers dominated the field through a combination of the high impact of their discoveries and the sheer volume of their output. While the U.S.'s position is being challenged in the twenty-first century by other countries that have begun to prioritize government investment in research—China, for example—American medical science still enjoys a quantifiable edge.[1]

It was not always this way. From the 1850s until the start of World War I, Germany was the undisputed leader in medical research, making a training stint there a rite of passage for any American serious about pursuing a research career. Prussian institutions, in particular, were destinations of choice because they linked laboratory work with education and because they had produced a steady stream of important discoveries with immediate clinical impact—from Röntgen's X-rays to Ehrlich's magic bullets. Ambitious Americans were eager to replicate Prussia's model.

Unfortunately, their own system was a shambles. Medical education in the U.S. was, at that time, a haphazard affair based on an apprenticeship model having little or no quality control; medical research was a minuscule enterprise supported mostly by private funding. In 1910, as part of its mission to improve education in the United States and Canada, the Carnegie Foundation engaged educator Abraham Flexner to evaluate physician training. To no one's surprise, Flexner's highly influential report recommended restructuring American medical schools to make them look more like

Germany's. In particular, he urged them to incorporate research into medical education and to integrate their faculties with those of America's best research universities.

The "Germanification" of American medical education had important consequences. Schools like Johns Hopkins, the University of Michigan, and later Harvard began to train legions of medical scientists who went on to lead the faculties of other medical schools where they replicated the research-based model and inculcated more acolytes with missionary zeal. Together, they fueled the rise of American medical science, allowing it to attain a level of prestige sufficient to fill the void left by the collapse of the German system after two wars and a fascist government's hostility toward science and scientists, especially Jewish ones. The new American system was a welcoming and familiar home for refugees from German medical schools.

While any number of salutary effects flowed from the incorporation of science into medical education—not least the production of more competent physicians—some educators became wary. They pointed to the critical importance of the humanistic side of patient care—the "art" of medicine—and expressed concern that it was being overwhelmed by the torrent of scientific facts being poured into medical students' heads. After a few decades, academic leaders at some schools deliberately and thoughtfully altered the balance of science and humanism in their curricula to ensure that they were training caring and compassionate physicians.

By the late 1980s, however, a revolution in biological sciences was underway. Advances in genetics and biochemistry were clarifying the molecular abnormalities responsible for human diseases, and that knowledge produced new and more effective drugs for formerly hopeless illnesses. Cancer was a perfect example: basic biological scientists had identified genes that control cell growth and, later, medically relevant researchers showed that cancers occur when these genes are altered. Drugs directed against those alterations had remarkable efficacy against otherwise untreatable cancers. That outcome was correctly perceived as a triumph of medical research.

The impact of this new science on patients convinced educators that properly educated medical students need to understand its principles. This led to a resurgence of a science-heavy pedagogy. Predictably, of course, a few decades later, the pendulum began its swing back toward humanism.

Medical research itself has experienced a similar oscillation between a focus on science and a focus on patients based on two complementary, but distinct, approaches to solving problems. One starts when a scientist observes a biological phenomenon, such as the inheritance of physical traits from one generation to the next, and designs experiments to explain how it happens. This is the kind of basic research that produced the revolution in genetics. The other starts when a physician observes a patient—a middle-aged woman, for example, with insufficient red blood cells, tingling in her feet, and a bright red tongue, a condition known as pernicious anemia—and tries to determine if a single underlying abnormality explains her signs and symptoms. This is the kind of patient-based research that uncovered the complicated system our bodies use to absorb vitamin B12, which is needed for normal blood production and nerve function. Both types of research have had enormous impact and both have been recognized with Nobel Prizes.

David Nathan, whose life spanned most of the twentieth century, witnessed firsthand the competition between these two approaches to medical education and research. Born in Boston and educated at Harvard, he started medical school during the first resurgence of humanistically focused training. At the same time, he was exposed to the practice of clinical research at legendary centers of mid-century medical science including the Thorndike Laboratories at Boston City Hospital and the new clinical center at the National Institutes of Health. These settings offered Nathan models for the kind of research that begins with observing patients. He also had plenty of exposure to basic biological research, but after experiencing the patient-based approach, he was all-in.

Much of Nathan's career in academic medicine can be read as a continual defense of, and advocacy for, the kind of patient-oriented research that had appealed to him during his training. As a faculty member, then division chief, then department chair at the Harvard-affiliated Peter Bent Brigham and Boston Children's Hospitals, his own research on diseases of red blood cells followed that paradigm: all of his scientific contributions were based on observing a single patient or, at most, a small number of patients. He also made sure that trainees—students, residents, fellows—were given opportunities to participate in that kind of research. Remarkably, he did this during an era in which basic research was ascendant. Despite the profession's shift away from patient-based research and the evaporation of government and foundation money to support it, Nathan was its tireless champion both locally within the Harvard community and at the level of national policy. His professional life thus provides a unique vantage point from which to view the competition between these philosophies of medical education and research.

But Nathan's patient-centric attitude extended beyond education and research to something even more important: as a physician, he was deeply committed to putting the patient first in all things. He spent his entire career in the milieu of teaching hospitals where, by definition, patients provide opportunities for medical education and research. However, these institutions are hospitals, after all, and their primary mission has to be providing the best possible care for the human beings in their trust. To Nathan, the best care meant comfort, ease, and emotional support as well as cutting-edge medical treatment. Even as he climbed to the pinnacle of the academic medical hierarchy at Boston Children's Hospital, he consistently worked to improve the experience of its patients and, in so doing, left a legacy of unparalleled pediatric care.

Nathan's patient-oriented philosophy culminated in his recruitment—his near conscription, in fact—to the presidency of Dana-

Farber Cancer Institute, Harvard's cancer hospital. The institute was renowned for its cancer research and its assets included a small inpatient hospital for providing care and running clinical trials of experimental treatments. In 1994, a horrific medical error resulted in the administration of an overdose of highly toxic chemotherapy to two hospitalized patients. One died and the other was incapacitated by damage to her heart. The young woman who died was a popular health reporter for the *Boston Globe* and the paper mercilessly excoriated Dana-Farber and its leadership in a series of front-page reports.

A central theme of the *Globe* articles, as well as the findings of two investigative committees, was that Dana-Farber had been guilty of overemphasizing its basic cancer research while neglecting its clinical responsibilities. This was, in microcosm, an example of the pendulum having swung too far from patient-focused medicine. Dana-Farber was in crisis and it is no exaggeration to suggest that the very existence of this freestanding cancer hospital, the dream of Sidney Farber, the father of chemotherapy, was threatened.

And so, to save the institute, Dana-Farber's trustees turned to Nathan. They saw in him a clinical scientist who understood and appreciated basic research well enough to gain the trust and support of its laboratory scientists. More importantly, though, they saw a clinically focused leader who could reorient Dana-Farber toward a philosophy in which the well-being and interests of patients would be paramount. In short, they saw someone who could restore trust in the institution. Nathan accepted the challenge. In five short years, he resurrected Dana-Farber, restoring its luster by making it a model for patient safety while enhancing its reputation for performing world-class clinical and basic research.

Nathan's career in medicine offers a model for the way academic leaders can balance the competing demands of basic *versus* patient-oriented research and education. In fact, a close examination of his life suggests that the competition may not exist. Nathan showed that the two approaches can be successfully integrated as long as the patient always comes first.

***

Nathan bore witness to another twentieth-century phenomenon: the gradual integration of Jews into the leadership ranks of elite academic institutions. By the time of his birth, in 1929, Nathan was part of the third generation of his Hungarian Jewish immigrant family to be born in the United States. His grandfather and great uncle had achieved financial success in their textile business, allowing Nathan, his sister, and their cousin to be reared in comfort. Family members were ambitious and one of the social markers they sought most avidly was education in the bastions of WASP privilege, especially Harvard.

Their timing was ideal. Charles William Eliot, president of Harvard from 1869 to 1909, believed that the university would benefit by educating students from diverse backgrounds. He was particularly welcoming to Jewish students. His successor, Abbott Lawrence Lowell, held a diametrically opposite position and, within a few years of becoming president, imposed strict quotas on the number of Jewish students admitted to Harvard. Fortunately for the Nathans, implementation of Lowell's plans was delayed just long enough for Nathan's father to be admitted to Harvard College's class of 1920. In another example of threading the timing needle, Lowell was succeeded in 1933 by the eminently rational James Bryant Conant. By the time Nathan was ready to apply to Harvard in 1947 much of Lowell's anti-Semitism had faded. Although his malign influence had not disappeared completely, the air was much cleaner and Nathan was accepted.

Nonetheless, a pall of early- to midcentury anti-Semitism persisted and extended well beyond Harvard College to include Boston's medical community. Harvard Medical School, Massachusetts General Hospital, and, to a lesser extent, the Peter Bent Brigham

Hospital had very few Jews on staff and essentially none in leadership positions. This state of affairs provided the rationale for establishing Boston's Beth Israel Hospital, a haven for Jewish medical professionals. But by the time Nathan was ready to mount the academic ladder at Harvard, barriers to Jews were falling at the medical school and its affiliated hospitals. The arc of history was tending toward tolerance, if not outright inclusion, and Nathan was able to participate in the change that produced a significant number of preeminent Jewish medical leaders in the Boston area.

Still, these individuals—viewed as arrivistes by the old guard—had grown up in a more restricted era and were sensitized by the exclusion they or their colleagues had experienced. This led, understandably, to a certain amount of tribalism. As individual Jews in Boston began to enjoy success in their fields, they were on the lookout for opportunities to help others of their faith when talent and opportunity coincided. Nathan benefited from this. For example, some of the trustees at Dana-Farber were among Jewish kids he went to school with in the Boston suburbs and they could personally vouch for him as the board considered his qualifications for president.

So, in addition to the themes of patient-oriented education and research, another constant in Nathan's life was his identity as a member of the upper middle class Jewish community of Boston. This environment and its people had an enormous impact on his approach to the world and its influence can be seen throughout this narrative.

$$***$$

I have woven together three distinct threads in this portrait of David Nathan. First and foremost are the circumstances, incidents, and people directly related to his life, with a focus on his family and his experiences in academic medicine. Second, to provide a richer context, I have described some of the key external factors that influenced him, such as the social hierarchy of private schools in Boston of the 1930s and 1940s and the Thorndike Laboratory where he was introduced to patient-oriented research. I have positioned these descriptions where they belong in the chronology of Nathan's life but have set them off in their own text boxes. They can be skipped without impacting the narrative. Finally, Nathan's research activities were a critically important part of his life and are described at the ends of Chapters 8 and 9. However, some of the descriptions border on the technical and readers who are less interested in these matters may skip them, too, without sacrificing their understanding of Nathan's life.

AUTHOR'S FOREWORD

I
n 2003, I was a midcareer physician-scientist at Dana-Farber Cancer Institute and Harvard Medical School. My work was going well and I was advancing academically. Barring some sort of professional implosion, it looked like I was on track to achieve tenured faculty status as a professor of medicine. Nonetheless, I was dissatisfied. Although I loved being at Dana-Farber and thought my work was interesting, I was having increasingly frequent "is that all there is?" moments.

Then I got a call to meet with David Nathan. I had been at Dana-Farber since the early 1980s and had lived through the medical error crisis in the 1990s that almost destroyed the hospital. I had also witnessed Nathan's masterful restoration of the institute. Although he had stepped down from Dana-Farber's presidency a few years earlier, Nathan was still a presence. But I hadn't interacted with him very much and the call to meet with him was unexpected.

Unsure of myself and the reason for my summons, I sat in Nathan's office while, with his back to me, he continued with some business at his computer. Nathan is an imposing man: six feet tall, solidly built, with a permanent and scary five o'clock shadow. Having finished whatever he had been working on, Nathan abruptly swiveled his chair to face me. I almost jumped out of my skin. He paused for a moment and then said, "Barrett, I've had my eye on you."

I had no idea what he meant. Should I be flattered? My initial impulse was to be worried—perhaps I had displeased the great man. Evidently not, because Nathan went on to say that the institute's new president, his successor, had decided to create a position to help him manage research at Dana-Farber: chief scientific officer, or CSO. Although no one was quite sure what the CSO would do, there was a consensus that it would be an important position. Nathan said that I would be the perfect first CSO.

Pretty well convinced that I would not be the perfect anything, much less chief scientific officer, I asked Nathan what had made him think of me. In response, he cited history. A few years earlier, Dana-Farber's experimental mouse colony had been ravaged by a viral infection. Many research projects were ruined, millions of dollars in research funding were jeopardized, and a large number of mice had to be euthanized. It was a disaster. At the time, I was serving as the head of the committee that makes sure that Dana-Farber's animal research meets the highest ethical standards. The task of ridding the colony of the virus fell to our competent veterinarian and her staff. My role was simply to provide status updates to the faculty, which I did through a series of town hall meetings.

Nathan said that my performance during the infection crisis made him think I'd be the right person to be CSO. When I pointed out that I had played no direct role in eradicating the infections, that all of the hard work was done by the veterinary staff, and that I was merely the front man, Nathan waved his hand and said none of that mattered. What did matter was that I could explain difficult situations to a constitutionally skeptical faculty and that my scientific background lent legitimacy to my explanations. Nathan insisted that only a small number of biomedical researchers had these talents that were so well-suited to the CSO position.

Rather than being flattered, I was devastated. In the world of Harvard Medical School, most of us believed that scientists who take administrative jobs in midcareer are, by definition, failed scientists. Was Nathan telling me that my research wasn't up to snuff and that I should switch careers?

I left Nathan's office feeling dejected. But over the next few weeks, something happened. Instead of thinking only about myself, I started thinking about Nathan. As I considered his career, I realized that he had singlehandedly populated most of the key leadership positions in pediatric hematology and oncology with his trainees, and they had all flourished. As a scientist, I've been trained to look at a collection of facts and generate a hypothesis to explain them. In this case, I realized that the explanation lay in Nathan's uncanny ability to intuit a trainee's unique skills and strengths and then find the job that matches them.

This alignment of skill set with job description is a rare talent. I realized that I would be an idiot not to take Nathan's advice seriously. I accepted the offer. I served as CSO for fifteen years and it was, by far, the best job I ever had.

Nathan's mentorship skill rests on his ability to see, hear, and understand the person sitting in front of him. I have come to realize that the same attribute underlies his research skill. Nathan has made several important discoveries in the field of hematology and all of them, without exception, were based on something he saw in a patient who was sitting in front of him. Even Nathan's impact on institutions like Dana-Farber or Boston Children's Hospital were grounded in his concerns for individual patients.

Having benefited personally from Nathan's unique approach to the world, I wanted to know where it came from. As I talked to him and interviewed his colleagues and family, and as I began to delve into Nathan's background and history, I kept finding more and more fascinating details. I think his story is extraordinarily compelling and I have dedicated myself to telling it.

Chapter 1

AN UNLIKELY SAVIOR

On February 8, 1995, a data manager at Dana-Farber Cancer Institute, one of Harvard's teaching hospitals, was transcribing information from a patient's medical record into a research database.[2] This was ordinarily a routine clerical task, but there was, as it soon became clear, nothing routine about this patient. She was Betsy Lehman, a health columnist for *The Boston Globe* and someone described by her editor as a "huge newspaper talent."[3] Lehman had developed breast cancer two years earlier at age thirty-seven. Despite her oncologists' best efforts, Lehman's cancer had become stubbornly resistant to conventional treatment and had spread to her lungs. Desperate to help her, Lehman's physicians enrolled her on an experimental study, clinical trial number 94-060. Lehman's experience on that trial would change Dana-Farber forever and thrust David G. Nathan, MD, a world-renowned hematologist and physician-in-chief at Boston Children's Hospital, into an unanticipated leadership role.

***

In the 1940s, pioneering oncologists discovered that a class of poisons known as alkylators could kill cancer cells. In clinical studies, these agents were found to be particularly effective against rare malignancies such as Hodgkin disease. But when they were tested against more common cancers, like those of the lung and breast, most tumors did not respond, a reflection of their innate resistance. But even when cancers did initially shrink, they resumed their growth later, indicating the development of acquired resistance. Thus, despite their early promise, alkylators seemed incapable of curing the most common and deadly cancers.

Research studies suggested that this might be a dosing problem: extremely high concentrations of alkylators could overcome resistance, whether innate or acquired, when tested on cancer cells in a petri dish or a mouse. Naturally, oncologists tried escalating the doses in patients, but their efforts were stymied by the toxic effects of these drugs on normal cells. The alkylators' most serious toxicities affected the bone marrow, the source of white blood cells, which fight infection, and platelets, which prevent bleeding. When patients were given high doses of alkylating agents, their white blood cell and platelet numbers dropped to dangerously low levels, putting them at risk of dying from overwhelming infections and uncontrollable bleeding.

One way to circumvent this problem is autologous bone marrow transplantation. Prior to receiving high-dose chemotherapy, a few ounces of liquid bone marrow can be harvested from the patient through needles inserted into their pelvic bones. The marrow, which contains the progenitor cells that give rise to white blood cells and platelets, can be preserved by freezing. The patients is then given ultra-high doses of alkylators in the hope of killing their cancer cells but with the certainty of killing their bone marrow cells. After the alkylator treatment is completed, the patient" stored marrow can be thawed and given back through a standard intravenous line. Remarkably, the progenitor cells migrate to their natural home in the bones, where they start churning out white blood cells and platelets. Thus, the patient is "salvaged" from the depredations of high-dose alkylators while benefiting, in theory, from their cancer-killing effects. This kind of transplantation is called "autologous" because the bone marrow comes from the same person to whom it is given. It removes the risk that patients might reject the marrow or, conversely, that marrow cells might attack their hosts, both of which are untoward outcomes that can occur when someone receives bone marrow that is not their own.

A cadre of Dana-Farber scientists had devoted their careers to investigating the use of high-dose alkylator therapy in "solid" cancers like those of the lung or breast (as opposed to "liquid" malignancies of the blood like leukemia).[4] Under the leadership of Dr. Emil Frei III, known to all as Tom, they created the Solid Tumor Autologous Marrow Program, or STAMP, a portfolio of clinical trials testing whether patients with solid cancers could be treated with marrow-killing doses of alkylators and then salvaged with autologous bone marrow. Frei's leadership of this program was auspicious: in the 1960s and 1970s, he had been instrumental in developing chemotherapies that converted deadly childhood leukemias into curable diseases.[5] He now hoped to replicate this success in adult cancers. STAMP protocol number 94-060 would determine if breast cancers resistant to conventional treatment might respond to very high doses of cyclophosphamide (brand name Cytoxan), a standard alkylator in common use at conventional doses. After treatment, these patients would be rescued by receiving their stored bone marrow.

This was the trial that Betsy Lehman joined in the fall of 1994. At first, everything went as planned: she received her first two rounds of high-dose cyclophosphamide a few weeks apart and powered through the usual side effects of nausea, vomiting, and hair loss—hardly a walk in the park but nothing unexpected. She was admitted to Dana-Farber for her third and final cycle on November 14, 1994, but this time, her side effects were much worse—"Am I going to die from vomiting?" she asked—but with help from an attentive and devoted nursing staff, she rode them out. Then, during discharge planning on the morning of December 3, with her bags packed, Lehman said that she felt unwell in a nonspecific way. She called a friend and left a message on her answering machine, "I'm feeling very frightened, very upset. I don't know what's wrong, but something's wrong."[6] A few hours later, while still in the hospital, her heart stopped and she died despite heroic attempts at resuscitation. Dead at age thirty-nine, Betsy Lehman left a husband and two young daughters.

Oncologists live with death—it is an inescapable part of cancer care. They spend much of their time preparing patients for their own deaths and families for the deaths of loved ones. But the savoir faire they display in the face of mortality relates only to expected deaths. Unexpected deaths in oncology are jarring and should trigger extensive self and system evaluations. It is surprising, then, that Lehman's death—which was entirely unexpected—did not provoke more than a perfunctory search for its underlying reasons. A review of the medical record was said to be unrevealing and an autopsy uncovered no specific cause of death,[7] which only reinforced her oncologists' complacency. In the end, they attributed Lehman's tragic outcome to an "idiosyncratic response" to chemotherapy, a formulation that physicians use when they don't understand something.

That's where things stood until two months later when Diane Warren, the data manager responsible for transcribing information from the medical records of patients enrolled on protocol 94-060, started working on Betsy Lehman's data.[8] She soon came to the section that documented the dose of cyclophosphamide Lehman's doctors had ordered for her. Chemotherapy doses are customized for every patient. In particular, they have to be adjusted for size: big patients require higher doses than small patients. The best measure of someone's size is body surface area, which is measured in square meters and can be derived from a formula that uses a person's height and weight.

As Warren analyzed Lehman's cyclophosphamide dose, she could see that the physician's order for the drug and the amount delivered from the hospital pharmacy were shockingly wrong. The correct dose should have been one thousand milligrams of cyclophosphamide per square meter of body surface area each day for four days, resulting in an overall total dose of four thousand milligrams.[9, 10] Based on Lehman's body surface area of 1.63 square meters, her customized dose should have been 1,630 milligrams of cyclophosphamide each day for four days, for a total of 6,520 milligrams. Instead, her orders had been written for 6,520 milligrams *each day for four days*—a fourfold overdose.[11] And that was the amount Lehman received.

One of cyclophosphamide's rarer toxicities is destruction of heart muscle,[12] rare because it occurs only after exposure to massively high doses. Thus, Betsy Lehman's heart was severely damaged and ultimately failed because of an incorrect cyclophosphamide order, which had been carried out to the letter. The data manager who discovered Lehman's overdose, found a second patient, a fifty-two-year-old teacher with breast cancer, who was similarly overdosed two days after Lehman.[13] She also developed devastating heart damage but somehow survived until she succumbed to her breast cancer in 1997.[14] The reappearance of her aggressive tumor just three years after treatment was a depressingly forthright demonstration that high-dose alkylator therapy had failed to achieve its primary objective: curing her underlying disease. Subsequent clinical trials have confirmed that this treatment does not cure breast cancer and the approach has been abandoned.

These fatal medical errors shook Dana-Farber to its foundations. The institute's leadership—its president, Christopher Walsh, PhD, a world-renowned chemist, and its physician-in-chief, David M. Livingston, MD, a prominent cancer biologist—took action. They placed several individuals on administrative leave, including the physician who wrote the incorrect order, another physician who was connected to the clinical trial, and three pharmacists who each had a hand in filling the order.[15] They also convened three investigative committees, two internal and one external, the latter led by Dr. Vincent DeVita, a former director of the National Cancer Institute.[16]

Meanwhile, a media firestorm had erupted after the institute submitted its mandatory notification about the overdoses to the Massachusetts Department of Public Health. The fact that it did so later than required by law did not help matters.[17] The *Boston Globe*, the newspaper Betsy Lehman had worked for, published a front-page article headlined, "Doctor's Orders Killed Cancer Patient,"[18] the first of twenty-eight front-page articles the *Globe* would publish about Dana-Farber over the next three years. Some were allegedly fueled by leaks of confidential internal information, an indication of the instability pervading the institute.[19] The news stories were often accompanied by opinion pieces, including one describing Lehman's overdose as resulting from "an appalling series of errors that would make The Three Stooges look like brain surgeons."[20] Descriptions of the tragedy soon made their way into national outlets like the *New York Times*.[21] Dana-Farber's reputation was in tatters.

The institute's troubles deepened during the spring of 1995. The Massachusetts Department of Public Health made a surprise inspection of Dana-Farber's clinical facilities on April 4 and later, in May, released a scathing "Statement of Deficiencies," which indicted the hospital's board as well as its management team.[22] On the same day as the Department of Public Health's visit, a national hospital accrediting body, The Joint Commission on Accreditation of Healthcare Organizations (now known simply as The Joint Commission) made its own unannounced visit and placed Dana-Farber on probation, a humiliating repudiation of a top hospital.[23]

Not surprisingly, a number of leadership changes ensued. The director of Dana-Farber's pharmacy resigned in May. The same month, David Livingston stepped down as physician-in-chief. Christopher Walsh continued as president but gave up his concurrent academic role as chair of the Department of Biological Chemistry and Molecular Pharmacology at Harvard Medical School in order, he said, to "devote all my energies to implementing the changes necessary to enhance patient care" at Dana-

Farber.[24] Walsh's second job had been a sore point for some time, with many wondering how running the institute could not be a full-time endeavor. Even the reviewers of the federal grant that supported the Cancer Center criticized him for keeping it.[25] But Walsh's move came too late. Dana-Farber faculty, staff, and trustees had lost confidence in his ability to lead through the crisis and, in September, he notified the newly elected chair of Dana-Farber's board of trustees, Gary Countryman, that he intended to relinquish the presidency.

By themselves, the overdoses and their sequelae would have been disruptive, but because they occurred at the same time that external forces were militating against Dana-Farber's clinical care model, the threat became existential. In 1995, the institute had fifty-seven licensed inpatient beds, which were housed on two floors of its Dana Building, an iconic black-glass tower that interns and residents in their enduring capacity for dark humor called "The Death Star." The rest of the building was filled with research labs, administrative offices, and a clinic. For several years, only about thirty of those beds were occupied at any one time and, although reimbursement rates from insurance companies for inpatient care were relatively generous, the low census generated insufficient revenues to cover the fixed costs of the inpatient service. This problem was exacerbated by a structural weakness unique to Dana-Farber: unlike other freestanding cancer institutes, Dana-Farber did not have its own surgery, radiology, or pathology services, all of which generate substantial revenue. Rather, the institute relied on the adjacent Brigham and Women's and Boston Children's Hospitals, a situation that was highly lucrative for them but not for Dana-Farber. Finally, the overdose crisis unfolded just as the institute completed construction of a two hundred seventy thousand square-foot research building. That risky expansion had occurred despite uncertainty about whether Institute scientists could attract sufficient research funding to support the building's operating costs. While other hospitals might use the margin from their clinical activities to cross-subsidize research operations, the squeeze on Dana-Farber's clinical revenues made this an unrealistic option. For all of these reasons, then, discussions about altering Dana-Farber's clinical model had already been broached even before the overdose occurred.[26]

In the late summer of 1995, the review panels that had been assembled in the wake of the overdose presented their findings to the trustees. Both the internal and external panels were united in their condemnation of Dana-Farber's inattention to its clinical enterprise.[27] Emblematic of the problem, according to the reports, was the fact that several senior leadership appointments had been made without due consideration for clinical expertise—the president was a PhD scientist with no experience in medical management and the physician-in-chief, although an MD, had spent his entire career in laboratory science. The panels pointed to the absence of a director of nursing, a position unfilled since November 1994, as an example of leadership's inattention to clinical needs. The popular press latched onto this idea: columnists wrote about the overdose as an expected consequence of clinically inexperienced scientists attempting to run a hospital. One went so far as to say, "It's obvious that Dana-Farber is more interested in research... than patient care."[28]

How did Dana-Farber, with its deep bench of brilliant and well-meaning staff, arrive at this dismal state of affairs? In part, it was an unintended legacy of the institute's founder, Dr. Sidney Farber. Dr. Farber is justly celebrated for establishing the tradition of combining clinical care and research in order to improve the lives of cancer patients. At the same time, though, he had strong isolationist tendencies. In particular, he had a vision for carving out pediatric oncology from the rest of the clinical activities at Boston Children's Hospital in order to create the Children's Cancer Research Foundation (CCRF), which, although still affiliated with Boston Children's, would be independent. The CCRF had its own patients, its own beds, its own faculty, and, importantly, its own money. Farber thought that the CCRF's primary focus should be on its outpatient clinics and that there ought to be little room in the budget or the floorplate of a cancer center for a true inpatient service. Farber was highly skilled at outpatient care and he developed what many considered to be one of the best pediatric clinics in the world, which he housed in the Jimmy Fund Building, named for the charity that supported his work.

When the National Cancer Act of 1971 provided funding for the creation of regional comprehensive cancer centers, Farber led the effort to expand the CCRF to include adults who had cancer, creating the Sidney Farber Cancer Center, the precursor to Dana-Farber. He also spearheaded planning for the new Dana Building. Several of the oncologists who cared for adults lobbied for inpatient floors. Despite his aversion, Farber reluctantly acceded to their request only because he thought they would be low-risk chemotherapy infusion areas for adults who might need several hours or, rarely, an overnight stay to receive their treatments.[29]

Over the next decade, however, as cancer care became more complex and cancer patients became sicker, this model was no longer tenable—the risks to patients were too great. Medical interns and residents who staffed the inpatient beds in the early 1980s were scared witless from the moment they walked into the Dana Building. If a patient required emergency medical intervention— cardiac resuscitation, for example—anesthesiologists and surgeons would have to run to the Dana Building from Brigham and Women's Hospital, a good ten-minute sprint. And if the patient needed critical care or surgery, the staff would have to call an ambulance to transport the patient across the three hundred yards separating Dana-Farber from Brigham and Women's. Like the economic challenges, the patient safety problems created by Dana-Farber's inpatient beds had been acknowledged prior to the overdose but not acted upon.

Now, however, as the trustees began their quest for a new president, they knew that they had to find someone—a physician, this time—who not only understood hospital finances, but also had a track record of prioritizing patient safety. Given Dana-Farber's preeminence in research, the new leader would have to appreciate science, too, and be enthusiastic about supporting it. And whoever they chose had to bring to Dana-Farber a personality that could inspire a deeply shaken and demoralized workforce. Plus, the decision had to be made quickly—there was no time to perform the usual prolonged international search. Of course, the quickest route to choosing a new president would have been to identify a qualified internal candidate, but that was out of the question. Fairly or not, any insider would carry a taint of complicity with the very culture that had gotten the institute into this mess. The new president had to be an outsider.

As the trustees mulled these considerations, a consensus began to form around offering the position to David Nathan. Nathan was a known and valued commodity in several respects. Trustees with long memories were aware of his work as chief of the Division of Hematology and Oncology at Children's Hospital and Dana-Farber, where he oversaw a superb clinical service and had run the world's foremost training program in pediatric oncology. Even more trustees knew him from his later service as physician-in-chief at Children's Hospital, where he had enhanced its overall clinical and research activities.

Despite Nathan's track record, the trustees were well aware that he was, in many ways, an unlikely choice. First, although he had trained in internal medicine and was a board-certified internist, Nathan had long since become a pediatrician and had not participated in the care of an adult in decades. Of course, Dana-Farber did have a vibrant pediatric oncology service—Sidney Farber's old Jimmy Fund Clinic—but the scale of its activity was minuscule compared with the adult oncology practice. Second, the overdoses and the safety deficiencies that caused them were the result of systems failures in a hospital, an operational environment where Nathan had little administrative experience. Although he had run the largest clinical department at Children's Hospital, Nathan's role was an academic one, focusing on training residents and recruiting and developing faculty. He had no experience overseeing the operations of a hospital: nursing, dietary, billing, human resources, maintenance, and so much more—an endless list of critically important functions. Third, Nathan was not an oncologist; he was a hematologist. His last exposure to cancer patients had been in the 1950s, when he cared for children with leukemia at the National Institutes of Health, an experience so traumatic that Nathan swore he would never give anyone chemotherapy again. But the problems at Dana-Farber had occurred on its cancer service, so a trustee might reasonably think that the institute would benefit from someone experienced in the proper administration and oversight of cancer care. Finally, David Nathan and Sidney Farber, both strong-willed leaders, had very different views about the way children with leukemia should be treated. This made them fierce combatants right up to Farber's death in 1973. It was hard to imagine anyone less likely to have been endorsed by the man whose name graced the institute. Despite these many caveats, Nathan's candidacy survived because the trustees also knew that he was strong-minded, smart, and fair.

Importantly, a few trustees, including Dick Smith, the recently retired board chair and one of the godfathers of Dana-Farber Cancer Institute, knew Nathan socially. In fact, the Nathan and Smith families had been friendly, and David and Dick had grown up in the same neighborhood. In a show of preadolescent generosity, Dick and the other neighborhood boys occasionally let David play football with them even though he was a few years younger.[30] This connection is an example of how important the relationships among the upper middle-class Jewish families of Boston were to Nathan's career. The constituents of this demographic who aspired to stature in the academic and social worlds of Boston, especially the Harvard-related ones, formed a mutually supportive community of sympathetic individuals who were civic-minded, generous, and highly ambitious. They felt that they could achieve their greatest collective good by promoting those within their circle who were capable of skillful leadership. Placing such people in key positions would enhance the status of Boston's Jewish community while ensuring that important institutions in the city would be managed for the benefit of all.

Dick Smith and David Nathan were deeply embedded in this tradition. Smith had known Nathan for decades and was convinced that he was the right person to be Dana-Farber's next president. Smith encouraged his successor as chair of the board, Gary Countryman, CEO of the insurance giant Liberty Mutual, to meet with Nathan. Well before the overdose, Countryman had grown frustrated with Walsh's waffling about the disposition of Dana-Farber's inpatient beds—should they stay in the Dana Building or be moved the Brigham—an uncertainty he ascribed to Walsh's inexperience in hospital administration.[31] In searching for Walsh's replacement, Countryman was now looking for someone who could be decisive about this and other matters. Countryman was immediately sold on Nathan during his interview when, in response to the question of what he would do with the inpatient beds, Nathan answered without hesitation that they would "have to go." After so many years of indecision, this straightforward declaration was a relief.

Smith and Countryman had their man. They liked the fact that Nathan was self-assured and had faith in his own judgment, traits that they thought would improve morale and get the institution moving again. In Nathan they saw an experienced leader both in clinical and research realms who was widely admired—at least, supporters outnumbered detractors by a considerable margin. Finally, Nathan knew Harvard medicine thoroughly so there would be no learning curve in dealing with political issues at the medical school and the university.

Countryman recommended Nathan to the Executive Committee of Dana-Farber's board, which, after an hour of deliberation, voted to offer him the job. Dick Smith was given the task of making the actual offer, so he called Nathan and asked him to his home in Chestnut Hill, a tony Boston suburb. Nathan was startled by the call, coming as it did on a Sunday morning, and decided that he had better make the drive across the Charles River from his own home in Cambridge. Soon after he arrived, Smith went right to the heart of the matter and asked Nathan if he'd be interested in becoming the next president of Dana-Farber. Nathan did not answer immediately. He hesitated because, at age sixty-six, he was about to step down from his position as physician-in-chief at Children's Hospital, in fulfillment of a longstanding pledge to his wife, Jean, that he would transition to semiretirement. He had promised her that his new life would include a bit of clinic and laboratory work but also, importantly, more time at the Nathan family home on Nantucket in the summer, more time in Florida during the winter, and, at long last, more time with Jean and the grandchildren. Nathan told Smith he could not immediately accept the offer.

Dick Smith's wife, Susan, was in the room. Nathan had known her, too, since childhood: as Susan Flax, she had grown up across the street from the Nathans in Newton, another Boston suburb. Like Dick, Susan had become an ardent supporter of Dana-Farber and was making her own mark by providing funding for research and care of women's cancers. She was tough, generally brooking no argument, and her response to Nathan's hesitancy was, "Well, what are you going to do about women's cancers when you're president?" She repeated this question at least once more during the conversation, indicating either that she had not heard Nathan's demurral, which seems unlikely, or that she was supremely confident that she and her husband would eventually convince Nathan to take the job. Seeing where matters stood, Dick Smith ended the meeting, suggesting to Nathan that he go right home and discuss the matter with Jean.

As Nathan drove back to Cambridge, he was dreading the tough conversation he was about to have—tough because he was inclined to accept the offer. Ever since the overdoses became public knowledge, Nathan had felt deep sympathy for the staff at Dana-Farber who, he thought, were talented and caring physicians and scientists. He had even written an open letter to the staff at Children's Hospital reminding them that "there but for the grace of God go we." But Nathan was a realist. He was keenly aware of the structural problems at Dana-Farber that had allowed this horrible error to occur, starting with the absence of strong clinical leadership. Nathan thought he could help. It would also be fitting to do so, Nathan argued to himself, since he had benefited so much from his association with Dana-Farber, and this would be a way to repay the institution. Finally, he knew in his bones that the inpatient beds had to move and this would be an opportunity to make that happen.

But Nathan's realistic side also made him wonder whether he was the right choice for the job. He was acutely aware that none of the experiences of his first sixty-six years had directly prepared him to run a hospital. Throughout his career, in fact, he had assiduously avoided dealing with the business side of medical care and research, thereby allowing him to be a passionate advocate for his faculty whenever he tried to wrest institutional resources from "the pencil pushers in their green eyeshades"—his caricature of hospital administrators. But Nathan also knew that he was financially literate and that, if the economics demanded it, he would have no trouble saying no to a supplicant. He also took comfort from the fact that, when it came to the technical intricacies of hospital finances, he would have a secret weapon in the person of Dorothy Puhy, Dana-Farber's chief financial officer. Puhy, who had been hired by Chris Walsh, had not only kept Dana-Farber solvent in the face of tremendous external financial pressures, but had maintained the institute's bonds at the top of the investment rating scale. By his own admission, Nathan "knew what [he] didn't know" about hospital finance but was sure that Puhy would hold his hand and teach him whatever skills he needed to have to make good decisions. Finally, Nathan was confident that he could woo another highly competent administrator, Jim Conway, from Children's Hospital to be his chief operating officer. As he thought about having this strong leadership team in place, Nathan's confidence grew.

So, he approached Jean about taking the job.

Nathan had anticipated that his wife might not be happy about his interest in becoming president of Dana-Farber, but he was unprepared for the intensity of her displeasure. As soon as he walked into the kitchen, Jean asked what Dick Smith had wanted. When Nathan told her about the offer of the presidency and his inclination to accept it, she became as angry as he had ever seen her in forty-three years of marriage. More than a little daunted, Nathan nonetheless laid out all of the logical arguments for taking the position, along with the sense of duty he felt to help an inherently fine institution that was facing such enormous difficulties. None of these arguments were persuading Jean. Eventually, though, she said, "Well, your father had such huge respect for Dick Smith's father. If Dick said you should do this, I can't stop you." And, with that underwhelming endorsement, along with Nathan's promise that he would spend his summers in Nantucket and commute to Boston as needed, Nathan accepted the job, a late-career opportunity to fundamentally reshape one of the world's premier cancer hospitals.

Chapter 2

OF HARVARD AND HOLLYWOOD: A TALE OF TWO IMMIGRANT FAMILIES

Throughout his career, David Nathan was an anomaly in the environments that mattered most to him: a clinical researcher surrounded by basic scientists at Harvard and MIT; a caring physician who was adamant about carving out time to learn about research; an administrator who disdained administration; a product of the Jewish middle class in the Brahmin worlds of Andover and Harvard. These contradictions never seemed to bother him. Nathan was protected from their unsettling effects by three fortunate attributes of character: an ambition that was boundless but not ruthless, a self-confidence that was complete but not overweening, and an impervious moral and ethical core shaped by deep sympathy for the suffering and downtrodden. How did these traits arise? Some may have been innate, but others were formed by his family: his parents, grandparents, and more distant relatives played a vital role in shaping the adult David Nathan.

1. THE NATHAN FAMILY

Emanuel Nathan, David's paternal great-grandfather, was a young man in Budapest in the late 1850s and at risk for conscription into Emperor Franz Joseph's army. Rather than fight for the Habsburgs, Emanuel left the Austro-Hungarian Empire to its fate and came to the United States, arriving in Boston in 1861 just as the Civil War was starting. Emanuel Nathan had no interest in fighting for his newly adopted country either and since, as he was supposed to have said, he had never met a Black person, he also had no interest in fighting for the abolition of slavery. So he decamped again, this time to the forests of western Pennsylvania where he waited out the war by "chopping wood," according to Nathan family lore.[32] Still, Emanuel must have spent some time in the civilized world because his first son, John, was born in Philadelphia in April 1861 (see Figure 1).

In 1866, with the Civil War safely over, Emanuel emerged from the woods. He and his wife had a second son, Jacob, and the young family moved to the growing metropolis of Cleveland, Ohio.[33] But just one year later, in 1867, Emanuel returned to Boston where, in a barn at the corner of Prentiss and Parker Streets[34] in the Roxbury neighborhood, he established the Roxbury Chemical Works, a textile soap factory.

A company with a similar name, the Roxbury Chemical and Color Manufacturing Works, had been founded in 1826 on the site of what is now the New England Baptist Hospital. Ideally located near railroad lines and the Stoney Brook (a source of water, which was something Emanuel Nathan's company would not have), the Roxbury Color Works, as it was often called, had been a great success—its 210-foot chimney was one of the tallest structures in Boston, a landmark that could be seen from downtown. By the 1850s, however, farmland around the factory began to be subdivided and sold to developers in an attempt to turn the neighborhood into a residential suburb. But when new homeowners moved in, they were confronted by the toxic fumes emanating from the factory and, in an early example of environmental activism, they convinced the city government to shut it down in 1856.[35] Nonetheless, the memory of the Roxbury Chemical Works lingered and it is possible, although no evidence supports the supposition, that Emanuel Nathan named his company in order to create associations, conscious or otherwise, with the earlier firm.

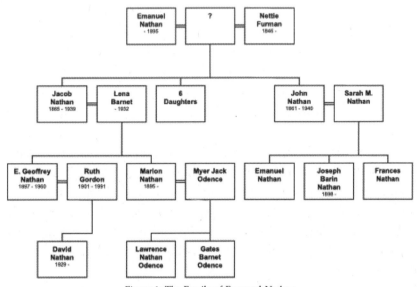

Figure 1: The Family of Emanuel Nathan

What did the Roxbury Chemical Works do? In the 1860s and 1870s, textile factories in the southern United States imported raw wool from Australia, which had to be cleaned before it could be processed and shipped to mills in the North. Companies like the Roxbury Chemical Works supplied tallow-based soaps for this purpose, and the company thrived thanks to considerable demand. John Nathan joined the business in 1873, followed by his brother Jacob in 1878, giving the company its alternative name, Emanuel Nathan's Sons. In 1876, Emanuel had sufficient cash to purchase the land and barn at 71 Prentiss Street from someone named Francis Ward for $18,000.[36] As the company expanded, Emanuel tore down the barn and built a larger factory along with two storehouses.

Roxbury Chemical Works flourished in the midst of the great Irish migration to Boston, and Emanuel Nathan deliberately tapped that population to fill its ranks. It was a bold decision since only a few years earlier, in 1857, the governor of Massachusetts, lieutenant governor, secretary of state, attorney general, all congressional representatives, all forty state senators, and all but three of the 379 state representatives were members of the adamantly anti-immigrant Know Nothing party. Using rhetoric redolent of our current age, Massachusetts governor Henry J. Gardner declared in his 1855 inaugural address that, "during the present decade...nearly four millions of aliens will probably be poured in upon us...[N]early four-fifths of the beggary, two-thirds of the pauperism, and more than three-fifths of the crimes spring from our foreign population."[37] To prevent further pollution of Gardner's America and, in his infelicitous phrase, to "Americanize America," he proposed that: immigrants must wait twenty-one years before naturalization; those naturalized citizens cannot hold public office; voters must be able to read and write English; and the Latin inscription at the speaker's podium in the State House be removed because it was not in English. (One of his goals was "to dispel from popular use every foreign language."[38] That a foreign language might be dead was irrelevant.)

It was in this atmosphere, so inimical to Irish immigrants, that Emanuel Nathan roamed the Boston waterfront looking for workers. Many did not have homes. Anticipating this, Emanuel purchased lots adjacent to his Roxbury factory and built more than a dozen houses where his new hires and their families could stay until they were able to afford lodgings of their own.[39] This material generosity, albeit in furtherance to commercial interests, was still on display two generations later for David Nathan to see. At age six, David met the foreman of the Roxbury Chemical Works, an Irish-born immigrant named Jerry Donovan, who told David how he had found employment with his great-grandfather.

"I come over on the boat," he was supposed to have said, "and was sitting on the dock. This big man come up to me and said, 'Paddy, what are you doing?' I said, 'Nothing,' and he told me to come work for him."[40]

Donovan was foreman at the Roxbury Chemical Works for forty-five years. In 1940, near the end of his tenure, he was asked whether he was still making soap the same way he had when he started. Covered in a burlap apron, mixing tallow in a large vat with a paddle, Donovan replied without looking up, "No, I'm improving every day."[41]

Not much is known about Emanuel's wife other than that she was said to have come from in Vienna and that, in addition to John and Jacob, she gave birth to six daughters. Very little material evidence survives to provide a picture of John's and Jacob's sisters other than David Nathan's recollection that "my grandfather's multiple sisters were bizarre and wraithlike figures in my childhood."[42] The only other certainty about Emanuel's wife is the sad fact that she died young. A few years after her death, during one of his frequent trips to New York City, the widower Emanuel met Nettie Furman, whose husband had died in 1890. Like Emanuel, Nettie was a Hungarian immigrant. They married in 1891 when Emanuel was sixty-five years old and Nettie was forty-five.

Roxbury Chemical Works had made Emanuel a wealthy man, which may have provided motive for his insisting that Nettie sign a prenuptial agreement, called an "antenuptial" in 1891. It stipulated that, upon Emanuel's death, his estate would provide her with a yearly income of $27,000 derived from revenue generated by his properties on Tremont Street in Boston and a lump sum of $5,000 in lieu of any other rights to the estate, which he had left to his children in his will. At the time of Emanuel's death in February 1895, his estate was valued at $400,000,[43] equivalent to $14.6 million in 2023 dollars. When Nettie saw that number, she sued the executors, John and Jacob Nathan, to have the prenuptial agreement set aside. She argued that she was not "conversant" in the English language, could not read English, and did not under-stand the true nature of the prenuptial agreement; she had assumed that the $5,000 she had received for her quitclaim had simply been a wedding present from her new husband. Nettie maintained that she had no idea that she was giving up her future rights to the estate.[44] A Justice of the county Supreme Court dismissed the suit.[45] It is notable that this family dispute was covered in the local press, which described John and Jacob Nathan as being "well known in Boston and the case for this reason is exciting much interest."[46] It had only been thirty years since Emanuel moved his family to Boston, but in that brief period of time, the Nathans had "arrived."

After Emanuel's death, his sons managed the business with John as president and Jacob as treasurer. According to David Nathan, his grandfather and uncle were inseparable. They turned the first floor of the Prentiss Street factory into a large office, where they played endless rounds of pinochle while bemoaning the ills of the world in a manner that Jacob's grandson found infinitely amusing. Their secretary, Rose Ryan, was described in a *Boston Globe* article about John Nathan as "a comely and attractive young lady who runs the soap business while [John] tours about."[47]

On Saturdays, after temple services, David would accompany his grandfather and uncle to the factory, where they would com-plain bitterly about everything the rabbi had said during his ser-mon. "Rosie, take a letter!" one of the brothers would shout.

Rose would dutifully type the brothers' withering denunciation until the torrent of invective became too much to bear, at which point Rose would stop typing and say, "Mr. Nathan! You can't talk that way about a man of the cloth!"

To protect themselves, the brothers never signed their names, using instead Jacob's drawing of a blind man being led by a dog. Whether any of these letters made their way to the objects of their scorn is not known.[48]

Soon after World War I, New England's manufacturing base began its decline, unable to compete with the lower cost of labor in the South and abroad. Although this trend significantly impacted the Roxbury Chemical Works' profits, the Nathan brothers were determined to provide a social safety net for their workers: they continued to house employees in the buildings they owned adjacent to the factory and kept wages at a reasonably high level even as the economics became infeasible. One example of their largesse involved the brothers' chauffeurs. Charles "Lenny" Lenhard was John's chauffeur; he drove him to the Prentiss Street factory every morning and home again to 429 Harvard Street in Brookline every night. At noon, however, a different chauffeur, John "Dinty" Hayes, took John to and from his home-cooked midday meal in a different car. The reason for this redundant arrangement was that Dinty had been Jacob's chauffeur, serving him for thirty-seven years. Jacob had watched over Dinty's welfare and had treated him well, even putting him in an adjacent hotel room during the brothers' frequent trips to Atlantic City. When Jacob died in October 1939, in the Roosevelt Hotel in New York City on the way back from one of those Atlantic City jaunts, John could not bear the thought of letting Dinty go. So, he continued to pay for two drivers and two cars.[49]

These kindhearted gestures, especially in the context of a dwindling business, took their toll on the Roxbury Chemical Works. The factory also suffered from not being sited near a river. Enormous amounts of water were needed for the soap manufacturing process and, rather than using natural sources of water like other factories, the Roxbury Chemical Works paid the City of Boston for its water. By 1921, the company's financial statement showed assets of only $90,930 while nearly all other textile concerns in Massachusetts had assets in excess of $1 million.[50] One possible, and curious, reflection of straitened circumstances was John's willingness to shill for an arthritis medicine called Kodicon (Figure 2).[51] The appearance of his testimonial in the local newspaper likely brought in some additional revenue. But it could not last—Kodicon Products was shut down by the Federal Trade Commission the following year for making false claims.[52] The fact that David Nathan's great uncle was a tout for an ineffective patent medicine is, of course, richly ironic.

The details surrounding the demise of the Roxbury Chemical Works are obscure, but what is clear is that the company, formally incorporated on June 26, 1914, underwent a sale and transfer of stock in 1940. In 1946, the new owners moved the concern from Boston to Fall River, Massachusetts, but to no avail: the Roxbury Chemical Works was finally dissolved on March 20, 1957, by order of the Supreme Judicial Court of the Commonwealth of Massachusetts.[53]

"KODICON IS WONDERFUL"

Mr. John Nathan. 71 Prentiss St., Roxbury, Mass., writes: "I have been a sufferer about 5 years—very painful at night. KODICON is indeed wonderful, causing me no stomach disturbance—no bad taste—great relief from pain."

Take KODICON for Arthritis

If other methods have failed don't give up hope. Many, many letters like the above testify to the marvelous relief that KODICON has been to sufferers from Arthritis, Rheumatism, Neuritis, Neuralgia, Sciatica and gout.

Price $1.00—At your druggist.

Figure 2: John Nathan's Endorsement of Kodicon

Long before the dissolution of the Roxbury Chemical Works, Jacob Nathan had married Lena Barnet, one of twelve children of Gates and Marion Barnet of Albany, New York. The Barnets were tanners by trade who had emigrated from Germany in the mid-nineteenth century. Being German Jews, they were of a higher caste than the Eastern European Jews who had fled the Pale of Settlement. However, according to David Nathan, a match with a Hungarian Jew like Jacob would have been acceptable because, "after all, his family might be Austrian!"[54]

Jacob and Lena moved out of the home Emanuel had built next to the Roxbury factory and into 215 Babcock Street in the Boston suburb of Brookline. In these upscale environs, they had two children: Marion, born on January 8, 1895, and Emanuel Geoffrey, known as Geoffrey, born on November 25, 1897. Jacob and Lena had high aspirations for their children, as did John Nathan and his wife, who had two sons and a daughter of their own. Both sets of parents enrolled their male children in the prestigious Boston Latin High School, where they acquitted themselves with honor. In 1911, Geoffrey won an award in Modern Studies[55] and, in 1914, an award for General Excellence in Conduct and Studies.[56] In his graduation year of 1916, Geoffrey won another award for Exemplary Conduct and Fidelity.[57] Not to be outdone, one of his cousins, Joseph, scored a hat trick of sorts: an award for Excellence in Classical Studies, something called the Franklin Medal, and a one hundred dollar scholarship.[58] His other cousin, Emanuel—both John and Jacob named their firstborn after their father—won an Honorable Mention for "Conduct Above Criticism" over his six-year course, surely a remarkable achievement despite the faint praise implied by its title.[59]

All three Nathan cousins went from Boston Latin to Harvard: Emanuel in the class of 1918, Geoffrey and Joseph in the class of 1920. Geoffrey was a member of Harvard's freshman track team and Emanuel was on the freshman crew which had the distinction of being the "huskiest" first year team on record, with an average weight of 178 pounds, five pounds heavier than the varsity crew. Emanuel Nathan was fifth rower, a position for the heaviest and strongest team members[60, 61] (Figure 3). When the Great War began, Geoffrey joined Harvard's Reserve Officers Training Corps, which was one of the first ROTC units to be formed and was the largest in the country, with 1,193 men enrolled.[62] Then, in 1918, he joined the U.S. Naval Reserve Force, one of three wartime naval schools at Harvard.[63] His training continued at a military camp at Plattsburgh, New York, but the war ended before he could be sent overseas. Geoffrey returned to Harvard, where he majored in chemistry, and graduated in 1920.

Figure 3: Harvard's "Husky" Freshman Crew Team of 1915. Top, posing on shore, Emanuel is fifth from the left. Bottom, posing on the Charles River, Emanuel is fifth from the bow. (Courtesy of David G. Nathan.)

HARVARD AND THE JEWS

Harvard's willingness to admit the Nathan cousins, second-generation Jews, might seem remarkable given the nature of the university's leadership in the early 1900s. For much of the prior century, 1869 to 1909, Harvard had been led by the liberal-minded Charles William Eliot. When his long tenure ended, the presidency passed to Abbott Lawrence Lowell, who would become infamous for his implementation of severe restrictions on the number of Jewish students admitted to Harvard. The full impact of his policies would not be felt until the 1920s when the disarmingly named "Committee on Methods of Sifting Candidates for Admission" provided Lowell with a means and a socially acceptable rationale for limiting Jewish admissions. Under his watchful guidance, a quota for Jewish students admitted to the College was instituted in 1926.[64] Lowell was so particular about the threat Jews posed to his vision of Harvard that his committee's report classified questionable applicants into three categories—J1 (conclusively Jewish), J2 (indicatively Jewish), and J3 (possibly but not probably Jewish)—in the belief that rigorous analytics might justify a baldly discriminatory policy that was abhorred by some faculty members as well as Lowell's predecessor.[65]

In fact, Lowell's vision for a homogeneous Harvard was only one instance of his larger vision for a homogeneous America. In an attitude reminiscent of the Know Nothings of fifty years earlier, Lowell worried that a new surge of immigrants from eastern and southern European countries was changing the nature of the United States and that securing America's future required policies that would protect its "original" homogeneity.[66] Putting his theories into practice, Lowell served, while president of Harvard, as vice president of the Immigration Restriction League, a Boston-based association dedicated to preventing an influx of undesirables. Among its most venerable members was Senator Henry Cabot Lodge, who proposed that prospective immigrants must pass a literacy test to gain entry into the United States. In support of the League's activities, Lowell wrote that "every nation is entitled to decide what additions from outside to its population it will receive."[67]

In stark contrast to Lowell, Charles Eliot, Harvard's previous president, supported the National Liberal Immigration League, which had been formed in 1906 to oppose a restrictive immigration bill introduced in Congress by Representative Augustus Gardner, Henry Cabot Lodge's son-in-law. At Harvard, Eliot had been a vigorous proponent of the notion that the College benefits from educating students of diverse backgrounds and he was particularly welcoming to Jewish students. Fortunately for the Nathan cousins, Lowell had not had time to fully transform Harvard by the time they were ready to attend. Even though Eliot's presidency had ended in 1909, the university was still acting in accordance with his enlightened stance that he could not "admit the doctrine that the United States should be reserved for the white race."[68] The proportion of Jewish freshman, which stood at 7 percent in 1900, continued to rise, reaching 21.5 percent in 1922.[69] In Geoffrey Nathan's class of 1920, 17.8 percent of admitted freshman were Jewish.[70] Thanks to Eliot's lingering influence, Harvard's record compared favorably to other schools—even in 1918, when overall Jewish enrollment at Harvard College was 10 percent, it was only 1.9 percent at Amherst, 1.9 percent at Bowdoin, and 1.4 percent at Williams.[71]

Once admitted, Jewish students in the decade from 1915 to 1925 found a thriving social environment, including Jewish fraternities such as Sigma Alpha Mu which Geoffrey joined[72] despite a membership of predominantly Eastern European Jews.[73] The Nathans also benefited from Eliot's endorsement of Boston Latin School as a feeder for Harvard College: it sent nineteen Jewish students to Harvard in 1918.[74] Combined with Jacob's and John's commercial success, which gave them the means to afford a Harvard education for their sons, this narrow window of Semitic tolerance made the Nathan cousins' matriculation at Harvard less unlikely than it would have been at almost any time other than the present.

While at Harvard, Geoffrey had decided to become a doctor, a choice consistent with the upward striving of the Nathan family. In fact, he had been admitted to Harvard Medical School's class of 1924, but his father forbade his matriculation. Jacob thought that medical doctors were "bums and loafers who come to your house and drink your coffee and then don't do a damn thing for you."[75] Surgeons were a different matter—Jacob thought that surgeons actually accomplished something and he had great respect for them. But Jacob was convinced that Geoffrey was not blessed with the attributes of a surgeon and, therefore, medical school was out of the question. At the same time, though. Jacob and John did not want some college-educated chemist telling them how to run their industrial soap factory, so joining Roxbury Chemical Works was also not a career option. Instead, Jacob steered Geoffrey to another corner of the textile manufacturing business. This led to a lifetime of professional unhappiness. To make matters worse, John and Jacob brought cousin Joseph into the business, a slap in Geoffrey's face, which led to a terrible falling out between them.

At a personal level, though, Geoffrey found happiness when he met Ruth Gordon and married her on March 31, 1925.

2. THE GORDON FAMILY

In the 1860s, the Gordon family lived in the villages of Soly and Smorgon in what is now Belarus.[76] However, they were close enough to Vilnius, the capital of present-day Lithuania, that later generations of Gordons claimed it as their ancestral home, perhaps because the Baltic states are more Germanic than Slavic Belarus— this counted for something among caste-conscious American Jewry. For most of the 1800s, this region was part of the Russian Empire, and Vilnius itself was home to a large Jewish community. Napoleon is said to have called it "the Jerusalem of the north" either on his way to or from Moscow in 1812.[77] Its Jewish population flourished throughout the nineteenth century, and by 1897 it comprised 40 percent of the city's inhabitants.[78]

Abel Gordon, Ruth's grandfather, was a "medical practitioner" of some sort; he and his wife Rosa had seven children, all of whom emigrated as the Russian Empire's tolerance for Jews eroded (Figure 4). Jacob, Ruth's father, came to Rochester, New York, in 1887[79] along with his brother Yale, known as Hyman. Like the Barnets of Albany (David Nathan's paternal grandmother's family), Jacob and Hyman Gordon were tanners and built a business in hides and leathers, making additional money by selling the meat by-products of their tanning works to local butchers.[80] Their enterprise, located at 128 Front Street, was soon incorporated as Jacob Gordon Sons.[81]

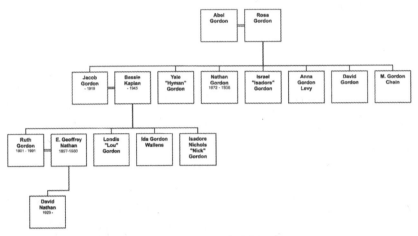

Figure 4: The Family of Abel Gordon

Jacob's brother Nathan had come to America earlier, in 1872. Alighting first in Connecticut, he promptly moved west, where he ran a variety of businesses in various locations, including a penny arcade in Denver, Colorado. In 1903, he and his brother Israel (known as Isadore) returned east to Worcester, Massachusetts, and set up a slot-machine picture business that evolved, in 1906, into the city's first nickelodeon. The business was wildly successful and Nathan Gordon expanded his holdings to become the largest operator of motion picture and vaudeville theaters in the northeast. In 1917, he partnered with another Russian immigrant, Louis B. Mayer, who had had landed in Massachusetts. Their Gordon-Mayer Theatrical Company distributed films from the Metro Pictures Corporation. Although Gordon's distribution company was successful, he and Mayer were feeling pressure from the distribution arm of Adolph Zukor's Paramount Pictures. In response, Gordon and Mayer formed First National Exhibitors Circuit, a group of independent theater owners whose numbers could counter the influence of Paramount.[82] In 1924, this entity became First National Pictures, which produced some of the most popular movies of the day until its acquisition by Warner Brothers in 1928.

As a major stockholder of First National, Nathan Gordon realized an impressive financial windfall.

Nathan Gordon also did very well on the theater side of his business. In 1908, he and Isadore convinced their brothers Jacob and Hyman to help them build a large theater in Rochester called the Gordon Olympia Theater[83] which would add to the vaudeville theaters they already operated—two in Worcester, one in Lowell, Massachusetts, one in Boston, and one in New Haven, Connecticut.[84] Permits and capital were slow in coming, but the theater, built exclusively with union labor as per the Gordons' orders, finally opened in 1912. It was so successful that, within a year, the Gordons created the Gordon Photoplay Company to incorporate the Olympia and other theaters.[85, 86] Ironically, Nathan sold his interest in the company to Paramount in 1925. This transaction plus the later sale of First National to Warner Brothers made Nathan Gordon a very wealthy man, whose philanthropic touch is still felt around Boston.

Meanwhile, as Jacob Gordon was building his leather business and dabbling in his brother's theatrical partnerships, he and his wife Bessie had four children: two sons, Londis (known as Lou) and Isadore Nicholas (known as Nick), and two daughters, Ida and Ruth (Figure 4). Like his famous uncle, Lou Gordon also went into the theater business. He partnered with Arthur Lockwood to create the Lockwood-Gordon Circuit, which owned and managed movie theaters in the northeast. Lou and Arthur will reappear later as two of the original supporters of Sidney Farber's Children's Cancer Research Foundation.[87]

Sadly, Jacob died a relatively young man in 1919. While he left Bessie a substantial estate of some $1.8 million in 2023 dollars,[88] he also left her alone with four children, so she moved her family to Brookline, Massachusetts, to a home on Dwight Street, to be near Nathan Gordon. Bessie's daughter, Ruth, had graduated from Rochester's East High School in the class of January 1919, several months before her father's death. Ironically, her yearbook picture

had been captioned, "Graceful lines and a marvelous complexion—
of course we mean her dad's car"[89] (Figure 5). In Boston, Ruth
Gordon matriculated at Simmons College, graduating in 1923
with a degree in social work. She began what was to be a life dedicated to social welfare by working at the Hecht Neighborhood
House, a vocational, educational, and service facility for immigrant
Jewish families located on Bowdoin Street in Boston's old West
End.[90] This was the Ruth Gordon who married Geoffrey Nathan
in her uncle Nathan's house on March 31, 1925.[91]

Figure 5. Ruth Gordon's High School Yearbook Picture.

Given their backgrounds, the union of the Nathan and Gordon
families seemed inevitable. While the class awareness of Germanic
versus Slavic Jews may have stoked some subtle differences, both
families shared a Mitteleuropa sensibility, including a deep-seated
dedication to philanthropy and social welfare. Although much
of their effort was focused on Jewish charities, their motivation
appears not to have been driven by religious feeling and, in fact,

their attitude toward religion was complicated. John and Jacob were observant Orthodox Jews and, by the time of his death, John had been president of his temple, Ohabei Shalom, for thirty-six years. David Nathan remembers watching Jacob pray in the morning adorned with yarmulke, prayer shawl, and phylacteries. But when he was done, he would turn to his grandson and say, "Now I will get dressed like an American and go to work." John and Jacob also had an aversion to people who they called "professional Jews"—those who wore their religion on their sleeves and engaged in special pleading with other Jews about their obligations to support coreligionists.

Unfortunately, events on the international stage compelled the brothers to embrace some of these obligations. In the mid-1930s, before Hitler's Anschluss made Austria part of the German Reich, a letter was sent from Vienna addressed only to "Emanuel Nathan, an der seifefabrik [at the soap factory], Boston, USA." Remarkably, the letter found its way to the Roxbury Chemical Works. Written by Charlie Winter, who claimed to be a distant relative of Emanuel,[92] the letter included twenty photographs of Winter family members along with an exhortation to sponsor their immigration to the U.S. During the period of 1933 through 1941, American immigration law required would-be immigrants from Austria and other middle-European countries to be sponsored by two individuals who were U.S. citizens or permanent residents, preferably close relatives. The sponsors had to provide six notarized copies of an Affidavit of Support and Sponsorship.[93] Through the efforts of Geoffrey Nathan and his friends, the necessary sponsorships were obtained and a visa was granted to Charlie's sister, Marianne, who traveled through England on her way to Boston. Marianne lived with the Nathans while she attended high school and, later, Hunter College. She went on to receive an MA and PhD from Bryn Mawr, and was professor and chair of the Department of Fine Arts at Boston College at the time of her death in 1989.[94]

Marianne's cousin Richard, a violinist, also made his way to the Nathan home, but he came the other way around the world—through Shanghai and Australia. David Nathan tells the story of Richard's first dinner with the Nathan family: When the meal was finished, Richard announced in his thick Austrian accent that it had been the duty of the Nathan family to save Austrian Jews because, after all, "We gave you Kultur."

In response, David's grandfather ground his cigar in the ashtray and said, "I'm going to bed." On his way upstairs, he was heard to mutter, "God damn their souls. They're all Nazis, every goddamned one of them."[95]

Like the Nathans, the Gordons were publicly nonobservant and fully secularized. Nathan Gordon's son, William, once said, "It came as a complete surprise to me that I was Jewish. My father and [Louis B.] Mayer could avoid temple together, if you know what I mean."[96] His statement was emblematic of the deracinated facade that both families worked so hard to show the public. Despite their posturing, however, abundant evidence shows that they willingly provided money and other support for Jewish causes beyond the kind of personal support that the Nathans offered to the Winter family: from contributing to the American Jewish Committee[97] to sponsoring benefits for the Palestine Orchestra Fund[98] to placing ads in the local paper offering to host Jewish soldiers on leave from the Great War who would like to celebrate Passover in an Orthodox home.[99]

The urge to help anyone in need ran very deep in both families, so much so that Jewish causes were, in a sense, merely vehicles for fulfilling a compulsion to give. For example, Emanuel Nathan's support of the Irish immigrant families whose fathers worked at the Roxbury Chemical Works had nothing to do with Jewish causes. Another notable example comes from an 1894 newspaper notice announcing the large, combined wedding of two young women who had been orphaned and were "wards" of Emanuel and his wife. Emanuel hosted the wedding and gave away both brides to their fiancées, who happened to be brothers.[100] These efforts, as well as those in support of Jewish philanthropies, arose from the families' attitude that the people who crossed their path, whether they were employees or Jewish immigrants or orphaned children, were part of the extended family. And, of course, one always helps one's family.

Chapter 3

A MODEL ACADEMIC CITIZEN

Ruth and Geoffrey Nathan's first child, a girl named Barbara, was born in 1926; David followed in 1929 (Figure 6). Ruth's commitment to social causes and the liberal outlook of both parents influenced planning for their children's education. Thus, David's academic career began at the Frances Stern Nursery School in Brookline, Massachusetts, described in its advertisements as "An all-day progressive school for children from two to six years."[101] One of his schoolmates was a distant relative named Richard Jackson Barnet, who became David's best childhood friend. Years later, Barnet cofounded a liberal think tank called the Institute for Policy Studies, which was sufficiently Left-leaning for the Heritage Foundation to call it an "avowedly radical organization."[102] This only further endeared Barnet to the Nathans. The sole surviving documentary evidence of Nathan's time in nursery school is a report card that reads, "David is a large child who uses his weight to his own advantage," an echo of his uncle Emanuel's fame as a member of the heaviest freshman crew in the history of Harvard College.

Nathan's elementary school education continued at the Runkle School, also in Brookline, which taught children from kindergarten through eighth grade. An architecturally striking six-room brick schoolhouse in the upscale Fisher Hill neighborhood, it was built in 1897 and named for John D. Runkle, the second president of MIT. It was demolished in 1963 to make way for a nondescript building characteristic of mid-twentieth century American public schools.

Figure 6. David Nathan, his father, and grandfather. (Courtesy of David G. Nathan.)

Nathan describes his time at the Runkle School in glowing terms. He recalls an environment filled with supportive women who encouraged him and made him feel responsible for his conduct and his schoolwork. An indicator of his happiness is the fact that, eight decades later, Nathan could remember the names of every one of his teachers[103] and even spoke warmly of the principal, Edith E. Wright.[104] After three years, however, David was uprooted when Geoffrey and Ruth moved their family, including David's grandfather, to a larger home on Hobart Road in Newton, Massachusetts, an affluent Boston suburb. While the move reflected upward social mobility, it also meant that David had to leave his beloved Runkle and enroll at the John Ward School, a public elementary school in Newton. But the setback would only be temporary. When his father heard that David's third-grade teacher at this so-called "progressive" school had instructed him to make a linoleum mat to sleep on during school, he was furious, proclaiming that a school room is not a bedroom. Geoffrey arranged for David's re-enrollment in the third grade class at Runkle. Jacob Nathan's chauffeur, presumably the same John "Dinty" Hayes who was introduced in Chapter 2, drove David back and forth between his new home in Newton and his old school in Brookline.

Two anecdotes help to illustrate Nathan's happiness at Runkle.[105] First, in the fourth grade his teacher chose him, along with his friend Richard Barnet, who had also transitioned to Runkle, to act in the tea party scene from *Alice in Wonderland*. Nathan was the March Hare and Richard was the Mad Hatter. Nathan recalls that they were so accomplished that a local radio station broadcast the performance. The second story involves the Good Citizenship Prize, which was awarded every year to one student in each class, the winner determined by a vote of the students. The same very good little girl had triumphed every year from kindergarten through fifth grade. This was to change in the sixth grade. She initially led the voting that year, too, but the teacher, Miss Taylor, made the undemocratic decision that the perennial favorite had won the prize too many times and therefore the award this year would go to the child who came second. When the ballots were tallied, twenty-two out of twenty-four had been cast for the usual winner. The two unaligned votes were from Nathan, who had voted for himself, and his friend Richard, who had also voted for Nathan. Thus, by means of a rigged election, did David Nathan win the Good Citizenship Prize from the Runkle School, which he proudly displays in his office.

The halcyon days of the Runkle School ended when Nathan graduated. For seventh grade, he was enrolled in the John Wingate Weeks Junior High School, a hulking public school in Newton built in 1930. Nathan was miserable there. He could not tolerate his classmates who, he thought, were not terribly intelligent. Many of them were unabashedly anti-Semitic and Nathan was getting into playground fights. To what extent his misery was the result of entering a new school environment as opposed to the objection-able nature of his classmates is unclear. What was clear, however, was his unhappiness.

The saving grace of the Weeks Junior High was Nathan's home-room teacher, who recognized his talent and urged his parents to send him to Roxbury Latin School where, despite having to repeat his current grade, he would undoubtedly thrive. Nathan enrolled in the seventh-grade class at Roxbury Latin at age fourteen.

THE LATINS: ROXBURY AND BOSTON

The Roxbury Latin School has played a prominent role in the academic and social history of Boston. Incorporated as "The Grammar School in the Easterly Part of the Town of Roxbury" in 1645 by John Eliot, minister of the First Church of Roxbury, and sixty-six of the town's richest landholders,[106] it was only the third educational institu-tion to be established in the colonies. The first two were Boston Latin School (1635) and Harvard College (1636). Roxbury Latin's boosters insist that it is the oldest school in continuous existence in America, blessed with the old-est charter.[107] Renowned for its rigor and requirement for aptitude in the classics, the school was established because, "in consideration of their religious care of posterity, [the founders] have taken into consideration how necessary the education of their children in literature will be, to fit them for public service in both church and commonwealth in succeeding ages."[108] The school's explicit goal was to pro-duce Christian citizens by providing "an education in Latin literature, training in moral character, and lessons in reli-gious or spiritual understanding."[109]

Notable alumni of Roxbury Latin include Joseph Warren, a Revolutionary War surgeon who died at the Battle of Bunker Hill, and his brother John Warren, also a surgeon and founder of Harvard Medical School; Frederick Law Olmstead, the designer of New York's Central Park and Boston's Emerald Necklace; Increase Sumner, three-time governor of Massachusetts in the late 1700s; James B. Conant, president of Harvard University (1933–1953); and Paul Dudley White, Dwight D. Eisenhower's cardiologist.

Renowned alumni notwithstanding, understanding why Nathan's otherwise progressive parents would consider sending him to the reactionary Roxbury Latin School requires an appreciation for its position in the academic ecosystem of early twentieth century Boston. It is especially helpful to compare Roxbury Latin, which was private, to Boston Latin, which was public. As at Harvard, a central question facing both schools was how to deal with the growing number of Jewish applicants.

For Roxbury Latin, the answer was simple: don't admit them. The school cleaved to its exclusionary policy well into the 1920s despite the demographic pressure exerted by the children of Eastern European Jews who, after immigrating to Boston in the 1890s and early 1900s, had become economically successful. Fortunately, these families had an alternative in Boston Latin. Not only did it lack an overtly anti-Semitic admission policy, but it was the one public school in Boston that efficiently fed its talented students to Harvard. This proved so irresistible to ambitious Jewish families that by the 1920s, the majority of students in Boston Latin were Jewish. As a result, the sociology of the two schools was strikingly different: Roxbury Latin served old Boston's refined gentility (in all senses of the word) while Boston Latin was home to the pushy Jewish newcomers.

The contrast is portrayed firsthand in a memoir by Francis Russell, a poet and historian who attended both schools in the 1920s.[110] Although Russell was of a generation just prior to Nathan's, his experiences and insights are relevant to the way Nathan's parents may have thought about the schools and, therefore, to their decision about where to send their son. This excerpt captures the Roxbury Latin sensibility:

> The boys [at Roxbury Latin] lived in a state of war with the masters but it was a genteel eighteenth-century type of warfare with its etiquette and truces and established rules for both sides. The members of each class formed a united front against their particular master. They pooled the results of their homework, they covered for each other. If anyone was unprepared it was the duty of the rest to help him out, to draw the master off the track of a difficult translation, to spar against time by asking long pointless questions. Some of us of course did better than the others, and for the cleverest there were prizes at the end of the year, but it was considered bad form to work hard at one's lessons, and even those who did kept the fact modestly concealed. The Roxbury Latin School did not admit Jews....[111]

Russell evokes the sense of entitlement that permeated all aspects of life at Roxbury Latin, including college planning:

> My own background was middle-class, Protestant, noncompetitive, like that of most Roxbury Latin boys. I had always taken it for granted that I should go to Harvard because my father in his time had

gone there; and I never doubted the possibility of this any more than I stopped to consider whether I really wanted to or not. That Harvard could be the goal of anyone's ambition never occurred to me.[112]

But Russell's family fell on hard times and his parents' straitened circumstances forced him from Roxbury Latin to Boston Latin. Russell writes, "Taken from my friends at Roxbury, suddenly thrust into a crowd of pushing little Jews, I was aware only of their unpleasantness, knowing nothing of the relentless grinding processes that had made them so different from the boys I had known."[113] Russell's misery is nearly palpable:

> To be imprisoned in the brick intellectual sweat-shop of Boston Latin gave me the feeling of being abandoned. At first I was appalled by the Jews... they were determined to get ahead. They worked far into each night, their lessons next morning were letter perfect, they took obvious pride in their academic success and talked about it. At the end of each year there were...prizes given for excellency in each subject, and they were openly after them.[114] There was none of the Roxbury solidarity of pupils versus the master. If anyone reciting made a mistake that the master overlooked, twenty hands shot into the air to bring it to his attention. They competed one against the other, and no one ever helped anyone as at Roxbury where we used to sit around the furnace in the basement each morning before school and construe Virgil. It was a fierce and grueling competition. To stay in it at all one had to work at least four hours each evening. Some of us

> in the Gentile rump were fair students, most of us lazy and mediocre ones, and by our very position at the foot of the class we despised the industry of those little Jews.[115]
>
> Other parts of Russell's essay recount the suffering of Jews through history and the multitude of opportunities that had been denied to them. Still, Russell has a hard time disguising his unhappiness about the advent of meritocracy and his lamentation for the passing of noblesse oblige. To contemporary eyes, his essay drips with faux sympathy in which nasty straw-man insults ("pushing little Jews") seem less an ironic and self-deprecating stance than an inadvertent display of his prejudices. Nonetheless, Russell the historian is adept at limning the contrast between the aristocratic Roxbury Latin and the hopelessly bourgeois Boston Latin.

For the Nathans, whose entire complement of second-generation native-born sons had attended Boston Latin and then went on to Harvard, true assimilation could no longer be realized simply by having the third generation go to Boston Latin, too. Harvard would always be the ultimate goal, of course, but now, the true measure of "arrival" would be enrollment at other bastions of WASP privilege like Roxbury Latin or, at a stretch, Andover. And so, despite having to repeat seventh grade, David Nathan entered Roxbury Latin's class of 1948 at fourteen.

His parents' choice complicated their son's life: it took him ninety minutes to travel back and forth from his Newton home to Roxbury Latin by public transportation every day. Undaunted by the cumbersome commute, Nathan loved the school. He reveled in its high academic standards and thought that the sports program was first-rate. He took pride in the strict requirement of six years of Latin and three years of Greek, for which absolutely no exception would be made. He also admired the headmaster, George Norton Northrop, a patrician art collector who had formerly been headmaster of the Brearley School in Manhattan.[116]

Unfortunately, family circumstances truncated Nathan's stay at Roxbury Latin after three years. His father, Geoffrey, had struggled to find professional focus after being excluded from the Roxbury Chemical Works by his own father and uncle. He puttered in various corners of the textile business but never found his métier. Although Geoffrey was an entertaining and endlessly amusing man—his son called him "uproarious"—he also experienced bouts of melancholy, which became much worse after his father's unexpected death. Eventually, it became clear that Geoffrey had a form of bipolar disorder that, despite occasional remissions induced by electroconvulsive therapy, became disabling. This outcome was particularly sad for his son. David thought that the only person in the world who could be as hilarious as his father was his grandfather, and when the two of them were living in the same house, the dinner hour was the greatest fun imaginable. His grandfather's death followed by the loss of his father to severe depression cast a terrible pall over Nathan's life at home.

During this difficult time, Nathan's source of support was his mother. Ruth Nathan had attended Simmons College, where she trained as a social worker. After graduation, she worked at the Hecht Neighborhood House, one of Boston's contributions to the settlement house movement, and then, during World War II, became vice chair of home services of the American Red Cross. After the war, she was director of the women's division of the United Jewish Appeal and, in that role, led fundraising drives for displaced Jews in Europe—she was quoted in the *Boston Globe* as saying, "We have no right to enjoy luxury while over a million of our fellow beings starve."[117] Later, Ruth continued her service activities as director of homemaker personnel for Family Service of Greater Boston and as a director of the Boston Lying-In Hospital. Ruth's combination of deep compassion and active leadership must have inspired Nathan, because he based his own life and career on these principles.

At home, Ruth was sensitive to the mixed feelings that Geoffrey's disability might elicit in her son. On one hand, she was deliberate in her efforts to preserve David's respect for his father. Her letters to him refer to Geoffrey Nathan's strong moral core—something he preserved even at his lowest ebb—and proudly aver that David had modeled his own strong moral character on his father's. On the other hand, she was concerned about the toll that living at home with an infirm father would take on David. She decided that it would be best if he were to complete his secondary education at a boarding school, where he could thrive without being subjected to daily reminders of his father's incapacity. To that end, Ruth made David spend the summer of 1945 taking English and mathematics courses so that he could skip tenth grade and use his advanced standing to apply to the eleventh grade, class of 1947, at Phillips Academy Andover. Although Nathan did as he was told and was accepted at Andover, he had no interest in leaving Roxbury Latin and begged his mother to let him stay. She adamantly refused, believing that her son needed to be spared the agony of watching his father's decline at close quarters.

The Nathan family now had a matriculant at Andover, arguably the American prep school that all other prep schools are measured against. Andover is another New England institution steeped in history. Established by Samuel Phillips in 1778, it claims to be the oldest incorporated boarding school in the U.S.[118] Three years after Andover's founding, Samuel Phillips's uncle John established Phillips Academy Exeter, which is independent of Andover. The Phillipses, uncle and nephew, descended directly from the Reverend George Phillips, who had sailed into Salem Harbor with John Winthrop and his Puritans on the *Arbella* in 1630.[119] Old New England does not get much older than that, and Andover's authenticity must have appealed to Ruth and Geoffrey Nathan. It would also not have escaped their notice that Oliver Wendell

Holmes—poet, physician, dean of Harvard Medical School—was an Andover graduate.

Although Nathan did become an Andover student, the barriers to his enrollment should not be underestimated. As late as the mid-1930s, Headmaster Claude M. (Jack) Fuess wrote to one of his colleagues that, "It is just too bad about the little Jewish boy, but I can't very well blame [Andover's dean of admissions] for trying to keep our school as predominantly Aryan as possible. If we once start to open our doors freely to members of that race, we shall be overwhelmed by applications."[120] The few Jewish students who did find themselves at Andover were often confronted by such overtly anti-Semitic behavior as being given the silent treatment by the other students in their dormitories. Despite residual pockets of prejudice, however, the attitude at Andover was changing in the 1940s, just as it had started to change at Harvard.

Nathan was not happy at Andover—he desperately wanted to go home and reenroll at Roxbury Latin. So he decided to misbehave, thinking that if he broke as many rules as he could, the school administration would be forced to have a sad but necessary talk with his mother about separation from Andover. Instead, a legendary assistant dean named James Ruthven Adriance, known as "Spike," saw what Nathan was up to. Spike Adriance was a Mr. Chips–like figure: a 1928 graduate of Andover and class president, he became assistant dean in 1934, went on to be director of admissions, where he had a salutary effect on the quota system, and continued to serve at the school until his retirement in 1971.[121, 122] Instead of sending the miscreant home, Adriance told Nathan to cut out the nonsense and get down to work. Nathan was impressed that someone in authority actually cared about him and it turned his attitude around. He became happier and, with time, found acceptance among the other students. Nathan's eventual integration into Andover life was so complete that by his senior year, his classmates saw him as a school leader.

When it came time for Nathan to plan for college, he found himself embedded in Andover's musty and anachronistic traditions. Until the 1930s, nearly all Andover boys went to the college of their choice, so no one on the staff worried much about college admissions.[123] Most students went to Yale—nearly 10 percent of the freshman class at Yale had come from Andover in 1936—followed by Harvard and Princeton, and then, in a different order each year, Dartmouth, MIT, Brown, and Amherst. But, in 1943, a new dean of students arrived with a fresh viewpoint. He was G. Grenville Benedict, known as GG or G-squared to students and Gren to faculty. His arrival coincided with a fundamental shift in the way Andover and other prep schools dealt with college admissions. Several factors compelled this change, the most important of which was the return to civilian life of World War II veterans. By the mid-1940s, as the number of college applicants swelled thanks to the GI Bill, the "Edwardian era" of college admissions, as Benedict called it, came to an end at Andover. Additional pressures came from colleges like Amherst, which had formerly been liberal about admitting Andover students but now wanted to limit the number of prep school students in its classes. In response, Benedict found ways both to maximize the number of Andover boys who got into at least one of their top college choices and to increase the likelihood that they would be happy when they got there. He accomplished this by taking a rational approach to college counseling and by broadening the spectrum of colleges that a student might consider. Of course, Andover continued to be a feeder to Ivy League schools. Oddly, and for unknown reasons, one of the effects of Benedict's policies was to reverse the order of colleges that accepted the most Andover students: by 1950, more students went to Harvard than to Yale.[124]

How did Andover's new philosophy of college placement affect Nathan? At this point in his young life, Nathan saw himself as a literary man and he was determined to fulfill his destiny by going to Amherst. But Benedict, taking a hard look at Nathan, quashed that idea and told him he would be going to Harvard. Nathan always suspected that this advice had something to do with Benedict's own loyalty to Harvard—G-squared prominently displayed a fob on his watch chain from the Owl Club, one of Harvard's dismayingly exclusive final clubs—but the historical context suggests that this was really a matter of steering Nathan to the school that would be more likely to accept him. David Nathan applied to Harvard and was accepted as a member of the class of 1951.

Before following Nathan to college, it is necessary to consider another profound influence on his development: the island of Nantucket. From the time Nathan was ten, his father would send him, his sister, and his mother there in the summers. Geoffrey spent his weekdays working in Boston but would join the family whenever he could.

It was on Nantucket that Nathan began his love affair with boats, starting with a wooden kayak that he would paddle just beyond the breakers. When David was fourteen years old, his father shelled out fifty dollars to buy a little sailboat that, as they soon discovered, leaked like a sieve around the centerboard. David and his father took it for repairs to a dockside boatyard run by Ernie King, who looked at the pathetic thing and told the Nathans that it was beyond repair. David was crestfallen. King took pity on the boy and hired him for the summer as a sort of dogsbody at a rate of fifty cents an hour. King was being big-hearted but he also needed the help since this was 1943 and most of the able-bodied men he would ordinarily hire were in the service. Nathan did a bit of everything: he cleaned boat bottoms, caulked open seams, and whatever else King asked of him. He got to the boatyard when it opened every morning and never left before closing time. Nathan admits that he worshipped King. He thought King was infinitely competent, quiet, honest, and kind. The next summer, King had him launch a Beetle Cat, a twelve-foot gaff-rigged wooden sailboat designed and built by the Beetle family of New Bedford,

Massachusetts. These boats now have tremendous cachet among wooden boat enthusiasts. Thus began Nathan's lifelong romance with sailing (Figure 7)

Figure 7. David Nathan sailing off Nantucket in 1946. (Courtesy of David G. Nathan.)

The other romance that began on Nantucket was with Jean Louise Friedman. Jean was the daughter of another striving Jewish family that had left Europe in the mid-nineteenth century. Her maternal great-grandfather, Louis Israel Aaron, was born in Mosina, Poland, in 1840. At age seventeen, Louis emigrated to the U.S., where he lived for a time in New York City and Atlanta,

Georgia, before ending up in Pittsburgh.[125] There, he founded Louis I. Aaron & Co. Malt House, a manufacturer of malt for the breweries of western Pennsylvania. The factory was located just behind the Eberhardt & Ober Brewery, which eventually became part of the Pittsburgh Brewing Company, brewers of Iron City Beer.[126]

In 1897, Aaron provided financial backing for the purchase of the Homer Laughlin China Company and became its co-owner with William Edward Wells, the company's bookkeeper. Homer Laughlin China, makers of Fiestaware, had been founded in 1871 by Shakespeare Laughlin and his brother Homer in East Liverpool, Ohio, on the banks of the Ohio River. Shakespeare soon sold out to Homer and then, when Homer decided to retire to California in 1897, he sold the concern to Aaron and Wells.[127] The company expanded so rapidly under its new owners that it outgrew its site in East Liverpool. To accommodate more kilns and worker housing, Aaron and Wells bought land on the other side of the river and founded a new town they called Newell, West Virginia. Newell became home to what was, at the time, the largest pottery plant in the world, and Homer Laughlin China began putting oatmeal bowls in every package of Mother's Oats.[128]

Louis Aaron and his wife Mina[129] had a son, Marcus Aaron (Figure 8), who eventually succeeded his father as president of Homer Laughlin China. Marcus received a law degree from the University of Pittsburgh and was one of the first members of Pittsburgh's board of education, serving from 1911 to 1947. He also played a key role in promoting legislation that established teachers' pay schedules. In a familiar theme, Marcus and his son, Marcus Lester, repeatedly petitioned immigration officials to allow their cousins, Magnus Neumann, his wife Dorothea, and daughter Else to emigrate from Germany to the U.S. Their petitions were successful in 1941.[130]

Marcus Lester Aaron received his law degree from Harvard and served as the next president of Homer Laughlin China. His wife, Maxine,[131] continued the Aaron family's interest in education by becoming the first female president of the Pittsburgh board of education.[132] Their son, Marcus Aaron II, known as "Pete," became the fourth generation of Aarons to lead Homer Laughlin China, and the last when he sold his interest to the Wells family.[133]

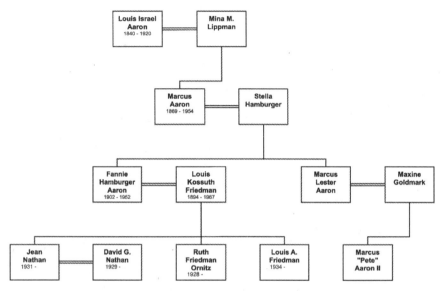

Figure 8: The Family of Louis I. Aaron

Marcus Aaron and his wife Stella[134] also had a daughter, Fannie Hamburger Aaron, who attended Vassar College from 1919 to 1923[135] and, for a time, taught English at University of Pittsburgh. Fannie married Louis Kossuth Friedman, whose mother Nina Loth Friedman had left Hungary for the U.S. at age ten.[136] Louis Friedman was brought into the family business and served as vice president and director of Homer Laughlin China. During the summers, Fannie and Louis would bring their three children, Louis A., Ruth, and Jean Louise, to Nantucket and there, on the island's beaches, is where David Nathan met his future wife (Figure 9). David became devoted to Jean and, after a few years, their attachment would continue even after the summer was over and the families had returned to their homes. During holiday breaks when they were in high school, Jean would invite David to dances in Pittsburgh, which he was thrilled to attend even though it meant miserable rides in freezing sit-up coaches on Boston-to-Pittsburgh night trains.[137] By the time he entered Harvard, Nathan thought that Jean Friedman was the only girl for him (Figure 10).

Figure 9. Fannie Friedman (left) and Ruth Nathan (right) sailing off Nantucket in 1946. (Courtesy of David G. Nathan.)

Figure 10. David Nathan (center) in Pittsburgh during Christmas break from Andover in 1947 flanked by Ruth Friedman (left) and Jean Friedman (right). (Courtesy of David G. Nathan.)

When Nathan matriculated at Harvard in the fall of 1947, the flood of returning World War II veterans had created a housing shortage so severe that the university could only provide on-campus accommodations for incoming freshmen who lived more than thirty miles from Cambridge. Some students met this challenge in inventive ways. One classmate from Nahant anchored his family's twenty-two-foot cabin cruiser in the Charles River near the university and rowed to shore each morning to attend class. Nathan was less enterprising and spent the fall semester of his freshman year living in his parents' home in Newton, which was only four miles from Cambridge. Of course, this undermined his mother's plan to keep Nathan out of the house during his father's illness, which continued its sad progression.

When spring of his freshman year arrived, Nathan was allowed to move into Harvard housing. Overpopulation still kept him from the traditional freshman experience of living in Harvard Yard, but there was room for him in Claverly Hall, a magnificent dormitory when it was built in 1892 along the stretch of Mount Auburn Street known as the Gold Coast because of its lineup of luxury apartments housing wealthy undergraduates.[138] By 1947, however, the building was run-down and far enough from the action on the main campus that Claverly was referred to as a "Mount Auburn Street Siberia."[139] As a Claverly exile, Nathan had a hard time meeting other students and making friends, although he did join the freshman crew in the tradition of his uncle.

Nathan also went out for football in his freshman year. During one scrimmage, he found himself lined up opposite Emil Drvaric, a 5'11", 195 pound, All-Ivy guard who had played at the Great Lakes Training School and was on the Navy All-Star team before transferring to Harvard.[140, 141, 142] The Nathan boys may have seemed large compared to most of their peers but they were no match for a real lineman. Seeing that Nathan was terrified, Drvaric told him, "Just step aside when the ball is snapped so you don't get hurt."[143] Nathan did as he was told and survived the encounter. Drvaric later applied to Harvard Medical School where, as the legend goes, an admissions officer asked Drvaric what he would do if he were not admitted. Drvaric replied, "I'd just beat the goddamned door down." This proved to be unnecessary since he was admitted to the school, graduated, and went on to practice obstetrics and gynecology for over thirty years in Milwaukee.

After finishing his freshman year, Nathan embarked on an unusual summer vacation. As an adolescent during World War II, he had been inspired by the Allies' Great Crusade against European fascism and Japanese imperialism. When he was a twelve-year-old Boy Scout in 1941, Nathan participated in air raid drills, riding his bicycle up and down the streets of Newton, warning the complacent citizenry to close their windows and have buckets of sand and water ready to protect their homes from Nazi incendiary bombs. While making his rounds on Sunday, December 7, Nathan remembers being scolded by a woman who shouted to him from her front door, "Go home, young man. We are at war."[144] Nathan did go home and, for the next four years, followed the war news with mounting pride and patriotism, an experience that evolved into an abiding desire to serve his country. And so, during the summer of 1948, at the dawn of the Cold War, Nathan joined the Platoon Leaders Class of the United States Marine Corps.

Platoon Leaders Class (PLC) was a feeder system designed to recruit young men with leadership potential from colleges and universities into the USMC officer class. Students spent six weeks at the Marine base at Quantico undergoing an abridged version of basic training. The full PLC course involved two summers: in their first, recruits were given the temporary rank of corporal and paid ninety dollars a month; those who completed both were commissioned as second lieutenants in the Marine Corps Reserve when they graduated from college. As reservists, they could join the regular corps, but only after they had gone through authentic basic training. When Nathan decided to go to medical school, however, he was discharged from the USMC Reserves because there were no doctors in the Corps, all of their medical needs being fulfilled by Navy personnel. Interestingly, Nathan's PLC experience echoed that of his academic hero, William Bosworth Castle (discussed in Chapter 4), who spent part of the summer after his junior year in 1917 at Officers' Training Camp in Plattsburgh, NY.[145]

A description of the PLC written in 1948, the year Nathan attended, provides a taste of what he experienced. The first week was "indoctrination," learning the duties of a battalion commander. The second and third weeks were spent on the rifle range, and the last three involved training in so-called "combat areas"

> ...where the future officers really began to broaden their knowledge and apply what they had learned. From early morning to late evening they moved from classroom lecture to field demonstration. This often meant covering five to ten mile distances from camp to impact range. They learned about machine

guns, mortars and flame throwers; the heavy armor and striking power of tanks, and the devastating destruction of artillery.[146]

The second-year group capped their experience with an amphibious landing on a Potomac River beach under simulated artillery fire.

In addition to overseeing these regular activities, the commandants were also dealing with logistical problems. In 1947, 433 students attended PLC; by 1948 that number had exploded to 1,540 young men from 220 different colleges and universities.[147] Some 40 percent of the 1948 group were World War II veterans, including Purple Heart recipients, whose presence lent credibility to the summer's activities for the younger students like Nathan. Still, the large number of participants who had to be accommodated during a short period of time led to problems, and this contemporaneous account describes the attitudes of regular USMC officers:

> Naturally with this large turnout, difficulties arose in the beginning of the course. Training methods had to be coordinated, minor revisions made in schedules and some misfits eliminated.

> ...This year's course was made more difficult than the last one in order to cover the entire schedule in the short time allotted to each subject. A few students who found it too tough went home, but no one missed them.[148]

The end of the course featured a graduation ceremony reviewed by a major general.[149]

PLC was an eye-opening experience for Nathan, who had led a sheltered life in the privileged environs of Brookline, Newton, Andover, Cambridge, and Nantucket (Figure 11). Quantico showed him that not everyone in United States was as broadminded or tolerant as the people who had surrounded him for the first years of his life. At one point during the summer, he hitchhiked to Washington, DC, on a weekend pass and was given a ride by the company commander. After a period of stilted small talk, the commander asked Nathan what he would do "if a nigger moved into your neighborhood." Thoroughly caught off guard, all Nathan could think to say was that he was uncertain. In response, the commander said Nathan should break the interloper's nose and helpfully showed him how he would do it with a belt buckle.[150] This exchange erased the romance of military service.

Figure 11. David Nathan in uniform at Platoon Leader at Platoon Leaders Class in 1949. (Courtesy of David G. Nathan.)

When Nathan returned to Harvard for his sophomore year, he lived in Winthrop House, the Kennedy brothers' dormitory. Winthrop had been formed by amalgamating two freshman dormitories, Standish Hall and Gore Hall. Standish was notable because it was one of the few freshman dorms that housed Jews, a tradition that continued after it was incorporated into Winthrop.[151] Now that Nathan was more fully integrated into undergraduate life, he could make friends and think about what he would study. He had entered Harvard imagining that he would become an English professor, so he majored in English literature. Characteristically, once he made that decision, Nathan threw himself into what he thought the life of an English major should be, including its obligatory accoutrements: tweed jacket with leather elbow patches, bow tie, and pipe.

In time, however, Nathan became disenchanted with his studies and unsure of his talent. Tellingly, he had started an honors thesis project on the late nineteenth century debate between the poet, Matthew Arnold, and the biologist, Thomas Huxley, on whether college curricula, which had traditionally focused on classical literature, should be expanded to include the natural sciences. Nathan had initially sympathized with Arnold's position advocating the primacy of the arts but, as his thesis neared completion, he began to see Arnold as an anachronism, hopelessly resistant to the idea that scientific literacy could play an important role in the life of a modern, educated person. Nathan took his concerns to his tutor, John Vincent Kelleher,[152] a scholar of Irish literature known for his wit, probity, and stammer. Kelleher was unable to hide his lack of enthusiasm for the subject of Nathan's thesis. Nevertheless, he agreed to a first meeting and then a second a week later. In the intervening seven days, Nathan's impatience with Arnold's narrow world view had only grown. He told Kelleher that he now hated his thesis and wanted to jettison anything having to do with Matthew Arnold. Kelleher regarded him sympathetically and said, "Oh, don't worry, boy. I can't bear the old bore either. So just forget about it— finish the damned thing and we won't discuss it at all."[153] Instead, Kelleher proposed that they meet every week at Hayes-Bickford, a Harvard Square cafeteria that served great apple pie. "We'll have pie and coffee, and I'll read you *Finnegans Wake*. You'll get your honors. I'll reward you not to talk about Matthew Arnold."[154] This is exactly what they did and Nathan graduated cum laude on the strength of a thesis that he claimed to have burned after graduation in Kelleher's honor.[155]

If English was not to be his life's work, then what was? Nathan found himself drawn to medicine. There were several reasons for this affinity, beginning with his father. Whether arising from his own frustrated ambition to be a doctor or because of a general admiration for the profession, Geoffrey had often urged his son to consider medical school. At the same time, his mother's sense of social responsibility had inspired Nathan to join the Phillips Brooks House Association, a public service and social justice organization run by Harvard College students. Nathan's experience as a community service volunteer confirmed his interest in helping those in need. Finally, in 1948, a Winthrop House suite mate of Nathan's named David Hanson developed tuberculous meningitis and died at a tragically young age at the Peter Bent Brigham Hospital, which was situated directly opposite Harvard Medical School. Nathan visited Hanson at the hospital and watched the bustling interns and residents in their white uniforms as they tried desperately to save his friend. Despite the futility of their efforts, Nathan was deeply impressed and could imagine modeling his life on these hardworking physicians.

Fortunately, some kind of premonition or, perhaps, simple parental urging had persuaded Nathan to take premed courses during each of his semesters at Harvard. In fact, despite being an English major, Nathan enjoyed his organic chemistry course, as opposed to his inorganic chemistry and introductory biology courses, which he found tedious. Thus, Nathan was a competitive candidate when he decided to apply to medical school in his senior year. Kelleher fully supported Nathan's decision.

In a bit of dramatic foreshadowing, back in 1946, when Nathan was on a school break from Andover and doing some homework at the Boston Public Library for his French language class, he decided that he would take a look at Harvard Medical School. He rode the trolley up to the campus and boldly walked into the imposing, marble-columned main administration building known as Building A. There, at the front desk, he saw Dorothy Murphy, who we will meet again later, and requested a catalog. He asked her how one gained admission to Harvard Medical School. Her reply was simple. "Go to a good college and get excellent grades." Nathan, of course, had followed her advice and, in the spring of 1951, he received a telegram from Kendall Emerson, the chair of the admissions committee at Harvard Medical School. Actually, Nathan did not receive the telegram himself. He was volunteering in Boston that evening as part of his Phillips Brooks House activities and called the Winthrop House night watchman, Mr. Rainey, to find out if a telegram had arrived for him. In fact, there was a telegram and Nathan begged Rainey to open it and read it to him. Although Rainey read poorly and slowly, the gist was clear. David Nathan had been admitted to the Harvard Medical School class of 1955.

Chapter 4

BECOMING A DOCTOR

When David Nathan enrolled at Harvard Medical School in the fall of 1951, American medical education was on the cusp of its second great revolution. The first had occurred in 1910 when Abraham Flexner, a schoolteacher from Louisville, Kentucky, published a detailed report that indicted the way physicians were being educated in America.[156] Prior to the Flexner Report, medical training was a haphazard affair that combined apprenticeships with public lectures for which students had to buy tickets. The system was proprietary and profit-driven, lacking any standardization or quality control, and it generated a glut of doctors with varying levels of competence and venality. While some who were called to the profession were selfless, dedicated, and brilliant, many others were decidedly mediocre.

This sorry state of affairs was exactly the kind of problem that drew the attention of Progressive Era reformers. In this case, the Carnegie Foundation for the Advancement of Teaching, one of six charitable organizations created by Andrew Carnegie in the early twentieth century, decided that improving American health care would be one of its central tasks, beginning with raising the standard of medical education.[157] Members had been impressed by Flexner's earlier book, *The American College: A Criticism*, which proposed a set of reforms for higher education based on his extensive in-person study of the great universities of Western Europe, especially Germany. The Carnegie Foundation engaged Flexner to do the same thing for medical education.

While it may have seemed odd to ask a nonphysician to undertake this task (Flexner himself thought he had been confused with his brother Simon, a physician who was the first director of the Rockefeller Institute), the Carnegie Foundation understood the project to be an analysis of education, not medicine. An educator would be more likely than a physician to make important pedagogic recommendations and, even better, a defensive medical establishment might be more inclined to take advice from an outsider. Flexner, whose motto was *ambulando discimus* (we learn by "walking" i.e., by gathering data),[158] enthusiastically took up the challenge—he personally inspected all 155 medical schools in the U.S. and Canada and toured the major medical schools of Europe.

At the core of Flexner's recommendations was his belief that medicine is a scientific discipline and that physicians must master its scientific underpinnings before embarking on their clinical training. He thought this was best accomplished by embedding medical schools and teaching hospitals within research universities. Flexner based his proposal on the German—or more properly, Prussian—model, recently adopted by William Welch at Johns Hopkins, in which students received two years of didactic teaching in classes led by university professors before going on to two years of clinical training in a university-affiliated hospital.

Flexner's report was immensely influential. State boards of medicine turned his findings into standards that nearly one-third of American medical schools could not meet; they were shuttered. His recommendations were endorsed by the great philanthropic foundations of the day, including Carnegie's and Rockefeller's, which provided the capital to build the laboratories and other facilities that would put science at the heart of medical education. Most importantly, the Flexner Report convinced universities of the importance of supporting full-time faculties of medicine. With salary lines for professors of medicine and surgery, those faculty could devote their attention to research and teaching without the distraction of having to manage a clinical practice to put food on the table.

By the time Nathan came to Harvard Medical School, Flexner's reforms had been in place for nearly forty years and the medical curriculum they inspired, once so innovative, had become routine. In their first year, Harvard students took didactic courses in anatomy, histology, physiology, and biological chemistry; second-year courses included pathology, bacteriology, and pharmacology.[159] The second-year curriculum also gently introduced students to patients by teaching the techniques of "physical diagnosis"—how to examine a patient. Tuition and fees came to $2,300, not including the obligatory cost of renting a microscope: Each student was responsible for acquiring his or her own, "preferably less than twenty years old" according to the student handbook. The microscope was used for examining normal and diseased tissues during the histology and pathology courses.[160]

Harvard provided rooms for students in Vanderbilt Hall, a well-appointed dormitory built in 1927 across the street from the medical school. Nathan, who had had his fill of institutional life as an undergraduate, wanted to live in his own apartment, although he would need financial help from his family to afford it. His father refused, adamant that only a married man deserved to live in an apartment or own a car, not for his own sake but for the comfort of his wife and family.[161] In fact, Nathan, already deeply in love with Jean Friedman, had begun his campaign to convince her to marry him when he was a senior at Harvard College. Jean had hesitated, telling him that her parents did not want her to marry until she had completed at least one year of graduate school at the Boston University School of Education. But Nathan shamelessly begged her to convince her parents to reconsider so that he (and she) could live in an apartment. Jean's parents relented and they married in Pittsburgh in September 1951. After a two-week honeymoon on Nantucket, they returned to Boston in time for the start of medical school. Nathan was one of only a small number of married students.

The Nathans' first apartment was at 1737 Cambridge Street, next to what is now the Harvard School of Design. According to his father's rules, Nathan, as a married man, was also entitled to a car, so he bought an old Plymouth and used it to commute across the Charles River to the medical school's campus in Boston. Nathan gave rides to some of his classmates who also lived in Cambridge, including Ann Birnbaum, a Sarah Lawrence graduate and one of only eight women in the class. Nathan was so taken with Ann that he introduced her to Richard Barnet, his childhood friend. Ann married Richard and both remained close to Nathan.

Ann Birnbaum Barnet, who became a pediatrician at Children's Hospital National Medical Center in Washington, DC, provided insight into the unwelcoming environment for women at Harvard Medical School in an essay she titled, "What Do Women Want, or the Couch in Building A."[162] She was referring to the fact that, because there were no accommodations for female students in Vanderbilt Hall, women had nowhere to grab a nap during grueling sixteen-hour days. When Ann tried to rest on a couch in the ladies' room in the basement of Building A, the medical school's very stuffy main administration building, she was rousted by a female administrator, who told her that the couch had not been put there for the comfort of medical students. As long as women composed only 7 percent of the class, it never occurred to anyone, male or female, to provide such straightforward facilities. Barnet's point was that the answer to the question, "What do women medical students want?" was often pretty simple.

Nathan's car gave him an opportunity to ferry other important people to and from the medical school, including Dorothy Murphy, the medical school's registrar. It was she whom Nathan, as a high school student in 1946, asked how one gets into Harvard Medical School. She had been hired in 1919 and through her service to four deans, became one of those legendary administrators who actually runs an organization.[163] She knew all the students, all their course selections, and all their plans. Nathan endeared himself to

Miss Murphy by driving her home to Cambridge whenever she needed a ride; as a result, he was granted his first choice for all elective courses and locations of his hospital rotations.

Another personal connection at Harvard Medical School was Helen Wendler Dean Markham, an assistant professor of anatomy who taught histology. Nathan thought the world of her teaching ability and admired her as one of the few female faculty members at the medical school. Tragically, she and her husband were named as Communist Party members during Senate testimony by Herbert Philbrick, the FBI informant who went on to write the red-scare potboiler *I Led 3 Lives*.[164] Markham herself was later called to testify before Congress and, as an unfriendly witness, refused to answer questions about her Communist Party affiliations.[165, 166] In response, the ruling body of the university, known as the Harvard Corporation, suspended her. Although her suspension was lifted after vociferous protests, the Corporation later stated that "new developments" had come to light and, as a result, "we can no longer reasonably believe that she is free from Communist domination."[167] What had incensed them was that Markham and her husband, against the university's advice, had issued a press release suggesting that Harvard had supported her decision not to answer questions about party membership. In retaliation, the Corporation decided that Markham would not be rehired when her appointment ended on June 30, 1954.[168] Sadly, the only recorded response from Markham, who was actively engaged in cancer research at the time, was that "somebody will have to continue my experiments."[169] This example of governmental overreach coupled with institutional cowardice made a huge impression on Nathan.

Meanwhile, the first year of medical school was an academic struggle for the would-be doctor. Although Nathan had taken the requisite premedical courses as an undergraduate, his experience as an English major had not prepared him for the rigors of coursework in quantitative medical sciences. Fortunately, the content of the stodgy first-year curriculum was highly repetitive.

Concepts introduced in the anatomy course would reappear in histology and then again in physiology and then again in pharmacology. For someone like Nathan, who was a hard worker and prodigious memorizer, this was a godsend. He could put his head down, absorb as much as possible, and earn passing grades even though his academic performance was not stellar.

Things improved during the second year. The courses—bacteriology, pathology, pharmacology—while still rather dry, were at least related to real medical problems affecting real patients. Bacteriology particularly appealed to Nathan because, in addition to the basic concepts of biochemistry and pharmacology, which appeared yet again, its unique precepts were framed within the broader context of medical history. Enough so that Nathan began to think of the story of medicine as a story of humans battling infectious diseases. This appealed to the humanist in Nathan, and it stimulated an engagement with the material that resulted in a better academic performance.

One of the benefits of a Harvard Medical School education in the 1950s was exposure to the luminaries of medical science who, at least in those days, devoted some of their time to teaching first-year students. They included Don W. Fawcett, a pioneer in the use of electron microscopy to discern the structures of tissues and the author of what is still the standard textbook of histology, and Clifford Barger, one of the foremost physiologists of his generation who discovered many of the mechanisms that underlie heart and kidney failure. Although Nathan admired these individuals and thought about emulating them, he worried that he did not have the creative spark or sustained interest to be a scientific researcher like these great men. Having come to this conclusion, Nathan's narrow goal was to get through the first two years of classwork so that he could finally interact with patients.

In their third and fourth years, Harvard medical students were taught the core specialties that make up medical care: medicine, surgery, pediatrics, and obstetrics/gynecology. They also took elective courses in more subspecialized areas such as infectious diseases or orthopedics. In an echo of the old apprenticeship model, students performed clerkships of one to three months at one of the Harvard-affiliated hospitals, where they would be assigned to a team of physicians in one of these disciplines. The teams were rigidly hierarchical with so-called attending physicians atop the pyramid. Attendings were fully licensed, practicing physicians who bore ultimate responsibility for patients under the team's care. But the real day-to-day work was performed by a resident physician and two or three interns who reported to the resident. The poor medical student was at the very bottom of the heap and the quality of his or her educational experience hung on the skill, interest, and whims of their interns, residents, and attendings. Patient care involves a tremendous amount of lowly but necessary detail work known as "scut." Some interns and residents dumped all of the scutwork on the student, leaving no time for learning. Others shouldered a little of the drudgery and used the time freed thereby to teach. Interns and residents who actually taught became legends to the students.

In the early 1950s, Harvard Medical School sent its students to fourteen different hospitals throughout greater Boston. Not surprisingly, the educational experiences they offered varied widely, even among different departments within the same hospital. Harvard students became adept at parsing the distinctions among learning environments at the various locations and passing that information on to the next class. It is disconcerting to consider how two students, despite having the same degree from Harvard Medical School, could have had strikingly different training experiences in, say, internal medicine or surgery. Only in recent years have attempts been made to standardize clinical education. But in the fall of 1953, these questions about medical pedagogy did not concern Nathan. Instead, he was nervously excited about beginning his first clinical rotation as a third-year medical student in internal medicine at the legendary Boston City Hospital.

BOSTON CITY HOSPITAL AND THE THORNDIKE LABORATORY/CURING PERNICIOUS ANEMIA

Boston City Hospital enjoys near-mythic status in the history of American medicine. Established by the City of Boston on June 1, 1864, to serve those who could not afford to pay for medical care, it was the first municipal hospital in America (Figure 7). Known as BCH, it opened with 180 beds and thirty-five physicians who staffed medical, surgical, and ophthalmic units.[170, 171] Harvard Medical School students began visiting BCH for their training and education soon after it opened. By the turn of the century, Boston's other medical schools—Boston University and Tufts—also sent their students there. Eventually, the wards at BCH were divided into numbered units which were independently managed by the three schools: the II and IV Medical Services belonged to Harvard, the I and III Medical Services to Tufts, and the V Medical Service to Boston University.

The value of a medical training experience can be measured, in part, by the variety of patients and illnesses to which a student is exposed. By this metric, BCH excelled. The citizens of Boston obliged their medical students by coming to BCH with a wide variety of diseases, some common, some rare. One veteran described the patient populations as "a mix of the desperately ill, the exotic, and the pathetic."[172] Generations of medical students, interns, and residents regarded their experiences at BCH as the ones that made them the physicians they became.

Figure 12: Boston City Hospital at its Founding.

This glorious melding of three medical schools in a single hospital with access to the most interesting and informative patients in the world worked well for a century. By the 1970s, however, Boston was experiencing the same general decline affecting most American cities, and the municipal budget could no longer provide the generous support for BCH that it had in the past. While a hospital with a simpler structure might have survived, BCH was dismayingly complex. A contemporary described it as "an administrative monstrosity...[T]hree independent medical and surgical services and a dozen or so semiautonomous fiefdoms, accountable to three deans of three medical schools. The BCH consisted for all practical purposes of three competing hospitals under one roof."[173]

Faced with diminishing resources from the city and a nonpaying patient population, the trustees of BCH decided to disaffiliate with Harvard and Tufts in 1973 and give Boston University (BU) School of Medicine sole responsibility for professionally staffing the hospital. While the decision was practical, it was also ironic—BU had been the last school to affiliate with BCH, some seventy years after Harvard. The delay was a consequence of the medical school's founding by a group of physicians who had been excommunicated from the Massachusetts Medical Society in the 1870s for practicing homeopathy; the Boston medical establishment, which controlled BCH, was not inclined to open its doors to those quacks. All was forgiven later, when BU joined the ranks of allopathic medical schools.

For a century before the disaffiliation, BCH had been home to some of the most famous names in medicine. An impressive number of medical school deans, department chairs, and authors of definitive medical textbooks trained at BCH. But the hospital was also known for the research performed by its doctors. These physician-scientists made profoundly important medical discoveries based on their direct observation of patients, a tradition that Nathan admired and internalized. It is worth considering one example in detail, namely pernicious anemia (PA), because its history illustrates how patient-oriented research worked at BCH and because the physicians involved in this research would later influence Nathan's career.

Anemia can be defined as a disorder in which the number of red blood cells circulating through the body is decreased. There are many types of anemia, but PA was distinguished from the others because it was untreatable, its course was relentless, and it resulted in death. Hence the descriptor "pernicious."

During the late nineteenth and early twentieth centuries, observant clinicians noted features that reliably accompanied the anemia of PA: numbness and tingling in the hands and feet; poor balance resulting in a gait that made people with PA look like they were drunk; and a sore tongue that lacked normal bumps and furrows. Microscopic examination of the blood from these patients showed that their red blood cells were much larger than normal. Physicians inclined toward wielding Occam's razor asked if there might be a single abnormality underlying these disparate signs and symptoms. BCH was the home of two figures who helped answered this question: George Richards Minot and William Bosworth Castle.

Minot was the son and grandson of eminent Boston physicians; his grandfather co-founded Massachusetts General Hospital.[174] A product of Harvard College and Harvard Medical School, Minot became a professor of medicine at Harvard and a leader of clinical research at Boston City Hospital. He also had a private medical practice in an office on Beacon Street, tending to the illnesses of his Back Bay neighbors. In fact, Minot had joined with two other physicians in one of the first examples of a medical group practice. This arrangement allowed the partners to cover patient care responsibilities for each other, which gave Minot the time he needed for his clinical duties at BCH and for his research.

In 1921, Minot developed diabetes. In fact, the diagnosis was made by Elliott Joslin, founder of the foremost diabetes clinic of the day, which still bears his name.[175] When Minot was diagnosed, the only way to manage his illness was rigorous dietary restriction to near-starvation levels. Minot adhered to his austere regimen until Joslin was able to procure insulin, which had been developed the year after his diagnosis. Even on insulin, though, Minot continued to monitor his diet obsessively. Motivated by his personal experience of the effect of diet on health, Minot tried treating his pernicious anemia patients with dietary supplements. His choice was influenced by a surgeon, George Whipple, who had reported that he could treat the anemia caused by blood loss in dogs by feeding them liver. Even though PA was a very different kind of anemia, Minot tried liver on his PA patients and found it to be highly effective. Blood counts rose almost immediately and, with time, all of the other manifestations of pernicious anemia also improved. The cure of this devastating disease was recognized by the Nobel Prize for Physiology and Medicine being awarded in 1934 to Whipple, Minot, and Minot's collaborator William P. Murphy.

Sometimes, Nobel Prizes are given for the wrong reasons. By chronically bleeding dogs, Whipple had induced what we now understand to be an iron deficiency anemia, similar to that caused by heavy menstrual flow. Liver is an abundant source of iron and it was iron that had improved the anemia in Whipple's dogs. The effectiveness of liver supplements given to humans with iron deficiency anemia can be highly variable due to differences in the rate of absorption of dietary iron into the bloodstream. In contrast, the effectiveness of liver supplements on PA is dependable and consistent. This led Minot to think that there must be some other substance in liver—something other than iron—that treated PA so effectively. Biochemical analyses eventually identified that substance as Vitamin B12, also known as cobalamin, which, by itself, could cure pernicious anemia and its associated symptoms. However, giving cobalamin by mouth did not work—it had to be injected. Why should this be so? After all, oral liver with its cobalamin worked just fine. Another BCH doctor, William B. Castle, who became Nathan's most important role model, answered this question.

Castle's father was a professor of zoology at Harvard University and was one of the first American scientists to study the genetics of mammals. But unlike Minot's family with its deep Brahmin roots, the Castles had been Ohio farmers until William's father came east to teach at Harvard. The younger Castle was a product of Harvard College and Harvard Medical School and entered Minot's orbit when he came to BCH for further training. Castle was more of a tinkerer than Minot—he kept the same Ford Model A running from 1929 to 1953—and wanted to understand exactly why cobalamin had to be injected rather than swallowed in order to work. What was the precise mechanism?

Castle's approach was informed by the fact that most patients with pernicious anemia are unable to make normal amounts of stomach acid. He reasoned that an interaction between normal gastric "juice" and food ought to mimic the effects of dietary liver on PA. The way he tested this idea was typical of his era and would be considered highly inappropriate today. Every morning during his ten-day experiment, Castle would eat three hundred grams of raw ground beef, wait an hour, and then induce vomiting by sticking a finger down his throat. He filtered out the solid matter from the regurgitated muck and administered the liquid via stomach tube to pernicious anemia patients. Blissfully unaware of the provenance of their treatment, the subjects experienced a remarkable recovery of their red blood cells counts—it was as if they had been injected with cobalamin.

The beneficial effects would not occur if Castle gave the patients his gastric juice before he had his ground beef breakfast or if he gave them ground beef alone; the two had to be mixed. He inferred that there must be two factors, one in the stomach itself and one in the meat. He called the first "intrinsic" factor—it came from within—and the second "extrinsic" factor. Extrinsic factor, of course, turned out to be cobalamin. Intrinsic factor was later shown to be a protein that binds to cobalamin and is needed for its absorption from the intestine into the bloodstream. Together with Minot's earlier discoveries, Castle's insights thoroughly neutralized the perniciousness of PA.

Minot and Castle did their work in a unit embedded within BCH called the Thorndike Memorial Laboratory. Established in 1923 as one of the hospital's internal "fiefdoms," it was the first clinical research laboratory in a municipal hospital.[176] Through a bequest in honor of surgeon William Thorndike by his brother George, a building was constructed which housed a seventeen-bed ward for studying patients, state-of-the-art X-ray facilities, and research laboratories. Its first director was Francis Weld Peabody, a Harvard professor who convinced the trustees of BCH that clinical research should be an integral activity of a city hospital. The ward was essentially a metabolic testing unit with adjacent kitchen services. In fact, Castle swiped his ground beef from the Thorndike kitchen.

Peabody was an inspiring leader who attracted some of the most prominent clinical researchers of the day. His own research covered many medical fields although he, too, began to focus on pernicious anemia when he was at the Thorndike. Sadly, Peabody died of stomach cancer a mere four years after starting the Thorndike. The directorship was then assumed by Minot and, when he stepped down in 1948, Castle became the third director. It is no exaggeration to say that modern hematology, Nathan's field, was born at the Thorndike Laboratory, where the practice of patient-centered clinical research was raised to its highest level.

Nathan thoroughly enjoyed his clinical clerkships. Exposure to real patients with real diseases gave him the feeling that he was finally doing something important. He reveled in the possibility that if he were any good at it, he would be improving people's lives. Nathan was so enamored with this idea that he decided he would become a general practitioner—his dream was to establish a prepaid multispecialty clinic in Cambridge, Massachusetts, that would cater to people of moderate means. Had he fulfilled his vision, Nathan would be remembered for starting the first HMO. Instead, he was exposed to clinical research at BCH and became so utterly captivated that he changed his mind and decided to make it his life's work. Characteristically, this happened through a direct encounter with a patient.

In the fall of 1953, Nathan was assigned with three of his classmates to their internal medicine clerkship at BCH. The students paired up, Nathan partnering with his friend Charles Keevil who, like Nathan, was one of the few married students in the class. Every Monday, each two-student team would take a medical history and perform a physical examination on a hospitalized patient. Then, each student would independently write up his or her findings, concluding with a presumptive diagnosis, citations of the relevant medical literature that supported their presumption, and a recitation of the laboratory or X-ray studies needed to confirm it. Each student would present his or her write-up to the attending physician, who would then examine the patient and critique the students' performance. The teams repeated the protocol every week for the three-month duration of the clerkship.

On one fateful Monday, Nathan and Keevil were assigned to examine a patient on the men's ward of the Harvard medical service. Keevil was sick that day, so Nathan was on his own. Excited and a little nervous about flying solo, Nathan made his way to the ward but found his would-be subject sound asleep. It was just after lunchtime, so Nathan waited for him to awake from what he assumed was the gentleman's postprandial nap. As the minutes ticked away, Nathan became uneasy; he'd have to get his history and physical exam done soon if he wanted to complete his write-up on time. Not wanting to be too discourteous, Nathan gently nudged the patient. No response. He pushed harder, raised his voice, shook the patient—still nothing.

With rising panic, Nathan realized that the patient was comatose. What was the problem? Was he in a diabetic coma? Had he fallen and hit his head? Nathan knew he needed help so he ran to the nursing station and begged them to page the resident physician. The nurses seemed singularly unruffled by this hyperventilating third-year medical student, but they indulged him anyway. They called the hospital operator requesting that she announce the resident's name over the loudspeaker system and instruct him to call the ward. Nathan paced nervously until he heard the blare of the resident's name. That was progress. He then waited an eternity for the resident's call, terrified that the very first patient for whom he had sole "responsibility" would die. What an inauspicious way to begin one's clinical career. The phone rang; it was the resident, at last. The nurses told him about the patient and the anxious medical student. He said he would be there directly.

When the resident finally ambled onto the ward, Nathan ran up to him and told him about the dire emergency. The resident smiled and replied laconically, "Oh, yeah. Don't worry. That guy always goes into a coma after he eats a big meal. Just wait. He'll wake up. Meantime, you can do your physical exam. He'll be cooperative!" The resident chuckled.

"But why does this happen?" Nathan asked.

"I don't know," said the resident, "but I heard about some new research from England saying that patients with cirrhosis of the liver can't get rid the ammonia that comes from meat in their diets. The Brits think that the ammonia is causing the coma."

"Is it?" Nathan asked.

"Well, unfortunately, there's no way to test the idea because there's no way to measure ammonia levels in the blood."

The resident walked away leaving Nathan to perform his physical examination, which revealed that the patient did, in fact, have the classical signs of chronic alcoholism and cirrhosis of the liver. So, the resident's explanation for the patient's coma made sense. What didn't make sense, at least to Nathan, was the inability to measure ammonia in the blood. How was it possible that no one could get a handle on something that was causing such a serious reaction—coma—in such a common disease—alcoholic cirrhosis? More important, how could doctors hope to make these patients better if they could not measure the very thing that was making them ill?

Something clicked. Here was an important clinical question that needed scientific research to provide an answer. Even though Nathan had not turned in a stellar performance in his undergraduate or first-year medical school science courses, he found himself stirred to do research on the relationship between blood ammonia levels and coma. The Harvard Medical School curriculum provided open times on Tuesday, Thursday, and Saturday afternoons for pursuing this kind of independent work and Nathan took full advantage of the opportunity.

His first project was a complete flop. Nathan remembered from his physiology course that ammonia in the blood is normally detoxified by the liver, which combines it with carbon dioxide and water to form urea. This is the elegant way the body captures a toxic gas—ammonia, a by-product of dietary protein—and locks it into a molecule that the kidneys can excrete in urine. Nathan also knew from his bacteriology course that bacteria have an enzyme called urease, which splits urea back into ammonia and carbon dioxide. Mammals do not have urease. Nathan thought that if he injected purified urease into rats, it would liberate ammonia and, if ammonia was truly responsible for inducing coma, the rats would become comatose, QED.

Nathan convinced the chair of the Pathology Department to give him five healthy rats and a big bottle of purified urease. Armed with the self-confidence of the naïve, Nathan injected urease into the rats. Nothing happened. In retrospect, Nathan realized that he had no idea what the right dose of urease might be or how often to give it or even if it would be active after being injected. Frankly, it would have been shocking if the experiment had worked.

As Nathan thought about his failure and contemplated how he might modify conditions for the next experiment—an early example of his characteristic resilience—he realized that he was missing an essential tool. Even if he were to increase the dose of urease, how could he know if it had done what it was supposed to do? The only way to be sure was to measure ammonia in the blood, something that his resident had already told him could not be done. He had come right back to the same problem.

Nathan knew he was stuck. So, he decided to tackle the problem directly by developing a method for measuring ammonia in the blood. As he dug into the scientific literature looking for clues about where to start, he discovered that an English biochemist had devised a way to detect gases like ammonia in various bodily fluids.[177] Unfortunately, it could not be applied to blood because red blood cells contain an enzyme, adenosine deaminase, which itself produces ammonia. Thus, any attempts to measure diet-derived ammonia in the blood would be confounded by the additional ammonia made by red cells. Nathan conferred with F. Lee Rodkey, a faculty member in the Biochemistry Department. Rodkey was a thoughtful scientist and, taking a step back, told Nathan that a successful method for measuring ammonia in blood would require the following: a simple apparatus to capture the gas, a color-based indicator that could be read by detectors in clinical laboratories, and a method to suppress ammonia production by red blood cells. Nathan threw himself into the work and, along with Rodkey, solved each one of these problems.[178] The result was Nathan's first scientific publication.[179]

Caring for patients on the medical wards and successfully pursuing a research question convinced Nathan that he wanted a career in academic internal medicine. But medical school offered a few more experiences that would test his conviction. For example, his surgery rotation at Massachusetts General Hospital (MGH) exposed him to a brilliant vascular surgeon named Robert Linton, a Scotsman who was one of the founders of his specialty. Vascular surgery can be harrowing: manipulation of brittle and sclerotic arteries often resulted in impressive amounts of bright red blood shooting across the operating room. Scenes like this could induce panic or, more often, fainting in medical students. Linton, however, would calmly hum a tune to himself and repair the leak. This deeply impressed Nathan—recall how his grandfather glorified surgeons—and made him question his decision to specialize in internal medicine. But after some careful soul-searching, Nathan realized that the Lintons of the world were successful because of their rare skills. Nathan told himself that, just as he didn't have the talent to play shortstop for the Boston Red Sox, neither did he have the talent to be a world-class surgeon. The insight was comforting and allowed him to worship surgeons for the rest of his career without pangs of jealousy.

Still, Nathan knew that, unlike surgery, much of internal medicine was spent managing routine and minor disorders with very little of the life-and-death drama that surgeons see. Would a placid existence in medicine be sufficiently satisfying? To test his resolve, Nathan chose to spend a month in the clinic that served Harvard undergraduate students. Here, he would be exposed to an unending parade of sore throats, coughs, urinary tract infections, depression, and, of course, the "worried well" who were physically fine but anxious enough to want to see a doctor. The health service was led by Dr. Dana Farnsworth, a psychiatrist who believed that the prevalence of psychiatric problems among undergraduates had been grossly underestimated and that "the amount of psychiatric time available [to students] determines the amount of use."[180] Farnsworth proved his point by developing a counseling arm of the student health service that was so extensively used it became known as the Farnsworth Hilton. Under his leadership, 11 percent of Harvard students would be seen by the psychiatric staff in any academic year, a proportion much higher than at other schools, where psychiatric services were smaller or harder to access.

Nathan's job was to take a history and perform a physical examination on the students and then present his findings to Farnsworth, who would develop recommendations for managing their problems. One day, Nathan presented a case of an undergraduate who, he suspected, was a drug addict. As it happened, one of Farnsworth's main interests was the harmful effects of drug use in the student population. Nathan's presentation gave Farnsworth an opportunity to expound on the pernicious influence of marijuana and other drugs. To illustrate his point, Farnsworth directed Nathan's attention to the building across the street from his office. There, in a window above a tailor shop, stood a disheveled and forlorn undergraduate. Nathan recognized the unshaved face—it was Andy, the roommate of Nathan's best friend, Richard Barnet.

"That's exactly what I mean, David," said Farnsworth, pointing out the window. "Look at that ruined young man. Drugs have likely destroyed him."

"Oh, don't worry, Dr. Farnsworth," Nathan replied. "That's just Andy. He doesn't bathe much."

Nathan had worried that the quotidian tasks of the student health service might discourage him from specializing in internal medicine. Instead, the work gave him a sense of clinical mastery and confirmed his decision. He was still debating whether his career would include clinical research but his mind was made up by something that happened to him as a fourth-year medical student, an experience which was also a harbinger of his interest in hematology.

During a month-long rotation on the obstetrics service at the Providence Lying-In Hospital in Rhode Island, Nathan became involved in the care of a young woman who, while in labor, had experienced a detachment of the placenta from her uterus. This can happen when the placenta develops so low down in the uterus that it covers the cervix; when contractions begin, it can be torn from the uterine wall causing life-threatening bleeding. The only treatment is an emergency Caesarean section. Nathan assisted the team during the operation.

As soon as the obstetrician made his incision, large amounts of blood welled up in the wound and the patient began bleeding from all of her orifices and from the intravenous lines in her arms. Why was this happening? Our bodies respond to bleeding by activating proteins in the bloodstream that gather around the site of the hemorrhage to form a clot. Occasionally, when the bleeding is acute or extensive, these clot-forming proteins can be completely used up in a vain attempt to stanch the flow. When that happens, the body has nothing left to make a clot and the result is a massive hemorrhage that can be fatal. As the patient went into shock, the anesthesiologist stubbed out his cigarette on the tank of the highly volatile anesthetic he was administering and, pointing at Nathan, barked, "Hey, you. Run up to the blood bank and get me three vials of Cohn fraction."

Nathan had no idea what the anesthesiologist was talking about but did as he was told. He later learned that Edwin Cohn, a biochemist at Harvard Medical School, had devoted his career to identifying and purifying proteins in blood, including those that produce clots. Using a variety of techniques, Cohn had separated some of these proteins into subgroups that he called "fractions." Cohn Fraction 1 contained fibrinogen, the immediate precursor of the main component of blood clots. Infusing Cohn Fraction 1 into patients with massive hemorrhage could replace the fibrinogen that had been consumed during the body's attempt to stop the bleeding. This can produce near-miraculous control of the hemorrhage, which is what happened in this patient. She and her baby survived, and Nathan was deeply impressed by the power that scientific discovery could have on the well-being of an individual patient. Clinical research would be his calling.

Nathan graduated from Harvard Medical School in June 1955. He drove with his parents to the graduation exercises in the medical school's quadrangle, a green expanse on Longwood Avenue bounded on three sides by the school's formally placed and forbidding marble buildings. The Nathan family parked their car by Vanderbilt Hall, the student dormitory opposite the quad. As they crossed the street, Nathan saw Dorothy Murphy, the school's registrar and his frequent automobile passenger, crossing in the opposite direction. When she caught sight of the Nathans she stopped in her tracks, stared at Nathan's father, and said, "Why, it's Geoffrey Nathan! Geoffrey, why didn't you come to us when we admitted you in 1921?" Nathan's family was astonished. Nathan later learned from Miss Murphy that his father's case had been so unusual that she recalled it as soon as she saw him.

Nathan had spent much of his third and fourth years in medical school trying to decide where he would most like to do his internship. Not surprisingly, he was leaning toward the Harvard Medical Service at Boston City Hospital. The outstanding teaching, the rich clinical material, the tradition of patient-focused research, and his own experience as a student made it an obvious choice. Another chance encounter changed his mind.

Nathan had done his third-year obstetrics clerkship (which predated his fourth-year elective in Providence) at the venerable Boston Lying-In Hospital. Part of his experience included being taught about the medical impacts of pregnancy by a resident from the Peter Bent Brigham Hospital named Buris Raye Boshell. Originally from Birmingham, Alabama, Boshell had come north to attend Harvard Medical School in the class two years ahead of Nathan's. Much later, after completing his residency, Boshell studied endocrinology under George W. Thorn, physician-in-chief at the Peter Bent Brigham, and diabetes under Elliot P. Joslin, founder of the eponymous clinic. Boshell was eventually lured back to the University of Alabama at Birmingham by Tinsley Harrison, the chief of medicine, who edited a definitive textbook of internal medicine along with Thorn.

But before all of that, Boshell had impressed Nathan with his deep empathy for patients and his masterful skill in caring for them. He was a skilled diagnostician whose notes in the medical chart were models of clarity. Nathan could not recall interacting with a similarly impressive resident at BCH. If the Peter Bent Brigham could produce a Boshell, perhaps Nathan ought to train there instead. To test the waters, he did his final clinical rotation in medicine as a fourth-year student at the Peter Bent Brigham. Occasionally, fourth-year students were given an opportunity to act as interns for a month, and this happened to Nathan when one of the actual interns became ill. Nathan's resident, Robert Petersdorf—later, a preeminent leader in academic medicine—appointed him acting intern. Nathan loved the experience, which convinced him to train at the Peter Bent Brigham—the fit just seemed right.

THE PETER BENT BRIGHAM HOSPITAL

Flexner's 1910 report on the sorry state of American medical education included a very specific criticism of Harvard Medical School. While acknowledging that its students benefited from exposure to the large number of patients at its affiliated hospitals, Flexner was surprised that Harvard University itself played little or no role in choosing or overseeing the instructors at those hospitals. In contrast to the university's authority to appoint laboratory-based scientists to the medical school's faculty, clinical appointments were made solely by the hospitals and were based on seniority and rank within those institutions. As Flexner put it, "the heir to the hospital service is heir to the university chair."[181] This disconnect prevented Harvard from applying its academic principles and quality control to the selection of clinical teachers. The tone of Flexner's assessment suggests that he was disappointed that "an institution of this rank" could not exert more influence over appointing its clinical professors.

Harvard Medical School's chastened response was to build a new hospital whose clinical faculty would be chosen using the same oversight and rigor that the university applied to its research faculty. To emphasize the hospital's academic bona fides, it would be located directly behind the majestic new medical school campus on Longwood Avenue, a decision enabled by the bequest of Peter Bent Brigham, a successful Massachusetts businessman, to establish a hospital for the "care of sick persons in indigent circumstances."[182] Brigham, who never married and died childless in 1877, instructed that his bequest not be spent until twenty-five years after his death. The timing was perfect—Harvard's new medical school buildings had been completed in 1906 and the open farmland behind them would be an ideal location for this new kind of hospital devoted to medical education and research.

Harvard intended to follow the Flexnerian model of staffing the hospital with professors who would be paid by the university, thereby reducing their need for an income-generating private practice. They would use the time thus freed for teaching medical students and performing research. Henry A. Christian, who had been appointed dean of Harvard Medical School in 1908 at the tender age of thirty-two, devoted much of his tenure as dean to designing the new hospital, supervising its construction, and organizing its medical staff. In 1912, Christian left the medical school to become the first physician-in-chief of the new Peter Bent Brigham Hospital (PBBH).

Every attempt had been made to create a physical facility that embraced modern concepts of patient care. "The Brigham," as it was colloquially known, was organized as a series of pavilions connected by an open-air walkway. The pavilions, which housed the patient wards, were built to encourage the free flow of fresh air. While this may have been a useful concept in the subtropical climates in which the architects had done their earlier work, it was a disaster in Boston. The pavilions and walkway were unprotected in the winter and became bitterly cold; the wards had insufficient airflow in summer and were stifling hot. One of the chiefs of surgery who had trained during this era said that the Peter Bent Brigham Hospital was "physically obsolete on the day it was opened."[183]

In 1920, just eight short years after its founding, the Brigham abandoned its pavilion model. Since then, it has undergone one hundred years of renovation and patching to accommodate advances in medicine, a growing staff, and an expanding patient population. When Nathan arrived, the Brigham was already a hodgepodge of crammed offices, dark corridors, and uncomfortable patient wards. Despite its physical limitations, a series of visionary leaders made the hospital a model of clinical care, teaching, and research. By mid-century, the torch of cutting-edge clinical research had passed from Boston City Hospital to the Brigham, leading one faculty member to observe that the Brigham hosted "the world's best medicine in the world's worst facility."[184]

Nathan began his internship at the Brigham in the summer of 1955. The schedule was punishing: interns had to be on the hospital wards every weekday, every other night, and every other weekend. The nighttime service was always busy, which meant that Nathan and his co-interns were continually sleep-deprived. In consideration for their work, interns received twenty-five dollars a month, hospital-issue white pants and coats that the hospital laundered, three square meals of dubious quality every day, and, when on night duty, Ritz crackers with peanut butter at midnight. Dormitory housing was available for the unmarried.

Nathan, of course, lived with Jean in Cambridge. At the end of his second year of medical school, they had moved to a rented house on Gibson Street near Mount Auburn Hospital, which is where they were living when their daughters, Linda and Deborah, were born in 1953 and 1955. Both girls were products of induced labor to accommodate Nathan's on-call schedule. (Their third child, Geoffrey, was born in 1958 when the family was in Bethesda, Maryland). It is difficult to know if Nathan's family was a comfort to him during his extraordinarily difficult internship year or if it was a constant reminder of responsibilities that his grueling schedule made him unable to meet. Either way, the marriage survived which is a testament to Jean Nathan's fortitude as much as it is to David Nathan's ability to balance his obligations.

The difficulties of that internship year were made worse by the way it started. Jonas Salk had announced the successful results of his polio vaccine trials in April 1955, and mass vaccination of American children began in May. However, a batch of vaccine made by Cutter Laboratories was contaminated with live poliovirus that, directly or through subsequent contacts, infected two hundred twenty thousand people, resulting in seventy thousand cases of muscle weakness, 164 of severe paralysis, and ten deaths.[185] Although the Cutter vaccine had been administered to children in western and midwestern states, the Commonwealth of Massachusetts suspended all of its vaccinations from May until the following January. The result was that the summer of 1955 saw the worst polio outbreak in Boston's history.[186]

This was a true medical emergency. The sudden surge of polio patients stretched the physical and professional capacities of Boston's hospital system to its limits. Nearly all of the wards at Boston Children's Hospital were repurposed to provide care to polio patients. Emergency rooms were so backed up that staff had to triage patients in their cars while they waited in lines that stretched for blocks. Physicians from one hospital were loaned to others that were short-staffed. This was why David Nathan, a brand-new Brigham intern, found himself beginning his internship at Massachusetts General Hospital overseeing its iron lung unit.

During the acute phase of poliovirus infection, some patients experience paralysis of the diaphragm, which makes them unable to breathe. In most cases, this paralysis lasts for about two weeks so that a person's ability to survive the infection depends on supporting their breathing during this period. The iron lung, which was developed by a physician at Boston Children's Hospital, consisted of an airtight metal chamber into which a polio patient would be sealed up to their neck. A bellows connected to the chamber periodically pumped air into and out of the chamber at a normal breathing rate. When the bellows pumped air into the chamber, the increased pressure forced air out of the patient's lungs; when the air in the chamber was removed, negative pressure forced air back in.

Although the iron lung saved lives, not all polio patients were so fortunate. Nathan had the unnerving experience of watching helplessly as a young man whom he had counseled for depression during his undergraduate clinic rotation with Farnsworth died from his polio infection. This was an utterly discouraging experience and Nathan credits his supervising residents with propping up his morale. One was Roy Vagelos, who went on to be the CEO of Merck and a major benefactor of the University of Pennsylvania and the Columbia College of Physicians and Surgeons.

Poliovirus can be transmitted easily from person to person and fear of contagion was rampant. Anyone caring for polio patients was at risk and, during the 1955 polio outbreak in Boston, several staff members at Boston Children's Hospital contracted the disease. Jean Nathan was worried that her husband might inadvertently bring the virus home, where it would infect their infant daughters. So, for the rest of that miserable summer, whenever Nathan finished one of his shifts and made his way home, Jean would meet him at the doorstep, force him to strip naked, put all of his clothes on a broom handle, and direct him into the shower. Jean would then dump all of the clothes into the washing machine. No one in the Nathan household developed polio.

Not only do interns take care of large numbers of patients, they are expected to do so while bone-tired. Cut off from family, friends, and other support systems by relentless work hours, theirs is a hermetic environment conducive to devising rules of engagement with little reference to the outside world. In particular, and of necessity, they evolve strategies for self-preservation, although the "self" is usually the tight-knit subgroup who are in the trenches together. For example, much effort is expended in the quest to convince some other subgroup to take care of a sick patient. A kind of heroism attaches to interns who successfully send these cases to a different service—they are proud to be called "walls." Disgrace follows interns who do not deflect them—they are "sieves." This plays out most starkly in the context of the tribal loyalties that internists and surgeons feel for their own kind, presumably because of the different way these specialists view the world. Confronted with a desperately ill patient, internists will debate endlessly about the precise nature of the disorder until they eventually devise a treatment plan. Surgeons want action—they want to cut the patient open right now and fix the problem.

As an intern, Nathan could find himself caught up in these parochial battles. One night in particular, he was called to the emergency ward to see an elderly man who had fallen in his kitchen and was unconscious; no other information was available. Although the possible explanations for the patient's coma were nearly endless, physical examination and lab work had led the emergency room staff to consider two likely possibilities: a stroke or bleeding around the brain. Either can cause loss of consciousness, but the distinction is critically important because removal of accumulated blood in the latter case can be lifesaving. Stroke victims, in contrast, need supportive care while they slowly recover. (These days, they might receive anticlotting drugs, making the proper diagnosis even more crucial than it was in 1953.)

Fully aware of this distinction and not wanting to be considered a sieve by his internal medicine colleagues, Nathan sought out the surgical resident and tried to convince him that the patient had bled and needed to be admitted to the surgical service so that the blood compressing his brain could be removed. In those pre-CT scan and pre-MRI days, the only diagnostic test for this kind of bleeding was a plain X-ray of the head to evaluate the location of pineal gland. This small organ in the center of the brain is calcified in older people, hence visible on an X-ray. Displacement of the pineal gland to one side or the other would be evidence for blood pushing on the brain. The surgeon wanted nothing to do with this patient, arguing that he'd had a stroke. But Nathan thought he had the surgeon dead to rights because the patient had such bad arthritis in his neck that he could not be positioned properly to do a standard skull X-ray. With no X-ray to disprove bleeding, the surgeon would be compelled to perform the one intervention that might save the patient.

Not to be outdone, the surgeon dragooned the X-ray technician and radiologist into jerry-rigging a chest X-ray setup so that it could produce a straight-on view of the arthritic patient's skull, perfect for the study. When it was finally completed, the X-ray showed a calcified pineal gland dead center, and the patient went to Nathan's internal medicine service.

The daily and nightly routines of interns are made up of skirmishes like these. But they are embedded in the serious business of evaluating and caring for a huge number of patients in a high-intensity setting. The result of their total immersion is that, by the end of the year, interns have absorbed enough medical expertise to bolster their self-confidence and engender an outright eagerness to apply their new skills. This was Nathan's experience: he was looking forward to starting his residency year.

Chapter 5

NIH CALLS AND A CAREER BECKONS

I n the spring of 1956, Nathan was basking in the exhausted self-confidence that surviving a year of internship brings. His trial by fire was nearly over and he was looking forward to taking on the broader responsibilities that come with being a resident. His hard-won medical competence also tempted him to revisit his plan to become a general practitioner in Cambridge, but he was diverted from that career path once and for all by a telephone call that came on an April morning after another sleepless night in the hospital. The caller was Gordon Zubrod, the newly appointed head of the division of cancer treatment at the National Cancer Institute (NCI), which was (and continues to be) the largest component of the National Institutes of Health (NIH), the federally supported biomedical research behemoth in Bethesda, Maryland. NIH had recently completed construction of a new clinical center, an enormous hospital devoted to clinical research, and needed medical residents with an interest in research to take care of its patients. To attract talented physicians in training, NIH created a two-year Clinical Associate program: in their first year, Clinical Associates would act as residents in the Clinical Center; in their second, they would perform research in an NIH laboratory. After two years, Associates would return to their home institutions to complete their residencies. Zubrod, who would become one of the pioneers of cancer chemotherapy, was offering Nathan a Clinical Associate slot for July 1956.

Nathan was flattered but surprised. How had Zubrod gotten his name? The answer was a magnificent example of unintended consequences that flow from governmental policy. Zubrod was desperate to find top-notch clinical trainees to staff his hospital but knew that it would be difficult to convince young medical superstars to move to Bethesda, a sleepy suburban town far from the illustrious centers of academic medical excellence. But Zubrod had an ace in the hole—the military draft. Despite the Korean War armistice in 1953, fears of Soviet expansion fueled ongoing American plans for military readiness. Among the preparations for manpower needs was the so-called Doctor Draft, which conscripted physicians to two years of military service upon completion of their internships. Like all male interns in the class of 1956, Nathan was likely to be drafted—his young family would not merit deferment, nor would his time in the Marine Corps' Platoon Leaders Class.

The NIH program offered an alternative. Because the NIH is a component of the United States Public Health Service, appointment as a Clinical Associate came with a rank of lieutenant commander in the United States Navy, which entitled Clinical Associates to basic pay, tax-free rental and subsistence allowances, full medical and dental care, and access to post exchanges.[187] But most importantly, the two-year appointment would fulfill military service requirements for those at risk for the Doctor Draft. Armed with these carrots, Zubrod had called the chiefs of the most prestigious medical training programs in the country and asked for names of interns who might make good clinical researchers. George Thorn, chief of medicine at the Brigham, offered up Nathan. Nathan was thankful—uprooting his family from Cambridge to Bethesda for two years seemed a small price to pay for not being sent to Korea. He eagerly accepted Zubrod's offer.

THE BALLAD OF THE YELLOW BERETS

In anticipation of American involvement in World War II, Congress passed the Selective Training and Service Act of 1940, which authorized the nation's first peacetime draft. When the war ended, military manpower needs decreased and the act was allowed to expire in 1947, thereby ending the draft. In short order, however, rising international tensions led to the Selective Service Act of 1948 (also called the Elston Act), authorizing a new postwar draft. The Senate version of the Act included "Special Calls for Doctors and Dentists" which would have required all physicians and dentists under age forty-six to register for the draft.[188] However, this provision was not in the House version and was removed in conference.

Two years later, as the Korean War loomed, Congress amended the Selective Service Act of 1948 to include the Doctor Draft. The new law required registration by all males under fifty-one who were in "medical and allied specialist categories" or "dental and allied specialist categories."[189] (Allied specialist categories included veterinarians.) If inducted, these individuals would be required to spend up to twenty-one months in active military duty. In practice, interns were not drafted but that only meant that, at the end of their internship year, newly minted residents found themselves confronted with the very real possibility of compulsory military service that could include tours of duty in Korea.

At the same time, there was a growing sense among government planners that medical research, especially clinical research, could contribute to the security of the United States. Some of this interest was stoked by fears of the medical consequences of nuclear war. Congressional appropriations for constructing the NIH Clinical Center, a process that began in 1946,[190] were tangible manifestations of these attitudes. However, because most physicians were unskilled in clinical research, explicit training in this discipline would be needed. This was the genesis of the Clinical Associate program, known formally as the NIH Associate Training Program (ATP). Its purpose was to create a cohort of clinical researchers who would fan out across the country to perform studies that would impact the health and well-being of the nation's citizens.

The ATP began in 1953, three years into the new Doctor Draft. Although selection of Associates would eventually involve formal review of applications,[191] its ranks were initially filled through an "old boy's network" composed almost exclusively of East Coast academic physicians—at one point, Harvard Medical School graduates made up 20 percent of the Clinical Associate group.[192] Thorn's recommendation of Nathan was a prime example of the process. In fact, including Nathan, six of the Clinical Associate class who started in 1956 were members of his Harvard Medical School class of 1955.[193] Technically, physicians recruited to the program were not exempt from the draft. Rather, once conscripted into a branch of the armed services, they were transferred to the U.S. Public Health Service (PHS) Uniformed Commissioned Corps, where they could serve at a variety of PHS stations, one of which was the NIH.[194]

During its first decade, the ATP was a somewhat esoteric option for draft-eligible physicians interested in learning about clinical research but uninterested in military service. Later, in the 1960s, the appeal of the program mushroomed, expanding in direct proportion to the risk that drafted doctors might be sent to Vietnam. From 1960 to 1973, as American involvement in the war escalated, the number of Clinical Associates increased from sixty-eight to 229.[195] Service in the PHS had been generally considered an honorable alternative to service in the armed military prior to the Vietnam era. By the mid-1960s, however, those serving stateside in the PHS were conflated with run-of-the-mill draft dodgers and given the derogatory nickname "Yellow Berets."

Despite the opprobrium, the Yellow Berets of the Clinical Associate program have had a profound impact on American medicine. Because they were culled from the nation's top university hospitals by personal recommendations of chiefs of service, the Associates were the smartest and most ambitious young physicians the country had to offer—destined for leadership. A survey taken in 1998 found that 24 percent of the professors of medicine at Harvard Medical School and 21 percent of those at Johns Hopkins had been Clinical Associates.[196] Former Associates have been 50 percent more likely to achieve the rank of full professor than non-Associates, twice as likely to be department chairs, and three times as likely to be deans.[197] One out of every six Nobel laureates in physiology or medicine from 1985 through 2007 are former Associates.[198] While the NIH might be inclined to infer that these impressive statistics were a consequence of the program's superb training, its selectivity may have simply attracted young physician-scientists who would have achieved greatness regardless of where they trained. Either way, the ATP has an impressive legacy.

It is worth noting, however, that because the ATP was commonly used as a means of avoiding conscription into the armed services, almost no women were enrolled. Some thought that giving a slot to a woman would remove a chance for a man to avoid risk to life and limb in Vietnam. Although documentation is sketchy, it has been reported that no women were admitted to the ATP until the late 1970s.[199] While this was hardly the sole cause of male overrepresentation in American academic medicine, it contributed to the absence of women in leadership roles in the 1960s and 1970s.

As noble as the goals of the ATP were, one of its important lessons is that powerful negative incentives can serve a higher purpose. Young, newly trained physicians, no matter how patriotic, were generally more interested in advancing their careers than spending two years in the military, with Vietnam adding an element of mortal peril. These considerations unintentionally, but directly, governed the ATP's fortunes. Its popularity peaked in 1973—the year of the Paris Peace Accords and the end of the draft—with 229 Associates. Just one year later, it had only 191 Associates. In 1976, that number had dropped to 108 and by 1980 there were only seventy-six.[200] The ATP finally closed in 1992, felled by a combination of a decline in the number of physicians interested in clinical investigation, the rise of high-quality training programs outside of NIH, and the disappearance of the old disincentives.

Soon after Nathan accepted the offer to come to NIH, his mother and wife went to Bethesda to investigate the housing scene. Ruth and Jean found a large, gracious home on Oldchester Road in the stately Whitehall Manor neighborhood. It belonged to a career military officer—a colonel of some sort—who had been posted to Japan. For a fraction of the rental prices they knew in Cambridge, the Nathans could occupy a four-bedroom house with grand living and dining rooms and a huge backyard for the girls to play in.

For Nathan, the good news about the house was tempered by an agreement the scouting party had forged during their travels. Ruth was convinced that the Washington, DC, area was a pestilential swampland during the summer months. She even repeated the legend—for which no documentation exists[201]—that members of the British Foreign Service used to receive hazard pay for Washington postings. Ruth insisted that Jean and the girls not spend their summers in Washington but rather stay with her in Nantucket. She had already rented a house for them close to the water. To David's chagrin, Jean readily agreed.

On June 1, 1956, the day after Nathan's internship ended, movers arrived at their Cambridge home to pack up their belongings.[202] Jean and the girls were already on Nantucket, so Nathan drove alone to the palatial rental in Bethesda, where he rattled around by himself for the whole summer.

The misery of being alone in a new city was mitigated by the excitement of working at the NIH Clinical Center. This gleaming new building—its first patient had been admitted in July 1953—could not have been more different from the Peter Bent Brigham. Designed to accommodate more than five hundred beds, the clinical wards were directly adjacent to research laboratories where the kind of clinical investigation that Nathan loved could be performed. With a nod to the Bethesda summers, it was fully air conditioned—an amenity that could only be dreamed of at the Brigham—and each room was wired for a bedside television set.[203] Even the elevators worked. Nathan thought he was in paradise.

The reality, of course, was that the first year of intense patient care responsibilities would keep Nathan nearly as busy as he had been as an intern. The experience was made even harder by the kind of patients he would oversee—his first assignment was on the childhood leukemia service. In 1956, leukemia was seen as a devastating disease that inflicted terrible suffering on its victims as they approached their inevitable demise. While this horrific image would change over the next ten years because of work done at the Clinical Center, Nathan witnessed only the initial stumbling and misery-laden steps.

CHILDHOOD LEUKEMIA

Leukemia is an uncontrolled proliferation of abnormal blood cells. All blood cells arise in the bone marrow, where early progenitors undergo an orderly maturation process until they are ready to be released into the bloodstream. In leukemia, a progenitor cell fails to mature and, instead, starts to divide and form more copies of itself. Eventually, these leukemia cells proliferate so aggressively in the bone marrow that they crowd out the normal progenitors, leaving leukemia patients with few mature blood cells: they become anemic, they cannot fight infections, and they cannot form blood clots. The tragic result is that these patients can die in many different ways, all of them horrible. Until the late 1940s, children with leukemia lived only four months and most physicians recommended that they be made as comfortable as possible and allowed to die without treatment since none was effective. This began to change in 1948 with Sidney Farber's discovery that a drug could reduce the number of leukemia cells in these children and, occasionally, make the cells disappear.

There are many different kinds of blood cells and there are just as many different kinds of leukemias. The most common involve white blood cells of which, again, there are many types. The most common childhood leukemia affects the progenitors of a white blood cell known as a lymphocyte, the cornerstone of the immune system. Another feature that distinguishes varieties of leukemia is the tempo of the disease. Some are characterized by the sudden appearance of leukemic cells that grow rapidly and lead to the patient's death in short order. These are known as acute leukemias to distinguish them from chronic leukemias, which have a more indolent course.

The most common leukemia of childhood is acute lymphocytic leukemia, abbreviated ALL, which is a rapidly progressive and fatal proliferation of lymphocyte progenitors. For decades, a child with ALL was considered a "hopeless case." Nonetheless, Sidney Farber suspected that ALL cells might have an Achilles' heel that could be attacked with drugs. His insight arose from two facts about pernicious anemia. One is that the red blood cell progenitors in the bone marrow of pernicious anemia patients look immature under the microscope in a way that resembles leukemia. Cobalamin not only cures the anemia, but it also returns to normal the leukemia-like appearance of the red blood cell progenitors.

The other fact, mentioned in Chapter 4, is that the red blood cells of pernicious anemia patients are much larger than normal. Examining blood from these patients under a microscope is one of the easy ways to make the diagnosis. But another kind of anemia also produces large red blood cells in the circulation and immature progenitors in the bone marrow—seen most commonly in pregnant women, it was first called "pernicious anemia of pregnancy" because of its resemblance to PA. However, a British physician working in India named Lucy Wills showed that, unlike patients with true pernicious anemia, these women have normal amounts of gastric acid in their stomachs. Following the lead of the physicians at Boston City Hospital, Wills tried giving her patients liver extract. Gratifyingly, this corrected the anemia of pregnancy but, in contrast to PA, purified cobalamin was ineffective. Wills hypothesized that there must be something else in the liver extract that reversed the anemia.[204] Searching for this "something else," she discovered that extracts from certain yeast cultures were effective. The unknown agent in the extracts was called "Wills factor" until the late 1940s when it was shown to be a vitamin called folic acid or folate (also known as vitamin B9). All pregnant women now benefit from this discovery through the addition of folic acid to foods.

Because folic acid cures the anemia of pregnancy, in which too many immature blood progenitors fill the marrow, and because children with ALL also have too many immature progenitors in their marrows, Farber thought that folic acid might cure ALL. While his reasoning made sense, the true underlying logic is not nearly so straightforward. Folic acid is required for making DNA, and DNA is required for cells to grow, so, in its absence, red blood cell production slows and immature progenitors accumulate. Replacing folic acid restores DNA synthesis, simulates maturation of progenitors, and therefore increases red blood cell production, correcting the anemia. Given this growth stimulatory effect of folic acid, it was surprising that experiments in the early 1940s had shown that excess folic acid could slow the growth of some tumors in animals. Farber used these paradoxical findings to bolster his rationale for treating childhood ALL with folic acid.

Still, the basic function of folic acid is to stimulate cell growth. Less surprising, then, was Farber's unfortunate observation that giving folic acid to children with leukemia produced what he called an "acceleration phenomenon" in which the number of leukemic cells abruptly increased and the children became much sicker.[205] This led Farber to reverse course and convince chemists at Lederle Laboratories to make a chemical compound that would block the effect of folic acid (i.e., a folic acid antagonist). The chemists named their antagonist aminopterin. During 1947 and early 1948, Farber and his colleagues gave aminopterin to sixteen children who had acute leukemia. Ten showed remarkable improvement and by the summer of 1948 when Farber reported his results, some were still alive and doing well.[206] This was wholly unprecedented.

Farber was careful to point out that six of his patients had not responded to aminopterin at all—they eventually died—and that, among those who had responded, improvements were only temporary. Farber wrote in his landmark paper that "[N]o evidence has been mentioned in this report that would justify the suggestion of the term 'cure' of acute leukemia in children."[207] The important message was that much more work needed to be done.

At this point, two divergent philosophies about curing leukemia emerged, each with its own partisan adherents. One camp was led by Farber, who believed that further chemical refinement of folic acid antagonists would produce a single compound able to cure leukemia with mild or, at least, tolerable side effects. The other was led by investigators at the NCI, who believed that cure could only be effected by combining drugs that attacked different pathways essential for leukemia cell survival, not just the folic acid pathway. Of course, each individual drug would have its own set of side effects and combining them would likely lead to profound toxicities. Nonetheless, the advocates of this approach believed that patients would have to be taken right up to the limits of those toxicities—just shy of death—to be cured. Farber thought this was barbaric, even immoral. He conceded that different classes of drugs might needed to cure leukemia but, if that were the case, they should be given sequentially to minimize side effects.

The champions of simultaneous multidrug combinations were Emil Frei III and Emil Freireich. The two Emils had been recruited to NCI in 1955 by none other than Gordon Zubrod, to run the leukemia service. During the war, Zubrod had worked on malaria and learned that the key to treatment success was concurrent use of different drugs having distinct mechanisms. He wanted to apply that lesson to leukemia. Research in mice and studies of cancer cells in the laboratory supported this approach. At the same time, drug companies were creating novel compounds that interfere with DNA synthesis or other cellular functions distinct from those antagonized by aminopterin. Frei and Freireich began testing combinations of these drugs in children with ALL. Each cocktail was rigorously evaluated in a clinical trial at NCI and in cooperative leukemia study groups around the country. A major improvement in survival, including some cures, emerged from a four-drug combination known as VAMP—**V**incristine, **A**methopterin (a less toxic derivative of aminopterin), 6-**M**ercaptopurine, and **P**rednisone. Decades of subsequent clinical research using other drugs and radiation of the brain and spinal cord—places where antileukemia drugs do not penetrate—have yielded 90 percent cure rates.

Curing nearly all cases of childhood ALL is a triumph of modern medicine, although one purchased at enormous cost—the severe toxicity and drug-induced deaths of children enrolled in the first trials. It is hard to imagine the courage and dedication of patients, family members, and physicians who persevered through the early days of combination chemotherapy. It is the rare individual who can increase the dose or add another toxic drug to a combination that had just killed a child. And yet, this was the recipe for success. Something special happened when the two Emils worked together. Zubrod said, "Freireich was hard-driving but highly innovative, and Tom [Frei's nickname] was always calm and kept a lid on things. But together they made a good team."[208] David Nathan had a front-row seat to medical history.

Nathan was more than a little frightened when he learned that his first clinical assignment at NIH would be the childhood leukemia service—after all, he had had no exposure to pediatrics since his clerkship in medical school. He wasn't alone. None of the other clinical associates who would spend time on that service were pediatricians and neither were the two Emils—Emil Frei III and Emil Freireich—who were running it. This would not be the last time that Nathan would see internists recruited to take care of children.

His inexperience with sick children and the horrific toxicities he saw on the leukemia trials made Nathan miserable. He could not know that this pain and torture were the first necessary steps toward curing the disease. What he did know was that children were being made to suffer by the drugs he was giving them and he could not shake the feeling that he was abetting their premature deaths. His experience convinced Nathan that he wanted no part of any clinical research program that had no hope of success, and he promised himself that he would never again be involved in clinical cancer research.

Near the end of his first year, Nathan met with Zubrod to map out his activities for year two. As an advocate for combination chemotherapy himself, and the man who brought the two Emils to NIH, Zubrod assumed that Nathan shared his excitement about this new field and would opt for clinical research in cancer or leukemia. Nathan quickly disabused him. Zubrod was surprised, but being a superb and empathetic mentor, he acknowledged Nathan's deep-seated reluctance and worked with him to think about alternatives. After some consideration, Zubrod decided to send Nathan to see Dr. Nathaniel Berlin.

Nathaniel "Nat" Berlin had graduated from Western Reserve University with a degree in chemistry and had gone to Long Island College of Medicine, now SUNY Downstate, for his MD. After his internship and residency, Berlin enrolled as a graduate student in the Department of Physics, Division of Medical Physics, at Berkeley where he studied under John Lawrence, a pioneer in the use of radioactive isotopes for medical research. Berlin's success in graduate school made him one of the earliest holders of both an MD and PhD. He joined the faculty at Berkeley only to be drafted—in the "regular" draft, not the Doctor Draft—and did his time in the Navy.[209] Berlin's expertise in radiation physics got him transferred to the Pentagon where he was in charge of preparing the Navy's response to nuclear accidents.[210] In 1956, Zubrod recruited Berlin to head the metabolism service in the general medicine branch of NIH.

Berlin was a brilliant researcher who knew his own mind. But like so many highly accomplished individuals, he also believed he knew the minds of others. Nathan met Berlin and told him about his interest in pursuing liver research, the field in which he had already made a small mark with his paper about measuring ammonia in blood. Berlin would have none of it. As both men tell the story,[211, 212] Berlin impatiently listened to Nathan while perched on an office chair with both legs tucked under him "like a Jewish Buddha."[213] After briefly considering Nathan's proposal to work on liver metabolism, Berlin decided that this would never do; Berlin knew next to nothing about liver disease. However, he did know quite a lot about red blood cells. Berlin decided that he would redirect the younger man's interests in an unambiguous way so he asked, "Nathan, do you know any math?"

"No, that's not my strength," Nathan replied.

"Well, if we were in uniform, how many stripes would you have on your sleeve?"

Nathan knew that Berlin was referring to their ranks in the uniformed Public Health Service and so, as a lieutenant, he replied, "Two."[214]

"And if I were still a commissioned officer in the Navy, how many would I have?"

"Four," replied Nathan, knowing that Berlin had been a captain.

"Correct. You *can* do math and you've just discovered why you are not going to study ammonia but instead work with me on the basis of anemia in patients with leukemia and myeloid meta-plasia [a preleukemia syndrome]. If you are desperate to work on ammonia, you'll have to find a way to do it after hours on your own time."

Berlin then climbed down from his chair and showed Nathan the laboratory space he would share with two of his Harvard Medical School classmates, Sherman Weissman and Thomas Waldmann, both of whom went on to their own high-profile academic careers.

Nathan was furious. He had assumed that Thorn and Zubrod knew about his interest in ammonia and liver disease and that their plan in bringing him to NIH had been to encourage his work in that area. But here he was, being ordered to study hematology. It felt like a bait and switch. Nathan calmed himself with the thought that at least he was not in Korea; instead, he was being given an opportunity to learn how to deploy the cutting-edge technology of radioisotopes in human medical research. He also reminded himself that his clinical research hero at Harvard had been William Castle, a hematologist—greater minds than Nathan's had found something compelling about red blood cells. He capitulated.

What Nathan learned from Berlin was the study of metabolism which, broadly speaking, is how the body uses chemical building blocks—proteins or sugars or fats in food, oxygen in the air—to make what it needs to function and grow. Metabolism research also reveals how diseases like cancer use these building blocks to fuel abnormal growth. Until the 1940s, researchers could only understand these processes in bulk. They could isolate pieces of liver or tumor and perform chemical analyses to determine how much of a given substance might be present. By comparing that to the amount of the substance's precursors that had been ingested or inhaled, they could infer something about how liver or tumor cells use the precursors to grow.

However, these are just inferences. What scientists really want to do is follow one of these metabolic precursors as it enters the body and identify the precise cellular structures into which it is incorporated. Radioisotopes allow them to do that. The elements that make up the molecules in our bodies are stable in the sense that their atoms have unchanging numbers of protons and neutrons. However, some elements have versions in which the numbers of protons and neutrons in their atoms are different from those in their stable counterparts. These are called isotopes and some are unstable: At a predictable rate, they change their nuclear structures and when that happens, they release a small amount of radiation which can be detected by sensitive instruments. These unstable atoms are called radioisotopes and, despite their radioactivity, share all of the chemical properties of their stable versions. That means that a radioisotope can be substituted for its stable counterpart in a precursor molecule without altering the behavior of that molecule. This radiolabeled precursor can then be administered to an organism by feeding or injection and its metabolic fate can be determined by measuring radioactivity in the new structures in which the precursor becomes incorporated.

Two radioisotopes were particularly useful in Nathan's work with Berlin. One was carbon-14 (abbreviated ^{14}C) which decays slowly, releasing radiation as it does. Carbon-14 is ideal for studying proteins, a major component of all cells and organs. Proteins are composed of linear strings of amino acids, of which there are twenty. One of these, glycine, is present in nearly all proteins, and a version can be made in which one of its stable carbon atoms is replaced by carbon-14. Berlin had used this tool to follow the fate of one specific protein, hemoglobin, the oxygen-carrying protein of red blood cells, and thereby measure how long red blood cells survive in patients with chronic leukemia.[215] Hemoglobin also contains iron, so iron-59 (^{59}Fe), a radioactive version, provided another way of tracking red blood cells.

Nathan spent his second year at NIH using these radioisotopes to measure the survival of red blood cells in patients with myeloid metaplasia, a bone marrow failure disorder,[216] and acute leukemia.[217] Both studies examined only a handful of patients, individuals who had been admitted that year to the wards of the Clinical Center for treatment. The problem with small numbers is that it is exceedingly difficult to draw firm scientific conclusions unless all of the subjects produce generally similar results. Nathan's studies showed just the opposite: the data were all over the map. Nonetheless, his papers were published in prestigious journals because they were a technical tour de force and because the radioisotopes outperformed the then-standard analyses of red cell survival.

While Nathan was mastering advanced technologies in Berlin's lab, he was also learning the ins and outs of clinical hematology by caring for patients on the wards. This combination of cutting-edge research and interesting clinical material was exciting, and it turned Nathan into a confirmed hematologist. He particularly warmed to the kind of clinical research being done in that field. It was different from research in oncology which seemed to be based on testing dangerous poisons in desperate circumstances. Research in hematology appeared, instead, to use new technologies and concepts to address challenging—but not hopeless—clinical problems. And those clinical problems were embodied in individual patients with whom he could interact. Nathan was sold.

But, before Nathan could pursue hematology in earnest, he had to decide where to complete his training. Having fulfilled his two-year commitment to the Doctor Draft, he now had options. One was to stay at NIH for more hematology. The other was to go back to the Brigham for a final year of internal medicine training as a senior resident. When he was a medical student and intern, Nathan had been filled with admiration for senior residents as they magisterially led their teams around the hospital. He wanted to do that, too. Fortunately, Thorn had just appointed Nathan's hero, Buris Boshell, as chief resident, and Boshell let it be known that he wanted Nathan back at the Brigham to be a senior resident. A return to the Brigham would also suit Jean Nathan, who hoped to get her master's degree in education from Boston University. So, in the summer of 1958, the Nathans returned to Cambridge, renting their house from a professor of anthropology at Harvard, one of only two tenured women in the Faculty of Arts and Sciences. Across the street was another Harvard professor, this one of fine arts, and around the corner was Harvard's chief marshal. Their house was only a few blocks from the Shady Hill School, a private day school, where they sent the children and where David Nathan served on the board with other parents in the neighborhood.

Nathan girded himself for another year of hospital call every other night and every other weekend. Jean made sure that the children would still recognize their father by driving them to the Brigham during his weekends on call, where they would meet on the ancient tennis courts that had been built with such good intentions on the hospital grounds in 1913. Nathan was happy to be back at the Brigham. He thought that his interns were terrific and he enjoyed his fellow senior residents, several of whom went on to important careers in academic medicine.[218]

Two stories provide a feel for the influences that surrounded Nathan as a senior resident. One involves Joseph Murray, the pioneering plastic surgeon who received a Nobel Prize for performing the first successful kidney transplants. Like the development of chemotherapy for childhood leukemia, the road to kidney transplantation was paved with failure and suffering. The procedure was dangerous because of the high likelihood that the donor kidney would have come from an individual who was immunologically different from the recipient. As a result, the recipient's immune system would perceive the kidney as a foreign invader, similar to bacteria or viruses, and would mount a vigorous rejection of the transplant. The result would be kidney failure, inflammation, fever, infection, and death. Of course, if a patient were to receive a donated kidney from an identical twin, the recipient's immune system would not see it as foreign and would not reject it. But the chances that a patient with kidney failure would have an identical twin are vanishingly small. And in any case, for kidney transplantation to be a more generally useful intervention, the donor would have to be a nonidentical sibling. That was what Joe Murray was trying to do, so far without success.

Just as he had on the leukemia service at NIH, Nathan developed an antipathy to a program that would dare perform yet another kidney transplant on yet another doomed patient so soon after the last one had died a horrible death—not to mention that a perfectly normal organ donor would now be left with only one kidney. One night when Nathan was on call, he was asked to see a patient who had been transferred from the Boston VA hospital. The patient had been scheduled to be Dr. Murray's seventeenth attempt at a nonidentical sibling transplant, but the patient's kidney failure was rapidly worsening and he needed emergency dialysis. When the patient arrived at the Brigham, he was in terrible shape: he was convulsing and vomiting and the high levels of potassium in his blood caused by his kidney failure were making his heart beat in a dangerously irregular way. Nathan noticed something else. In 1958, there were no blood tests that could predict immunological compatibility between an organ donor and recipient. Instead, Dr. Murray would remove a small patch of skin from the recipient and place into the wound a similar patch of skin from the donor. He reasoned that, if the recipient tolerated the donor's skin patch without rejecting it, then the recipient might not reject the kidney. This patient had one of Murray's skin patches. Nathan saw that the patch had turned black, a sure sign of rejection.

Nathan and his team slaved over the patient. They dialyzed him and corrected his blood abnormalities so that, by morning, he was relatively stable. But during that long night, Nathan had promised himself over and over that he would not let this man die a pointless, painful death—he would not become Murray's seventeenth victim. Nathan summoned all of his faux authority as a senior resident and confronted Dr. Murray, the chief of plastic surgery. Nathan said that the skin graft clearly indicated incompatibility and he could not condone the operation. He insisted that the patient be given morphine and allowed to die in peace.

To Murray's great credit, he could see that his junior colleague was deeply troubled. He told Nathan that he understood his concerns and offered to transfer the patient from the medical to the surgical service. Nathan gladly did the paperwork for the transfer and thought no more about this unhappy encounter until three months later when he saw the face of this same young man on the cover of *Life* magazine—he was being introduced to the world as the recipient of the first successful kidney transplant from a nonidentical twin. The patient and the donor had been immunologically compatible after all—the skin graft had failed for technical reasons. Like the two Emils, Murray had pressed ahead to do something that he believed would be successful even when the available evidence argued against it. This was an important lesson for Nathan about the hubris of youth and the dedication of clinical researchers.

The second story involves another patient Nathan saw as a senior resident. Mr. Zhangi had emigrated from Italy as a child and lived most of his life in Boston's North End, home to many immigrant Italian families. Now, at age seventy, he had come to the emergency ward at the Brigham because his skin had turned a jaundiced yellow color and he was anemic. A chest X-ray showed masses in his lungs and he was presumed to have cancer of the pancreas, which often causes jaundice, with spread to the lungs.

Nathan disagreed and thought he had a way to prove he was right. One of the most cost-effective clinical tests ever devised is examining a patient's blood after smearing it on a glass microscope slide. Precise diagnoses can be made based on the size and shape— the morphology—of the red blood cells. However, the effectiveness of the blood smear as a diagnostic test depends on the skill and experience of the person peering through the microscope, which is why teaching the subtleties of blood cell morphology to trainees is a time-honored tradition in hematology. During his second year at

NIH, Nathan learned how to analyze blood smears from legendary figures like George Brecher, the chief of the hematology section at NIH, who had emigrated from Czechoslovakia to England in 1939 and to the U.S. in 1942. Nathan became a highly accomplished morphologist and passed this skill on to generations of his trainees.

Being a hematologist at heart, even as a senior resident, Nathan would routinely look at the blood smears of his patients. When he examined Mr. Zhangi's, he saw something unexpected. The physicians in the emergency room had presumed that Mr. Zhangi's anemia was caused by cancer-associated blood loss or poor nutrition, either of which would produce an iron-deficiency anemia with small, pale red cells. Nathan saw some of these in the smear but he was sure that he also saw, mixed among them, cells characteristic of another type of anemia, namely thalassemia. As will be discussed in Chapter 6, thalassemia is a family of diseases in which genetic mutations cause problems in red blood cell production. These mutations are more common in people from Mediterranean countries, like Mr. Zhangi. However, thalassemia is ordinarily diagnosed in childhood and the seventy-year-old Mr. Zhangi carried no such medical history.

Still, Nathan's eye for morphology gave him enough confidence to bring the blood smear to the most eminent hematologist he could find. Louis Diamond had created the world's first pediatric hematology research program at Boston Children's Hospital, right across the street from the Brigham, where he studied thalassemia and other rare anemias of childhood, some of which bear his name. If Nathan were correct about Mr. Zhangi's diagnosis, there could be no one better to confirm it.

Diamond looked at the smear and agreed with Nathan: Mr. Zhangi had thalassemia, which meant that the masses in his lungs were not cancer at all. They were actually his body's attempt to make more red blood cells to compensate for his chronic anemia—they were clumps of red blood cell precursors that ordinarily live in the bone marrow, which, in Mr. Zhangi's case, was already completely full. Further, his jaundice was not due to cancer but was rather a consequence of the fact that the red blood cells in thalassemia are misshapen and destroyed by the liver. This releases their cellular contents, including hemoglobin, which the body converts into a molecule called bilirubin. In thalassemia, bilirubin released from destroyed red blood cells can accumulate to such an extent that it forms deposits in various organs. Because bilirubin is yellow, it causes jaundice when it builds up in the skin.

There are few things in medicine more satisfying than coming up with a diagnosis that, first, was missed by everyone else and, second, explains a panoply of seemingly unrelated symptoms and signs. Nathan was justifiably proud and presented the case at grand rounds. Interestingly, one of the senior physicians who heard his presentation was Chester Jones, a gastroenterologist at Massachusetts General Hospital who happened to have seen Mr. Zhangi several years earlier At the time, Jones had thought that Zhangi's anemia and enlarged spleen were due to Banti's syndrome, a rare disorder caused by obstruction of the blood vessels that drain the spleen and liver. On his recommendation, Zhangi's spleen had been removed. Because the spleen destroys red blood cells in thalassemia, the severity of his true underlying disease was blunted and the diagnosis delayed until his eighth decade.

Nathan's triumph led to two important career outcomes. The first was a decision to focus his clinical research on the thalassemias, a family of diseases whose patients provide material and insights that could help Nathan reveal the underlying mechanisms responsible for their clinical problems. The second was more practical: Dr. Diamond had noticed him. Recognition by the world's leading pediatric hematologist, who happened to be based at Boston Children's Hospital, would play an important role later in Nathan's life.

Meanwhile, Nathan had to decide what to do when his senior residency was over. The path of least resistance would be to join the faculty at the Brigham as a hematologist, which would allow him to stay at Harvard and his family to stay in Cambridge. This was by no means preordained—the Brigham was one of the premier research hospitals in the world and Nathan would have to convince Thorn to hire him. In Nathan's favor was the fact that he was a known quantity. He had been an intern and senior resident at the Brigham and Thorn had thought highly enough of him to recommend him for the ATP at NIH during his junior resident year. In fact, having a graduate of that program on the faculty would be a feather in the Brigham's cap.

Also working in Nathan's favor, ironically, was the fact that Thorn had little interest in the kind of clinical research Nathan wanted to do and even less interest in hematology as a specialty. In fact, Thorn actively promulgated the idea that the future belonged to physician-scientists who could perform research on the molecular basis of disease.[219] As for his division of hematology, Thorn had hired Frank Gardner to be chief. Gardner had been at Boston City Hospital's Thorndike Laboratory under Castle, who was happy to have Gardner spread the hematology gospel at the Brigham. Although Gardner was a solid clinical hematologist, he was not an accomplished investigator. His appointment was consistent with Thorn's strategy of not building a strong division of hematology, preferring instead to forge closer ties with Sidney Farber, who was developing the Children's Cancer Research Foundation and the Jimmy Fund Clinic. Farber was a masterful fundraiser and Thorn thought that an alliance with him might enable the Brigham to attract money for the new hospital it so desperately needed to build.

An indirect result of these machinations was Thorn's offer of a faculty position in the division of hematology at the Brigham starting July 1959. Although Nathan's laboratory space would not be available for a year, he was eager to accept because Gardner was willing to share his own lab in the interim. However, two events foreshadowed an unhappy outcome. First, while he was weighing the offer, Nathan was summoned to the long central hallway in the Brigham, known as the Pike, by Samuel A. Levine, a world-famous cardiologist who happened to be a friend of Nathan's parents. Levine told Nathan that joining the Brigham would be a huge mistake, that Thorn would use him to make money for the hospital by forcing him to see an endless stream of patients and then discard him without a thought for his career. To Levine, the only way a physician could afford to do research was by having the financial security of a private practice. Operating a full-time research laboratory and seeing patients in a hospital clinic would be madness. Levine said that he had discussed the plan with Nathan's father, Geoffrey, and both of them thought it was "stupid." Nathan listened politely but was not dissuaded.

The second event was the death of Geoffrey Nathan from complications of diabetes and atherosclerosis on the day that David Nathan opened his laboratory in 1960.

Chapter 6

THE MALICE OF A DIVERTED BLOOD—THE THALASSEMIAS

Imagine meeting a seven-year-old boy whose small size makes him look like he's only three. His skin is pale with a yellowish tint and his large forehead protrudes over prominent cheekbones, putting you in mind of a chipmunk even as you chide yourself for the thought. His arms are too short for his body and they, along with his legs, are contorted by what his mother describes as a litany of broken bones. Pain appears to be limiting his movements. Mom tells you that another of her eight children had the same problems as this child and died of heart failure complicated by diabetes before her twelfth birthday. She shakes her head in frustration because both children had appeared completely normal when they were born; their troubles began only after their first birthdays. The story devastates you and, out of sympathy, you ask about the extended family. Not only do cousins on both sides have the same affliction but she also knows of sick children from unrelated families who live in the same Syrian city where she grew up.

What is wrong with this child? Analyzing his blood offers some clues. First, he is anemic, meaning that he has fewer red blood cells than he ought to have. But the real tip-off comes from looking at his blood smear through a microscope. Normal red blood cells have a monotonously regular shape: they are round, red discs of uniform size with a slight depression in their center. This child's cells look strikingly different: They are smaller than normal and vary in size; they are pale pink instead of red; some have bizarre shapes; there are even what appear to be mere fragments of cells. It almost looks as if the child's red blood cells are being torn to pieces.

These abnormalities indicate that he has thalassemia, the disease to which David Nathan devoted much of his clinical and scientific career. Understanding why this disease occurs and why it produces these particular clinical manifestations is a triumph of biochemistry, structural biology, and genetics. Familiarity with this scientific context is needed to fully appreciate Nathan's contributions.

The cells in our bodies need oxygen to survive. For multicellular creatures like humans, the challenge is getting it to all of their cells. This cannot happen by simple diffusion from the air: At best, oxygen can penetrate only a few cell layers, not even all the way through the skin. Evolution solved this problem by developing a network of blood vessels that could, in principle, transport oxygen from the lungs to cells in every recess of the body. But there is another problem—only a small amount of oxygen can dissolve in water. So, even if blood vessels can reach every cell in the body, they cannot deliver enough oxygen to keep those cells alive if all they carry is water.

The solution is hemoglobin, a molecular machine that efficiently picks up oxygen from air in the lungs and releases it in body tissues where it is needed. Some of the earliest and most elegant achievements in biochemistry revealed how this works. Hemoglobin has two components: heme, which is a molecular cage for an iron atom, and globin which is a protein. Proteins are made up of strings of amino acids, their precise order dictated by that protein's gene. Normal adults have two kinds of globin, alpha and beta, whose slightly different structures are determined by their alpha-globin and beta-globin genes. In fact, humans have four alpha-globin genes, two inherited from each parent, and two beta-globin genes, one from each parent. The globin proteins encoded by these genes are attached to one heme molecule apiece to form hemoglobin. The final molecular entity that actually carries oxygen from the lungs to the tissues has four hemoglobin molecules: two alpha-globin chains with their hemes and two beta-globin chains with their hemes. This form of hemoglobin is called hemoglobin A, abbreviated HbA.

A drop of blood contains several different cell types but the one relevant to thalassemia is the red blood cell, technically known as an erythrocyte from the Greek roots ερυθροσ meaning reddish, and κυτοσ meaning a vessel or container or, in this case, a cell. Mature erythrocytes are sacs filled with hemoglobin, their membranes protecting the protein from being degraded by enzymes in the blood. In the lungs, where the amount of oxygen is high, the four hemoglobin chains of HbA have a three-dimensional shape that favors the binding of one molecule of oxygen to each of the iron atoms in the four hemes. Hemoglobin with bound oxygen is called oxygenated hemoglobin. When the erythrocyte with oxygenated hemoglobin reaches tissues, where the concentration of oxygen is low, the four hemoglobin chains change their shapes. Although the shift is subtle, it is sufficient to loosen the heme iron's grip on its bound oxygen. This releases the oxygen which diffuses out of the erythrocyte so that it can be taken up by tissue cells. The erythrocyte then travels back to the lungs where hemoglobin again changes its shape, re-binds oxygen, and restarts the cycle.

This is a complex but robust system that elegantly solves the problem of delivering oxygen to tissues. Sometimes, however, things go wrong. Every time a cell divides, it must copy all of the DNA in each of its forty-six chromosomes so that a full complement of genetic material can be transmitted to the new cells. This requires a faithful replication of all three billion subunits that form the DNA in each of our cells. Not surprisingly, errors occasionally occur. Sometimes, just one DNA subunit in a gene might be copied incorrectly leading to what is called a point mutation. This can change the blueprint for the structure of the protein encoded by that gene. Sometimes, an entire segment of a gene might not be copied at all, leading to a "deletion" of that gene. The result is a complete absence of the protein encoded by the gene. And sometimes, DNA sequences adjacent to the gene which control how much protein it makes might be damaged or mutated. In these cases, despite the presence of an apparently normal gene, no protein is made.

The child introduced at the beginning of this chapter has mutations in both of his beta-globin genes and, as a result, produces almost no beta-globin protein. This leads to a condition called beta thalassemia major, also known as Cooley's anemia, named for the Detroit hematologist who systematically described it. Essentially every aspect of this child's clinical picture is explained by the absence of beta-globin:

Anemia with small, pale red blood cells—Erythrocytes are bright red when they contain normal amounts of oxygen-bound hemoglobin. When no beta-globin protein is made, there is no HbA. Although humans have other globin genes which produce other types of globins, they are either made in low amounts or do not bind oxygen well. Low amounts of fully functional hemoglobin in an erythrocyte, or high amounts of poorly functional hemoglobin, result in less oxygen-bound heme which produces a pale pink cell. A correct balance of alpha- and beta-globins is also essential for hemoglobin to function normally. In the absence of beta-globin, the excess alpha chains try to form a four protein complex in imitation of HbA but these complexes are not soluble and form solid aggregates in the red blood cell (a discovery Nathan contributed to). This has two consequences: (1) the erythrocyte precursors containing these aggregates are destroyed in the bone marrow resulting in "ineffective erythropoiesis," which simply means that the marrow is not making erythrocytes at a normal rate; and (2) the small number of aggregate-containing red blood cells that do escape the bone marrow are destroyed by the spleen which is responsible for removing red blood cells that are misshapen or have solid clumps in them. The result is fewer red blood cells in the blood—anemia—along with fragments of destroyed cells.

Pale, yellow skin—What we call a healthy skin color comes from the reddish tinge of oxygenated hemoglobin in erythrocytes flowing through the skin's blood vessels. Decreased numbers of erythrocytes in thalassemia patients and poor oxygenation of the non-HbA hemoglobin in those erythrocytes combine to produce pallor. The yellowish tint, called jaundice, is a consequence of the spleen's destruction of abnormal erythrocytes. When the spleen rips apart a red cell, hemoglobin is released into the bloodstream where enzymes degrade globin thereby freeing heme. Through transformations in the liver and elsewhere, heme is converted to bilirubin which is yellow. Ordinarily, bilirubin is collected in the gall bladder which transports it to the intestine to be excreted with feces. But, when red blood cell destruction by the spleen is as extensive as it is in beta thalassemia major, the gall bladder excretion route is overwhelmed and bilirubin accumulates in the blood. This bilirubin is deposited in several organs including the skin where it imparts a yellow tinge.

Skeletal abnormalities—Rapid growth during fetal and early neonatal development requires oxygen and, therefore, a high demand for erythrocytes which is met by expanding the bone marrow. Because the need for erythrocytes is so substantial during this period, nearly every bone in the body is stuffed with marrow. Later, when oxygen requirements decrease, fewer erythrocytes are needed and their production becomes restricted to the marrow of the pelvic bones, the vertebrae, the long bones of the arms and legs, and the skull, while the marrow that had been active in other locations disappears. In beta thalassemia major, however, the body is chronically starved for oxygen. In response, tissues release hormonelike signals, which stimulate the bone marrow to expand in an attempt to make more red cells. Bone marrow soon re-establishes itself in places that had once housed fetal marrow: facial bones and the smaller bones of the arms and legs. Because the abnormal hemoglobin in beta thalassemia functions so poorly, the body's demand for oxygen is never satisfied; the need for more erythrocytes never goes away and marrow continues to grow. As it expands, it pushes the surrounding bone outward. In the skull, this produces "frontal bossing," the technical term for a protruding forehead; in facial bones, "chipmunk" cheeks; in the bones of the extremities, bowing and contortion of the arms and legs. As bone is pushed further outward by the marrow, it becomes thinner and more susceptible to fractures.

Expanding marrow explains most of the skeletal abnormalities in beta thalassemia major but not short stature. One's height is determined by the age at which the ends of the long bones of the arms and legs close off, preventing any further lengthening. For unclear reasons, this closure occurs quite early in patients with beta thalassemia leading to their diminished stature and foreshortened arms.

Endocrine abnormalities—Although this little boy does not have problems with his endocrine glands yet, his older sister had diabetes. This, too, is related to beta thalassemia major, albeit indirectly. Without treatment, most children with beta thalassemia die by age five. The reason this child and his sister lived longer is that they received blood transfusions. The erythrocytes in transfused blood carry oxygen to the body's tissues, relieving some of the pressure on the bone marrow to make more red cells. However, every molecule of hemoglobin in transfused erythrocytes has an iron atom in its heme and as those cells age and are destroyed during the normal life cycle of a red blood cell, the hemoglobin is degraded and its iron is released. Repeated transfusions eventually overwhelm the body's capacity to remove iron. At the same time, ineffective erythropoiesis—the bone marrow's failure to make sufficient numbers of erythrocytes—sends a signal to the stomach and intestine to absorb more iron in food. Together, these forces lead to a state of iron overload in which the metal accumulates in tissues such as endocrine glands. When too much iron piles up in the pancreas, insulin-producing cells are destroyed, leading to diabetes; too much iron in the thyroid can cause hypothyroidism.

Heart problems—Beta thalassemia major patients often die from progressive heart failure, a weakening of the heart muscle so severe that it cannot effectively pump blood. Two insults lead to this terrible outcome. First, the same iron overload that damages endocrine organs also damages the muscle fibers of the heart. Second, when tissues are starved for oxygen, as they are in thalassemia, they send signals to the heart to pump harder and faster in an attempt to deliver more oxygenated hemoglobin. This constant overwork leads to weakening of the muscle which, when combined with the damage caused by iron deposition, produces deadly results.

Why did this disease appear in two of the mother's children and in the children of unrelated families who live in her Syrian hometown? The answer lies in the genetics of the thalassemias. Recall that people have two beta-globin genes, one inherited from each parent. In patients with beta thalassemia major, both of their beta-globin genes are abnormal. So, in order for the little boy and his sister to have beta thalassemia major, they would have to inherit one abnormal beta-globin gene from their mother and another from their father. This could happen if both parents had one normal and one abnormal beta-globin gene. Each beta-globin gene, the normal one and the abnormal one, has an equal chance of being passed on to a child. Therefore, the probability that the mother could pass her abnormal beta-globin gene to a child would be one in two or 50 percent. The probability that the father could pass his abnormal beta-globin gene to a child would also be 50 percent. The chance that both parents could pass their abnormal genes to the same child would be the product of each of the parents' individual chances: one in four or 25 percent. It is no surprise, then, that two of the eight children in this family had beta thalassemia major.

Someone with one normal and one abnormal beta-globin gene, like these parents, is said to have beta thalassemia minor. Although individuals with beta thalassemia minor may have a mild anemia with slightly small and pale red cells, they have no symptoms and lead normal lives. Nonetheless they are carriers of the beta thalassemia gene which could have important implications for family planning. One additional subtlety is that some mutations in beta-globin genes cause only mildly decreased production of beta-globin protein rather than outright loss. This causes a disease known as beta thalassemia intermedia, the severity of which lies between the extremes of beta thalassemia major and minor.

What about alpha-globin genes? They can also undergo mutation or deletion, which results in thalassemia syndromes of varying severity. Because people have four alpha-globin genes, the possibilities are more complex than they are with two beta-globin genes. Loss of only one alpha-globin gene is well compensated by the other three and individuals with this condition, known as alpha-thalassemia minima, are clinically normal. However, loss of two alpha-globin genes begins to cause detectable abnormalities because of the imbalance of alpha- and beta-globin proteins. These individuals have alpha thalassemia minor (or alpha thalassemia trait) and, like those with beta thalassemia minor, a mild anemia with small, pale erythrocytes, but they are clinically normal.

Things get worse when three alpha-globin genes are deleted. Now the balance between alpha- and beta-globin proteins is so out of whack that the beta-globins start to form four-membered complexes called hemoglobin H, or HbH. HbH has such poor capacity for binding oxygen and is so inefficient in delivering whatever oxygen it does carry, that it causes a severe disease that looks like beta thalassemia major. Individuals with three deleted alpha-globin genes are kept alive by the tiny amount of alpha-globin made from their one remaining gene. We know this because deletion of all four alpha-globin genes causes fetal death, a condition known as hydrops fetalis.

Fetal death due to wholesale loss of alpha-globin genes occurs late in gestation. The delay is explained by the transient appearance of functional hemoglobin subtypes during embryologic development, a phenomenon that has important implications for the work Nathan did in sickle cell disease. Initially, a normal fetus has no beta-globin, making instead a different globin called gamma. Gamma-globin in the fetus works like beta-globin in the neonate: it contributes to a four-membered hemoglobin molecule containing two alpha- and two gamma-globin chains called HbF, for "fetal hemoglobin," which functions nearly as well as HbA. At about thirty-two weeks of gestation, gamma-globin production declines and beta-globin production commences. By twelve weeks after birth, gamma-globin levels are very low and beta-globin has nearly reached its adult levels, as has HbA.

If a fetus lacks all four alpha-globin genes, then the gamma-globin proteins form a four-membered hemoglobin called HbBarts, named for the London hospital—St. Bartholomew's—where it was discovered. Although four gamma-globins are not as functional as two alphas and two betas, they are far more functional than four betas. That is why a fetus missing all of its alpha-globin genes can survive for some time in the uterus. But when the normal shift from gamma-globin to beta-globin production occurs, the fetus has no functional hemoglobin left and dies shortly before birth.

Individuals with severe beta- or alpha-thalassemia major almost never reach reproductive age. Why hasn't Darwinian natural selection removed these devastating mutations from the human genome? The answer lies in geography. If one were to draw a band on the globe starting from the lands that ring the Mediterranean, then extend it eastward through the Levant, and further eastward through the Indian subcontinent, southeast Asia, and the Malay archipelago, one would have identified areas with a high prevalence of thalassemia. In fact, the name thalassemia was proposed in 1932 by George Whipple (introduced in reference to pernicious anemia Chapter 4) because all of the cases that had been described up to that time came from families whose origins could be traced to countries near the Mediterranean or "the sea"—θαλασσα in Greek.[220]

These are the same geographic regions that have the highest prevalence of malaria. Similar to sickle cell anemia, another disorder of mutated hemoglobin, the abnormal hemoglobins of the thalassemias make red blood cells resistant to infection by the malaria parasite. For unknown reasons, alpha-thalassemia erythrocytes are more resistant to malaria than beta-thalassemia erythrocytes but both types of thalassemia are protective. Thus natural selection for malaria resistance provides the counterweight to the evolutionary pressure that would otherwise rid the human population of these harmful globin mutations.

Nathan decided to dedicate his career to the thalassemias. The molecular abnormalities underlying these diseases combine principles of genetics and biochemistry which allowed him to learn some basic science and apply the concepts to human disease. The complex clinical manifestations gave him an opportunity to use the expertise in hematology he had gained during his two years at NIH. Most importantly, though, the disease disrupted the lives of children and adults and Nathan wanted a chance to interact with these patients. He was convinced he could help them.

Chapter 7

STARTING OUT: HEMATOLOGY AT THE PETER BENT BRIGHAM HOSPITAL

Nathan's first faculty job began in the summer of 1959 in the Division of Hematology of the Department of Medicine at the Peter Bent Brigham Hospital, where he was expected to see patients in the division's outpatient clinic and serve as an attending physician overseeing the care of patients on the hospital wards for one month every year—finally leading one of those teams of residents, interns, and medical students that he had joined at Boston City Hospital as a lowly medical student. During the eleven months when he was not attending, he would provide consultation services for physicians who needed advice on the care of patients with hematologic problems. Nathan's position came with an appointment as an associate in medicine at Harvard Medical School, where he was asked to teach in the hematology course for second-year medical students, a setting in which he imparted the skills for assessing blood smears that he had learned at NIH. Nathan's participation in the Hematology course would continue for nearly sixty years.

As a young faculty member with a steady income and growing family, Nathan decided that he deserved a new house. Even though he was working in Boston, he still had a deep affinity for the Cambridge community on the other side of the Charles River. Accordingly, Jean and Ruth found the ideal place at 192 Brattle

Street,[221] directly behind what would later become the official house of Harvard's president. Ruth sold the home she had shared with Geoffrey in Newton and moved to Wyman Road, a fifteen-minute walk from the Nathans. The Brattle Street house had been built in 1908 for Arnold Dolmetsch, one of the founders of the early music movement. Dolmetsch oversaw a workshop that produced period instruments such as viols, lutes, recorders, and harpsichords. In fact, the house at 192 Brattle is notable for carved cutouts of viols decorating the balustrade. After Dolmetsch, it became home to the poet Josephine Preston Peabody and later to Felix Frankfurter, associate justice of the Supreme Court, when he was at Harvard Law School. The Brattle Street house suited the Nathans so well that they stayed there for fifty years.

To Nathan, the most exciting aspect of his new job was the opportunity to direct his own research program. As the most junior member of the division, he was assigned a minuscule amount of research space in what was known as the Richard C. Curtis Hematology Research Laboratory. Unfortunately, the Curtis Laboratory's grandiose name belied its meagre amenities. It was housed on the second floor of an ancient three-story structure called the Fanny Tackaberry Laboratories, which had been built adjacent to the Brigham shortly after the main hospital opened. A creaking flight of stairs led from the Curtis Hematology Lab down to the pathology department, which was chaired by Gustave Dammin, known to all as Gus, who became famous for his contributions to the science of organ transplantation. Whenever one of Nathan's experimental setups sprang a leak, the flood always seemed to target Dammin's desk on the floor below.

Even by the standards of 1959, Nathan's lab space was woefully inadequate. To reach it, he and his assistants had to pass through an outer laboratory where three hematology fellows were busy doing their own research. Beyond that gauntlet was Nathan's postage-stamp lab. It had just enough room for a benchtop and a fume exhaust hood where experiments with noxious chemicals could be performed. In the adjacent administrative area, Nathan shared an office with other young faculty members. The Curtis Laboratory's small footprint also included the hematology division's clinical laboratory, which performed analyses on blood samples from patients in the clinic or the hospital. Four technicians were squeezed into the that lab, making the space even tighter. The only member of the hematology division not shoehorned into the Curtis space was Frank Gardner. As division chief, he was privileged to have an office in the main hospital where he also saw patients in his private practice.

Just one year earlier, Nathan had been working in the palatial air-conditioned luxury of the new NIH clinical center with its sparkling research laboratories. Although frustrated by the Spartan provisions of the Curtis Laboratory, Nathan energetically embraced his new opportunity. His enthusiasm was an example of the trade-offs ambitious faculty members often make in order to work in an exciting environment surrounded by world-class colleagues. In the future, Nathan would exploit this willingness to compromise when, as division chief, chair, and hospital president, he recruited his own new faculty to less than ideal facilities.

One of the more serious challenges posed by Nathan's tight research space was its inability to accommodate a piece of equipment he deemed essential—a whole-body radiation detector, an instrument that measures the distribution of radioactive materials after injection into a research subject. Nathan had learned how to use this technology when he was with Nat Berlin at NIH and now wanted to apply it to his own research. Because it was too big to fit in his lab, he wedged it into an open area across the hall. Soon enough, though, Nathan needed yet another piece of equipment, one that precisely measures radioactivity in small biochemical samples. This large and unwieldy instrument, called a liquid scintillation counter, would not fit anywhere in the Curtis Laboratory. Fearing that Nathan might abandon the hematology division for a job elsewhere if he could not have his new "toy,"

Gardner bought a trailer which he parked between the Brigham and Children's Hospital. Nathan put his liquid scintillation counter in the trailer and, while he was at it, moved his office there. In that pretransistor age, the instrument ran on over one hundred vacuum tubes. Fortunately, when he was at NIH, Nathan had become adept at the care and maintenance of liquid scintillation counters. As the technology spread to more laboratories in the Harvard Medical Area, he became the *de facto* serviceman for these instruments—he had his own tube tester and was on call for labs whose machines were on the fritz.

With his laboratory and fancy equipment in place, Nathan now planned his research—what scientific questions would he ask? What area of hematology would be most interesting? What would have the greatest impact? Ever since his encounter with Mr. Zhangi, Nathan had been thinking about thalassemia, his growing fascination coinciding with a period of stunning break-throughs in the biochemistry and genetics of hemoglobin. Max Perutz had just determined the physical structure of hemoglobin,[222] Nobel Prizewinning work that confirmed the four-protein com-plex predicted by Linus Pauling.[223] The single amino acid change in beta-globin that causes sickle cell disease had been identified a few years earlier,[224] rounding out the picture of what Pauling called the first "molecular disease." (Pauling, a brilliant physical chemist with little exposure to medical research, had started working on sickle cell hemoglobin at the suggestion of Nathan's hero, William Castle.[225]) Geneticists were determining the number of alpha- and beta-globin genes in the human genome and their chromosomal locations. Hemoglobin was a hot research area, one full of limitless potential for an ambitious, young physician-scientist.

Nathan was embarking on his research career at the same moment that the thalassemia field was struggling with a critically important question: how does the deletion or hobbling of a globin gene lead to the myriad clinical problems that affect thalassemia patients? There are two ways to think about this question and David Weatherall, one of the giants of thalassemia research and, later, a close friend of Nathan's, elegantly described the choice:

> Once it was realized that the thalassemias result from defective alpha- or beta-chain production, thinking about their pathophysiology moved in two different though often overlapping directions. On the one hand, workers in the field wanted to understand how mutations at the alpha- or beta-globin gene loci could result in the widespread clinical manifestations which seemed to affect nearly every system in the body and which were not confined to the red cells in which the globin genes are expressed. On the other, it seemed equally important to try to determine the different kind of mutations that might underlie the defective production of alpha and beta chains.[226]

Both approaches would be necessary in order for hematologists to develop a full understanding of the thalassemias but Nathan became an adept of the first. He decided to devote his research to understanding why thalassemia patients suffer the particular signs and symptoms that they do (Figure 13)

At the outset, one curious fact drew his attention. The facile explanation for the low red cell numbers in thalassemia was that genetic loss or malfunction of globin genes leads to decreased production of hemoglobin, which, in turn, leads to decreased production of red blood cells. However, direct examination of the bone marrow, where these cells are made, showed something else. Surprisingly large amounts of hemoglobin are produced in the marrow of thalassemia patients, but then, much of it is rapidly destroyed. This is the setting for "ineffective erythropoiesis," the inability to produce mature red blood cells. Why does this happen?

Figure 13. Left to right: Sir David Weatherall, David Nathan,
Edward J. Benz (Courtesy of David G. Nathan.)

Some patients with mild thalassemia, or thalassemia intermedia, appear clinically normal despite their abnormal hemoglobin
A (HbA) because, even as adults, they produce fetal hemoglobin
(HbF). As described in Chapter 6, HbF contains two alpha- and
two gamma-globin chains while HbA contains two alpha- and two
beta-globin chains. At birth, gamma-globin production normally
stops and beta-globin synthesis ramps up. The result is loss of
HbF coincident with the appearance of HbA. For reasons that were
unknown at the time, some thalassemic patients with abnormal
globin genes continue to make gamma-globin, which is incorporated into HbF. The amounts are small but enough to mitigate
some of the clinical effects of chronic anemia. Nathan wondered
if the fetal hemoglobin in these patients was distributed evenly
among their red cells or if, instead, some red cells had lots of HbF
and some had nearly none. If the latter, then perhaps, the balance between HbF and abnormal HbA determined red cell survival:
those with little HbF and lots of abnormal HbA were destroyed

while cells with plentiful HbF and less abnormal HbA survived to carry oxygen to tissues.

Nathan reasoned that if this were the case, then red cells with high amounts of HbF should persist in the bloodstream of thalassemia intermedia patients longer than cells with low amounts. He tested this using the radioactive tracer technology he had learned from Nat Berlin at NIH. By injecting radioactive building blocks of hemoglobin into thalassemia patients and normal volunteers, Nathan could measure the rates at which the two types of hemoglobin were being produced and how long they lasted. If his hypothesis were correct, HbF should enjoy a longer lifetime in the bloodstream of thalassemia patients than HbA.

While the experiment was conceptually simple, making these measurements in the early 1960s was a tall order. In particular, quantifying the amounts of radioactivity in HbF and HbA would depend on physically separating the two hemoglobins, a biochemical task that was far from routine at the time. However, as with so many medical advances, the solution was provided by a new technology. Scientists in Sweden had invented a technique called "column chromatography" that could reliably and cleanly separate individual proteins in a complex mixture like blood. It was the ideal tool for isolating the different hemoglobins. Unfortunately, like most brand new technologies, column chromatography was not yet widely available or commonly used. The Swedes were the only true experts.

Nathan's deus ex machina was his Harvard Medical School classmate, Tom Gabuzda. After finishing his internship and residency at Massachusetts General Hospital, Gabuzda had gone to the Karolinska Institute in Stockholm where he mastered the intricacies of column chromatography. Armed with that rarified knowledge, Gabuzda returned to Boston and joined Nathan's fledgling research group. Nathan was thrilled. Now, if he were to inject his radioactive material into thalassemia patients and then draw their blood sometime later, Gabuzda could separate the hemoglobins, which would allow them to measure the radioactivity in each type. Nathan could then determine the rates at which HbF and HbA were being made and destroyed.

The other bit of luck for these studies was the referral to Nathan of two adults with beta thalassemia intermedia from Dr. Louis Diamond, the head of hematology at Boston Children's Hospital, and his fellow, Park Gerald, who would later become a major force in clinical genetics. Nathan eagerly recruited the men, Steven and Joe, into his research project. They agreed to let Nathan inject them with radioactive material that would eventually find its way into their newly synthesized hemoglobin. At regular intervals over the next several weeks, Nathan drew their blood, which he handed off to Gabuzda, who separated the two hemoglobins using column chromatography and then quantified the amount of radioactivity in each using Nathan's liquid scintillation counter.

A contemporary reader might blanch at the thought of Nathan deliberately injecting radioactive material into humans solely for research purposes. The same reader might then try to assuage his or her concerns by assuming that the men had been told about the risks of the experiment before they signed on. Nothing could be further from the truth. The subjects in Nathan's experiments simply followed their doctor's orders and did not provide anything close to what we would now recognize as informed consent as a precondition for their participation. In later years, Nathan recognized this deficiency. Looking back ruefully, he said that, in those days, informed consent consisted of a physician telling a subject to "lie down over there on that exam table."

Clinical research in the 1950s and 1960s had a Wild West feel. Nathan would inject his subjects with radiation and then send them back home to mingle with their families. He took a similarly casual approach to their blood samples. One of the men, Steven, lived in Framingham, a community about twenty miles west of Boston. Because his work schedule precluded his coming all the way into Boston, he would meet Nathan in the parking lot of the newly built Shoppers World, one of the first suburban shopping malls in the United States. Sitting next to Steven in his car, Nathan would draw his blood in full view of shoppers and, once, a Massachusetts state trooper. Occasionally, Nathan would bring his eight-year-old daughter Deborah with him and involve her in the proceedings saying, "Debsie, you can help since you have small hands. Put the caps on these test tubes."[227] Nathan would bring the capped tubes of blood home with him to Cambridge and store them in the kitchen refrigerator until he took them to the lab the next day. This laissez-faire attitude toward research subjects, radiation, and human blood samples is nearly inconceivable today.

Questionable ethics aside, the blood Nathan drew from these subjects and others generated unambiguous results, which were published in three papers over the next few years.[228, 229, 230] As Nathan had predicted, HbA lasted a much shorter time in their blood than did HbF. The reason was not obvious but Nathan had a straightforward idea. Perhaps red cells with lots of HbA and little HbF survived only a short time as opposed to red cells with little HbA and lots of HbF, which survived longer. The differential destruction of the two types of erythrocytes might explain the differential persistence of the two types of hemoglobin. Nathan devised an experiment to test this idea. If HbF protected red blood cells from premature destruction then cells with lots of HbF should live longer than cells with lots of HbA. Cells that live longer should be older and therefore, if Nathan was right, older red cells should have a higher proportion of HbF than younger red cells. Erythrocytes can be separated by age after spinning blood in a centrifuge: old cells are dense and go to the bottom of the centrifuge tube while young cells stay near the top. When Nathan and Gabuzda tested blood from the thalassemia subjects, they found that most of the HbF was in old cells. This told them that HbF survived longer than HbA in thalassemia because red blood cells containing lots of HbF survived longer than red cells containing lots of HbA.

This was an important observation but it left a key question unanswered: how were the red cells with abnormal HbA marked for destruction? Surprisingly, the explanation came from an old-fashioned, low-tech analysis: looking at red blood cells through a microscopic. Phaedon Fessas, a hematologist working in Athens, reported in 1963 that a high proportion of red blood cells in thalassemia patients contain clumps of material not present in normal red cells.[231] Based on their absorption of specific dyes, he inferred that they were made of hemoglobin. Because the patients whose blood he examined had beta thalassemia, he thought that these clumps must be comprised of alpha-globin chains that, in the absence of their beta-globin partners, had aggregated into insoluble precipitates. As expected from Nathan and Gabuzda's results, the clumps were present mostly in younger cells, the ones with shorter survivals. Taken together, the observations from Fessas and Nathan suggested that the anemia of beta thalassemia is not so much a consequence of the specific abnormalities in mutated beta-globin chains as it is an *imbalance* between alpha- and beta-globin chains. Of course, mutations in beta-globin genes are the underlying cause of the disease but it is the absence or underproduction of beta-globin protein in the setting of ongoing alpha-globin synthesis that causes the clinical problems. Without their beta-globin partners, alpha-globins are forced together, causing them to clump, and their clumping marks red cells for destruction.

When Nathan went back and reexamined blood from his study subjects with thalassemia intermedia, he saw alpha-globin clumps in their red blood cells and confirmed that they were mostly in younger cells. However, their blood also contained misshapen red cells and cell fragments, suggesting that the erythrocytes were being destroyed. This all made sense. There are a variety of medical conditions in which red blood cells containing clumps of any kind—so-called "inclusion bodies"—are destroyed by the spleen and the bone marrow. Microscopic examination of the blood from those patients also shows misshapen and fragmented red cells. Ironically, both subjects had had their spleens surgically removed in what, for that era, was a standard treatment for thalassemia intermedia. Without spleens, the red blood cells with clumps could survive longer, giving Nathan a much better opportunity to observe them.

That the clinical manifestations of thalassemia are the result of unbalanced globin synthesis rather than underproduction of a particular globin is a subtle but important distinction. If the syndrome of beta thalassemia, for example, were caused solely by decreased production of beta-globin, then its clinical picture would consist only of an anemia characterized by low numbers of small, pale red blood cells—pale because of their lack of hemoglobin. Instead, the imbalance between alpha- and beta-globin production leads to a relative overabundance of alpha chains. Without a matched number of beta chains, the alpha chains bind to each other, become insoluble, and turn into the clumps that mark red cells for destruction. It is precisely this destruction of red blood cells with release of their heme that leads to the dire complications of beta thalassemia: severe anemia with skeletal abnormalities caused by the bone marrow's futile attempt to produce more red cells, plus jaundice and organ damage due to high levels of bilirubin derived from free heme.

This is the kind of medical insight that Nathan loved. Part of its appeal was that it came from a way of thinking about disease that was distinct from the molecular approach then dominating hematology. So much of the excitement about thalassemia and sickle cell disease had been stimulated by the genetic, structural, and biochemical discoveries relating to globin that were fueling a revolution in the biological sciences. Even today, many hematologists choose to study the thalassemias by focusing on globin genes, trying to understand precisely how and why they are abnormal. That productive line of inquiry has revealed many of the fundamental mechanisms that control gene expression, with relevance far beyond globin. In contrast, Nathan and his ilk began their inquiry with the signs and symptoms they saw in their patients. They asked how the loss or alteration of a beta-globin gene could lead to the panoply of clinical abnormalities that beset those patients and found that the answer did not lie solely in the loss or alteration of globin genes but rather in the resulting imbalance between globin proteins. That is a discovery that requires an understanding of the patient at a "systems" level, one that integrates genetics and molecular biology with physiology.

In 1966, Nathan and one of his medical students, Robert Gunn, wrote a definitive journal article about unbalanced globin synthesis in thalassemias.[232] Although it presented little new data, it consolidated the new ideas about thalassemias and explicitly defined the unbalanced globin model. In addition to being a useful reference work, it was also a canny bit of academic self-promotion. All subsequent work on thalassemia would now have to cite the Nathan and Gunn article, making Nathan the de facto expert in unbalanced globin synthesis even though others, like Fessas, had also made important contributions.

Dr. Diamond, who had sent the young men with thalassemia intermedia to Nathan, was very impressed with what his junior colleague had accomplished. So much so that he began sending other clinical puzzles across Shattuck Street to Nathan's lab at the Brigham. The conduits for these consultations were Diamond's fellows. After Park Gerald, who brought those first subjects to Nathan, Diamond's go-to fellow was Frank Aram Oski. A Philadelphia native, Oski had gone to Swarthmore, where he was a blocking back on the varsity football team, and then to the University of Pennsylvania School of Medicine. After training with Diamond at Boston Children's Hospital, he joined the pediatrics faculty first at Penn and then SUNY Upstate in Syracuse. He eventually became chair of pediatrics at Johns Hopkins, where he served for ten years until his death in 1996. He and Nathan spent decades editing the definitive textbook on childhood hematology and oncology—now in its eighth edition—which is known to everyone as "Nathan and Oski."

When Oski was a fellow at Boston Children's, he played a crucial role in Nathan's next clinical discovery. Michael P., a child with unexplained anemia, had been admitted to Diamond's service for evaluation. His red blood cells had an unusual appearance under the microscope, and Diamond dispatched Oski to solicit Nathan's opinion. Nathan used his own microscope to examine the blood smear and saw a sea of red cells with spiny protrusions that made them look "crinkled." He was sure that this was an artifact caused by poor slide preparation so he sent Oski back to Children's Hospital telling him to return with a properly processed smear. Within minutes, Nathan's telephone rang—it was Dr. Diamond. Nathan sprung out of his chair and stood by his desk; he always stood in the presence of Dr. Diamond.

"Did you tell Dr. Oski that Miss Neveska can't make a slide?"

Diamond was referring to the hematology technician at Children's Hospital, Josephine Neveska, who had more than twenty years of experience preparing blood smears. It is a well appreciated but little examined fact that all of the great hematology technicians in teaching hospitals have been women.

"No, Dr. Diamond," Nathan replied. "I wasn't criticizing Miss Neveska. I simply found the slide uninterpretable."

"I don't pay you to comment on slide technique," growled Diamond. "I pay you to give me your opinion. Dr. Oski will return with that slide."

Which he did. On more careful examination, Nathan—along with Oski and Diamond—thought that Michael P.'s crinkly red blood cells looked like those from individuals who are deficient in pyruvate kinase, an enzyme needed for maintaining an erythrocyte's structure. In essence, red blood cells are concentrated solutions of hemoglobin wrapped in a cell membrane. A healthy, pliable membrane gives them their characteristic disc shape and allows them to squeeze through capillaries half their diameter. Both their shape and their ability to be reversibly deformed require energy—

without it, red cells would be spheres incapable of snapping back into form after squeezing through narrow passages.

The source of energy for red blood cells is adenosine triphosphate, or ATP. There are two ways for cells to make this molecule: one is to metabolize glucose to lactic acid through a series of enzymatic steps that generate ATP; the other also begins with glucose but uses oxygen to go down a different pathway, one that generates even more ATP. The latter, oxygen-dependent process takes place in subcellular structures called mitochondria. However, red blood cells are unique in their stripped-down functionality. To transport as much hemoglobin as possible, they have jettisoned any cellular structures that do not contribute directly to their mission. So, red cells have no nuclei—DNA is not necessary for carrying hemoglobin through the bloodstream—and they have no mitochondria. The lack of mitochondria in red cells is ironic: the cells that carry oxygen to other cells throughout the body to meet their energy needs cannot themselves use oxygen to generate ATP.

For decades, hematologists had recognized an inherited form of anemia in which spherical red cells, which they called "spherocytes," are destroyed by the spleen. This disorder, hereditary spherocytosis, is caused by mutations in any of several genes that specify structural components of the red cell membrane. However, other individuals who are also born with anemia due to red cell destruction by the spleen may have few if any spherocytes. They are said to have congenital (present at birth) nonspherocytic (no spherical red cells) hemolytic anemia (low red cell counts because of destruction). Unlike hereditary spherocytosis, in which removal of the spleen is uniformly effective in correcting the anemia, congenital nonspherocytic hemolytic anemia responds to splenectomy in unpredictable and inconsistent ways. Because of this variability, hematologists thought that there might be distinct subtypes.

One variety is an anemia caused by deficiency of glucose-6-phosphate dehydrogenase (G6PD), an enzyme responsible for the first step in a metabolic pathway that protects erythrocytes from oxidative stress. Children with this disorder rarely have symptoms unless they are exposed to things that produce that kind of insult such as certain antibiotics or foods—fava beans are a common culprit. In 1961, hematologists in California described three patients with congenital nonspherocytic hemolytic anemia whose G6PD, surprisingly, was completely normal. Instead, they were deficient in the enzyme pyruvate kinase, which contributes to the last step in the non–oxygen-dependent metabolic pathway that generates ATP from glucose.[233] Because red blood cells have no mitochondria, they are uniquely dependent on this pathway to generate energy. Thus, systemic abnormalities in the non–oxygen-dependent system will disproportionately affect red cells compared to other cells, nearly all of which can use the oxygen-dependent one. That is why patients with pyruvate kinase deficiency (PKD) are unable to generate enough ATP to keep the membranes of their red blood cells intact. Instead, they have red cells with crinkly membranes that are destroyed by the spleen, thereby producing anemia, but they do not have energy abnormalities elsewhere in their bodies. After reporting these three cases, the California group described seven more in 1962 and showed that the disease has a recessive inheritance pattern, meaning that the parents can be asymptomatic carriers.[234]

Diamond realized that the red cells in Michael P.'s blood smear looked like those in the PKD patients from California. He and Oski searched through the records at Children's Hospital and found two more cases of crinkly erythrocytes. In 1963, they proved that these children also had PKD and confirmed the recessive inheritance pattern of the disorder.[235] They asked Nathan to perform more tests on Michael P.'s blood and then dragooned him into a field trip to find potential carriers of pyruvate kinase mutations in Michael P.'s family.

Most of the extended family lived in upstate New York. Because Diamond was a terrible driver, Nathan proposed that they fly to Saranac on Allegheny Airlines, an old regional carrier. Shortly after takeoff, Oski became airsick, making him a target of Diamond's derision. Upon landing, Diamond ordered Nathan and Oski to carry his bags while he greeted the medical dignitaries on the tarmac. After a brief stop at their hotel, the two young doctors began driving around the county to draw blood from Michael P.'s family members. They interrupted their chores only for as long as it took to attend a dinner in Dr. Diamond's honor. At the end of that very long day, an exhausted Nathan and Oski finally crawled into their beds.

At the crack of dawn, the great man, clad only in his union suit, shook Nathan and Oski awake telling them they had more blood to draw. They finished their rounds and caught an afternoon flight to Boston. Back at Children's Hospital, Nathan and Oski stayed up all night measuring pyruvate kinase levels in the blood samples. Their results were published in 1964 and confirmed the earlier reports from California.[236] A few years later, Nathan used his radioactive labeling expertise to show that the spleen plays a major role in destroying PKD red cells and that its removal in this form of nonhereditary spherocytic anemia could be beneficial.[237] This would be one of the last papers Nathan would coauthor with his boss Frank Gardner.

The experiments Nathan performed for that paper would have personal legal and medical consequences for him. To test whether the spleen might be responsible for destroying PKD red cells, Nathan had collected red cells from PKD patients and marked them with radioactivity. He then injected them into volunteers who did or did not have spleens and measured how long the transfused cells lasted. If the spleen were responsible for destroying PKD erythrocytes, then the radioactive red cells should survive longer in recipients who didn't have one.

The normal recipients—those with spleens—included one of the hematology division's laboratory technicians and Nathan himself. The paper did not identify those individuals but did describe them as "informed normal subjects."[238] However, as with the young men with thalassemia whom he'd studied, Nathan's practices for assessing experimental risks and communicating them to research subjects were far below contemporary standards. And the risks were very real. Within two years, the technician developed hepatitis and sued Nathan. This was a shattering experience and one that Nathan feared would end his career. Ultimately, the technician settled the suit for $25,000, which was the liability limit of Nathan's personal policy.[239]

Nathan himself developed hepatitis C some thirty years later. His infection was presumed to have come from the same source since he had no other known exposure and, occasionally, the diagnosis can only be made years after the initial infection. One of the triumphs of twenty-first century medicine is the development of highly effective drugs that inhibit the hepatitis C virus and cure the disease. Unfortunately, Nathan became sick before their advent— the only treatment available to him was a prolonged course of interferon, a drug with miserable side effects, and a nonspecific viral inhibitor that, when given together, have about a 50 percent chance of curing someone. Fortunately, he was in that 50 percent and fully recovered.

Clinical investigators in Nathan's generation romanticized the image of the lone researcher who bravely expanded the boundaries of medical knowledge by performing daring experiments on himself. William Castle's studies on pernicious anemia are a perfect example. However, Nathan's experience with hepatitis stripped away much of this mythology and made him a staunch advocate for the ethical conduct of clinical research and the careful oversight of clinical trials. This was a critically important attitude that he brought with him much later when he became president of Dana-Farber.

PHYSICIANS FOR SOCIAL RESPONSIBILITY

One of Nathan's coauthors on the paper describing pyruvate kinase deficiency in Michael P. and his family was Victor W. Sidel, another Harvard Medical School/Brigham residency/NIH ATP product. Sidel contributed expertise in membrane biophysics to the project, but Nathan already knew him from their work in a very different area. In the spring of 1961, Sidel, Nathan, and a few other young physicians were called by Bernard Lown, a cardiologist at the Brigham and a faculty member at the Harvard School of Public Health. Although Lown would soon become famous for inventing the direct-current defibrillator, a device that has saved countless lives, his primary interest was in preventive health. After hearing a lecture on nuclear disarmament,[240] Lown became convinced that an organized society could not survive nuclear war. He thought that the federal policy promoting bomb shelters was misguided, providing only false hope for a postapocalyptic world.

Lown applied his public health expertise to the problem. If the "disease" of nuclear Armageddon cannot be treated, then the only rational approach to survival is prevention, by which he meant disarmament. Lown proposed publishing a series of objective articles about the medical consequences of nuclear war in order to steer the national discourse toward disarmament. The young physicians he recruited to a planning meeting in his Newton living room included Nathan, Sidel, and others who would go on to have enormous impact in social medicine.[241] One outcome of that meeting was the creation of Physicians for Social Responsibility, an organization with chapters around the world that advocates for multilateral disarmament and a ban on nuclear testing.

The other outcome was the publication of four articles on the medical consequences of nuclear war in the May 31, 1962, issue of the *New England Journal of Medicine*. They were preceded by an Introduction written by the "Special Study Section of the Physicians for Social Responsibility" consisting of Nathan, Sidel, H. Jack Geiger, and Lown. It set the stage by asserting that the papers would scientifically demonstrate the futility of Civil Defense planning for surviving nuclear war and, therefore, that "prevention is the only effective therapy."[242] There followed two absolutely harrowing articles. The first, which Nathan coauthored, described the "human and ecological effects" of a twenty megaton bomb exploding over Boston and an eight megaton bomb exploding over nearby Bedford Air Force Base (now known as Hanscom).[243] In cold, dispassionate terms, it modeled the thermal and radiation impacts at various distances from ground zero. Human survival was estimated to be impossible within a radius of twenty miles from the detonation site. Short-term fatalities from the atomic blast and its heat were expected to number two million two hundred fifty thousand. Additional deaths were anticipated later due to exposure to radioactive fallout. The second article described the physician's role during the period after the attack.[244] Again, in stark clinical terms, the authors estimated that of 6,560 physicians who worked in greater Boston in 1962, only nine hundred would survive; medical supplies would be woefully inadequate; competition by survivors for whatever services remained "would be likely to raise new problems"; and physicians would face demands from patients for euthanasia on an unprecedented scale. The third article was a glossary of terms related to radioactivity and radiation biology, the fourth a discussion of the psychiatric and social implications of fallout shelter utilization.

Although the horrendous scenarios described in these articles can still produce a visceral response sixty years later, it is difficult to know what their impact on the U.S. strategy for nuclear survival might have been. Nathan always thought that this special issue of the *New England Journal of Medicine* contributed to the dismantling of the nation's bomb shelter–based Civil Defense policies and took pride in the role he played. Lown, for his part, would go on to cofound with his Russian counterparts International Physicians for the Prevention of Nuclear War, which would receive the Nobel Peace Prize in 1985 for its disarmament efforts.

Chapter 8

TRANSITION: HOW AN INTERNIST BECOMES A PEDIATRICIAN

Academic medicine—a catch-all designation for the educational and research enterprise at medical schools and teaching hospitals—can sometimes look like a world in which autocratic professors and department chiefs jealously guard their fiefdoms. Their internecine battles can be fierce, even destructive, with junior faculty serving as cannon fodder. Ironically, the lower the tangible stakes, measured in dollars or real power, the more intense the fighting.

This was the state of affairs in the 1960s at the Peter Bent Brigham and Boston Children's Hospitals. George Thorn was the powerful chief of medicine at the Brigham where he oversaw several clinical divisions including the division of hematology led by Frank Gardner, a gentler soul. Charles Janeway was the nearly-as-powerful chief of medicine at Children's. His division of hematology was led by Louis Diamond who, unlike Gardner, was a force to be reckoned with. Meanwhile, everyone thought that cancer was such a hopelessly untreatable disease that both hospitals left it to Sidney Farber, the chief of pathology at Children's. Although pathology traffics in tissues and dead bodies, Farber took over the care of children and adults with cancer both at Children's and the Brigham. Farber was a skilled marketer with a national reputation and used his singular status to create the Children's

Cancer Research Fund, a money-raising powerhouse that eventually became the Jimmy Fund.

Battle lines were drawn. Thorn had no respect for Gardner and wanted him gone. His dream was to align with Farber in the hopes that the latter's prowess in attracting philanthropy would enable Thorn to build a new tower at the Brigham. The Brigham surgeons—an extraordinarily powerful group because of the money they brought to the hospital—also wanted Gardner out because his division did not provide the kind of medical services the surgeons needed for their cancer patients.[245] Farber did.

At Children's, Diamond and Farber hated each other because of their fight over who deserved credit for the world-changing demonstration that drugs could induce remissions in childhood leukemias. Diamond's name did appear among the authors of the famous 1948 *New England Journal of Medicine* paper describing the breakthrough, but it was in second position behind Farber's.

Nathan understood that he was merely a pawn in these power games. He also knew that if Thorn were to succeed in getting rid of Gardner, Nathan would lose his protector. And, if Farber's ascendancy continued, Nathan would be in further jeopardy because Farber would perceive him as one of Diamond's boys—which he was. Nathan's fears were realistic: Thorn would sacrifice the young hematologist in an instant if it meant staying in Farber's good graces.

Even beyond the personalities and infighting, Nathan knew that Thorn did not share his vision for the way medical research should be performed. Thorn had become a vocal advocate for expanding basic science research in departments of medicine. Nathan, of course, had cast his lot with clinical researchers whose ideas flow from patients they care for. In the long run, Thorn would be unlikely to support Nathan and his research style. All of this meant that, by 1963, Nathan figured that he had no future in the division of hematology at the Brigham and that it would be better to leave of his own accord than to be pushed out.

But where could he go? Motivated by his family's deep roots in Boston and their comfortable home in Cambridge, Nathan scouted local opportunities first. Beth Israel, another hospital affiliated with Harvard, seemed like a reasonable possibility. A brilliant thirty-eight-year-old named Howard Hiatt had just been appointed chief of medicine and was energetically building a research-oriented faculty. However, Hiatt had done his scientific training at the Institut Pasteur in Paris with Jacques Monod and Francois Jacob, who would receive the Nobel Prize in 1965 for their work on the molecular mechanisms of gene expression. With that strong background in basic research, Nathan thought that Hiatt's hiring preferences would be similar to Thorn's and that he would never consider Nathan for a job. Ironically, Hiatt's interests later drifted away from basic science and, after leaving Beth Israel, he became dean of the Harvard School of Public Health.

An option outside of Boston was the University of California at San Francisco. UCSF is now a clinical and research powerhouse, but in 1963 it was a sleepy medical backwater without much of a research portfolio. Nonetheless, California's natural beauty and the opportunities it provided for sailing attracted the Nathans—David more than Jean. He was being recruited to UCSF by an immunologist named H. Hugh Fudenberg, who later became notorious for promoting the thoroughly discredited ideas that childhood vaccines cause autism and that the influenza vaccine causes Alzheimer's disease.[246] A visit to the campus left Nathan unimpressed, and since Jean was reluctant to leave Cambridge anyway, he turned down the offer.

With no other viable options and the clock ticking, a white knight appeared in the form of Dr. Diamond. From the moment Nathan came back to the Brigham from NIH, Diamond had recognized his unique combination of skills in clinical hematology and biochemistry and had solicited his opinion on puzzling anemia cases. The collaboration had been productive and mutually gratifying—together, Nathan and Diamond unraveled the causes of several unusual diseases of red blood cells. Diamond had also been helpful in supporting Nathan as he established his research and academic independence from Gardner. Not only did the cases from Children's provide a means for publishing scientific papers that did not include Gardner's name on the author list—a sine qua non for career advancement—but Diamond also helped Nathan receive grants to support his research. Financial self-sufficiency further contributed to Nathan's independence. By 1963, Diamond had arranged for Nathan to have an appointment at Children's as an "associate" concurrent with his Brigham appointment.

Unfortunately, Diamond would be of no help if Thorn were to dismantle the division of hematology at the Brigham—his influence did not extend across hospitals. Besides, Diamond was approaching the then-mandatory retirement age of sixty-five and would soon leave Children's. Paradoxically, this worked in Nathan's favor. Charles Janeway, as chief of the department of medicine, was aware that he had to find a replacement for Diamond to lead the division of hematology and some people had whispered Nathan's name in Janeway's ear. One was Diamond himself. Another was Fred Rosen, a junior faculty member at Children's who had trained in pathology with Farber but switched to pediatrics and was now running Janeway's laboratory. Nathan had met Rosen in 1961 and forged an instant bond. Rosen went on to become a prominent immunologist and one of Nathan's closest friends. But even by 1965, he had formed a sufficiently favorable impression of Nathan that he recommended him to Janeway as a replacement for Diamond.

While it might seem odd to recommend an internist for a leadership position in pediatric hematology, Janeway was receptive to the idea because he, too, had been trained as an internist. In fact, he had been a faculty member in the Department of Medicine at Peter Bent Brigham Hospital before moving to Children's as physician-in-chief, so the path from Brigham medicine to Children's pediatrics was familiar. Another virtue of making Nathan division chief was that it would cost Janeway, who was notoriously cheap, much less money than recruiting someone more senior from the outside.

So, Janeway summoned Nathan to his office to discuss the job. Although the physical plant at Children's was even more rudimentary than the Brigham's, Nathan was entranced. He respected and admired Janeway from the moment they met and those feelings never faded. Nathan also liked the idea of being based in a children's hospital since the research projects he most enjoyed were the ones that began with an unexplained anemia in a child. To make this his life's work, he would need to be near a major pediatric hospital that could attract odd and difficult cases from around the world. He could not be any nearer than to be employed by one.

A few days after meeting Janeway, Nathan received a letter offering him the job—he would be made chief of the division of hematology at Children's and an Assistant Professor at Harvard Medical School as of July 1, 1966. His salary would be $15,000 which, like all research-based faculty members, he would have to raise himself from grants and career development awards. Nathan would be in charge of hematology while, to his relief, cancer would continue to be directed by Sidney Farber in his Jimmy Fund Clinic. He would be given a laboratory and an office in the basement of the newly built Fegan Building, where there would be sufficient space for the precious liquid scintillation counter and a multi-headed microscope that Nathan could use to teach blood cell morphology to trainees. Best of all, his friend Fred Rosen would be down the hall.

As attractive as it all seemed, Nathan had nagging doubts about moving to a pediatric hospital. He was not trained as a pediatrician and the last time he had taken care of a child was on the dismal leukemia service at the NIH ten years earlier. How could he suddenly pretend to know how to provide medical care to kids? How could he ever earn the respect of the card-carrying pediatricians who would be working for him? Janeway dismissed his concerns—after all, he was not a pediatrician either. Not feeling particularly comforted, Nathan raised another objection: as an internist, he had passed the certification test of the American Board of Internal Medicine, but he did not carry that seal of approval in pediatrics. He was not a "board-certified" pediatrician and never could be since applicants for board certification must have completed a pediatrics residency. Janeway batted that concern away, too. He said that after five years as chief of medicine at Children's Hospital, the American Board of Pediatrics allowed him to take the certification exam, which he easily passed.

"All well and good for Janeway," Nathan thought. "He's a genius; I'm not."

In desperation, Nathan turned to his mentor from his time at Boston City Hospital, William B. Castle. He described his concerns to Dr. Castle, who said that he had only one question.

"Does the idea of going to the Children's Hospital make you happy?" asked Castle.

Nathan replied that it did but he was afraid of failing.

"Well," replied Castle, "most of the people who come to see me are unhappy. If I were you, I'd go to Children's."[247]

Nathan said that this was the best advice he ever received. He decided to move to Children's.

Of course, nothing is simple and Nathan faced several problems right out of the gate. One was the fact that at the same time he decamped to Children's, Gardner was finally pushed out of the Brigham. This made Nathan the only full-time hematologist in the Longwood Medical Area—the cluster of hospitals near Harvard Medical School. So, in addition to seeing patients with blood disorders at Children's every morning, he was being called almost daily to consult on medical and surgical patients back at the Peter Bent Brigham, on rheumatology patients at the Robert Breck Brigham (an arthritis specialty hospital), and on obstetrics patients and newborns at the quaintly named Boston Lying-In Hospital. The aerobic benefits of running between these hospitals were nullified by the relentless demands of evaluating patients during days, evenings, and weekends. This was not what Nathan had signed up for.

Fortunately, by the end of that first summer, Gardner's replacement as chief of the division of hematology at the Brigham had been identified. He was Bill Moloney, a native Bostonian who was chief of hematology at Tufts Medical Center. Sidney Farber had strongly pushed for the appointment and Thorn was happy to make Farber happy. Moloney knew Nathan and took pity on him, offering to start consulting on hematology patients at the Brigham before his official start date. This was a godsend. When Moloney arrived at the Brigham for good, he assumed responsibility for all adult hematology patients in the Longwood area. Nathan ceded the adults to Moloney with relief but also with a twinge of regret—it made his abandonment of internal medicine for pediatrics final.

Meanwhile, Nathan felt blindsided when he was told that his responsibilities included the clinical hematology laboratories at Children's. This is where all of the blood tests relating to hematology are performed for all of the patients in the hospital or the clinics. This had not been described in Janeway's offer letter. Nathan had no experience running clinical laboratories and absolutely no interest in gaining any. Even worse, the four lab technicians who performed the tests occupied some of the space that had been promised to Nathan for his research. The situation was unacceptable—Nathan needed his research space and he did not want to be responsible for clinical lab testing. At the very least, he had to find a way to move the technicians.

His first idea was simple: transfer hematology lab testing to the hospital's central clinical laboratories. The central labs were overseen by another physician, Henry Schwachman, who was an expert in cystic fibrosis but, unlike Nathan, had been trained in clinical pathology, the medical subspecialty that does lab testing. But when Nathan ran the idea by Dr. Diamond, who was still at Children's, he strongly urged Nathan to keep the clinical labs himself. Diamond insisted that central labs know nothing about hematology tests and he convinced Nathan that their quality would suffer if they were performed outside of a division of hematology.

Frustrated in his attempt to move the clinical labs out of hematology, Nathan hoped at least to find someone else in the division to oversee them. He was thwarted again when his financial administrators reminded him that, first, a portion of his salary came from hospital funds and, second, the hospital funding was explicitly tied to his oversight of the clinical hematology labs. If he were to foist the responsibility onto someone else, he would lose that component of his salary and be forced to replace it with money from external grants. As uninterested as Nathan was in learning how to run a clinical lab, he was even less interested in writing more grant applications.

Bowed but not broken, Nathan had another idea. Perhaps he could physically transfer the four technicians to the central clinical laboratories while still guaranteeing quality control through the division of hematology. Nathan visited the central lab to test his idea, but the technicians who worked there—all of whom were women—seemed to have been forewarned about this internist interloper who knew nothing about their work. They, with Schwachman's support, turned him down flat. Discouraged and unsure of his next step, Nathan went to his scheduled clinic where he was told that a Sister Mary Jo Hipp was waiting to see him. "Sister," as she came to be known, was not a patient; she was chief hematology technician at a hospital outside Boston and wanted to learn the latest procedures from the technicians at Children's.

Nathan had a brilliant idea. Perhaps Sister would have the diplomatic and organizational skills to run clinical hematology testing in Children's central labs. By including Sister in his proposal, he made it more palatable for Schwachman and, importantly, for the technicians in the central labs. They agreed both to Sister's oversight role and the move of the four clinical personnel from Nathan's research space to the central labs. Sister did a superb job and, except for a brief hiatus, worked at Children's Hospital until the 1990s.

Sister's hiatus happened when her order sent her to rural Kentucky to serve the poor. Before she left, Nathan introduced her to his younger daughter, Linda, who was in high school and active in the antiwar movement. Linda had the same highly developed commitment to social justice that her mother and grandmother had and she decided to join Sister in Kentucky during the summers. Sister left her order after a few years and returned to Children's.

Having solved the clinical laboratory problem, Nathan turned his attention to the clinics themselves. The division of hematology at Children's had been run much like the division at the Brigham. In the same way that Gardner would see his private patients in an office separate from the general hematology clinics, Diamond saw his private patients in his office in the Hunnewell Building, an elegant Classical Revival structure topped by a copper dome tinged with verdigris. Unfortunately for Nathan, that is where the patients with interesting and research-worthy disorders went. The general hematology clinic was, instead, overrun by worried mothers and their children who all had benign, largely self-limited problems like hemolytic disease of the newborn in which the mother's blood type differs from her child's. These children have jaundice and low blood counts, which generally resolve on their own but the standard approach in the hematology clinic had been to give blood transfusions. Nathan thought this was unnecessary and instituted a new rule: children with this disorder would be transfused only if they had trouble feeding. While the pediatricians were put off at first by this internist's meddling, the newborns did fine and most were spared repeated needle sticks.

Another outcome of Nathan's policy was that fewer clinic hours were spent on children who did not really have to be there, creating room for other kinds of patients. The timing was perfect. Dr. Diamond left Children's for San Francisco in 1966 and all of the patients he had been seeing in his private office could now come to the general hematology clinic. Diamond's departure also meant that Nathan could move into his roomier and more private office.

Nathan's next challenge was to obtain grant funding. For himself, he would need money to pay for his research activities and most of his salary. For the division, Nathan wanted to secure a training grant from the National Institutes of Health to support the clinical and research education of hematology fellows, physicians who have completed their internships and residencies in general pediatrics and now want subspecialty training in hematology. Fellows perform essential functions in hospital divisions that have clinical and research missions: they participate directly in patient care under the supervision of senior physicians and they learn how to do research by working for two to three years in laboratories where they take on projects under the guidance of the faculty lab chief.

Because fellows are trainees, they cannot bill directly for their clinical services and are not yet accomplished enough to compete for their own research grants. That is why a training grant is so important. But there is a catch. Standard research grants like those awarded to Nathan or other faculty are given directly to individuals. Training grants, in contrast, are awarded to institutions that manage disbursement of funds to their fellows. Therefore, granting agencies like the NIH require applicant institutions to make an explicit commitment to provide the infrastructure needed to manage the grant and the fellows. This pledge comes from an "institutional official" who has the authority to approve submission of the grant application and the obligations it entails. At Children's Hospital, that official was Sidney Farber whose animus toward Diamond was now directed against his protégé and successor. Farber was also opposed to any grant that might go to a hematology program that competed with his cancer program. If hematology at Children's were to receive a large training grant, talented fellows who would otherwise go to Farber's cancer program might go to hematology instead—another example of academic fiefdoms battling over small potatoes.

Farber reluctantly allowed Nathan to submit the training grant application, aware that he could still scotch it during the site visit if he wanted. In those days, the NIH required an on-site review of institutions applying for training grants in order to assess the quality of the resources and the fellows. Review teams were composed of experts from first-rate hematology programs around the country. For Nathan's grant, the chair of the site visit team was Helen Ranney, a hematologist from Albert Einstein College of Medicine in New York. She had made key discoveries about the genetic basis of sickle cell disease and would go on to become the chair of the department of medicine at the University of California, San Diego, the first woman to lead a major department of medicine.

By the time of the site visit, Farber had raised the money for, and completed the construction of, the Jimmy Fund Building, the home of his cancer program. The site visit meeting occurred in a conference room on the top floor of the building adjacent to Farber's palatial office. Despite his disdain for Nathan and the division of hematology, Farber was on his best behavior. He was not effusive but neither did he actively undercut the program. It was not until later that Nathan learned that Bill Moloney, Farber's hand-picked choice to lead Brigham hematology, had told Farber that he would leave the Brigham if he ruined the site visit.

The site visitors thought little of the physical plant at Children's but they were deeply impressed by Janeway. They also decided that Nathan was well positioned to lead a research-based pediatric hematology division despite his internal medicine training. All was going well, heading toward a successful denouement, when Dr. Farber, in his pompous manner, asked Dr. Ranney if she had any final questions.

"Yes," she said. "May I keep my Jimmy Fund pencil?"

Farber was furious but maintained his composure. Nathan got his training grant.

With the grant in place, Nathan got down to the work of running the division, supporting the fellows, and doing his own research. In what felt like the blink of an eye, he finished his first five years as division chief. Janeway reminded him that he was now eligible to take his board examination in pediatrics. Although Nathan never thought that board certification was a reliable marker for clinical skill—he used to say that anyone can pass a test if they study hard enough—he knew that the fellows in his program were eager to have him pass his boards. They seemed to feel that there was something improper about the head of a pediatric hematology division not being a board-certified pediatrician. So, Nathan arranged to take his board exams and his fellows helped him cram. They tried to fill his head with every last bit of pediatric minutiae they could think of.

The board exams consisted of written and oral portions. Nathan passed the written test without difficulty. The orals, for which he had to travel out of town, tended to focus on rare syndromes. The fellows knew this and prepped Nathan by showing him picture after picture of children with unusual disorders—pediatricians are expected to make these diagnoses simply by glancing at the facial features of affected kids. Nathan, however, was not particularly adept at facial recognition, a fact that became painfully obvious to the frustrated fellows.

Deciding that he was as prepared as he would ever be, Nathan packed a bag and went to his oral exams. As predicted, his examiner began by showing him a picture of a child with a nearly absent chin and asked him to name the syndrome. Nathan recalled the exchange[248]:

> "Hmm," I said, struggling to remember if this child looked like any that the fellows had shown me. "Hmmm...a bird-like face..."
>
> "Yes," whispered the examiner. "Like a bird..."

"Sparrow?" I tried hopefully.

The examiner shook his head.

"Hawk?"

He shook his head again.

"Robin?"

"Yes!" the examiner cried as he leapt to his feet. "Pierre Robin Sequence. You pass!"

With a little nudging, Nathan had "identified" this developmental abnormality, named for the French dental surgeon who first described it, in which newborns have a small jaw and displacement of the tongue toward the back of the throat. Nothing to do with birds. But Nathan was now a certified pediatrician and his staff breathed a collective sigh of relief.

On his return to Boston, Nathan took up one of the most difficult challenges he would face as division chief—the management of childhood leukemia. Two groups at Children's with starkly different philosophies had been battling over the care of these unfortunate children. In the department of medicine and division of hematology, Janeway and Diamond believed that children with leukemia were hopeless cases. Rather than torture them with toxic and ineffective therapy, the staff were instructed to make them comfortable as they died. Nathan's experiences as a clinical associate at the National Cancer Institute initially made him sympathize with that approach.

In contrast, Sidney Farber had assembled a team to practice his philosophy that childhood leukemia was treatable—perhaps even curable—with the right drugs. Farber's demonstration of transient remissions in response to folic acid antagonists was, to him, proof that his concept was correct and he was happy to take the children that the division of hematology did not want to treat.

After a few years, children with leukemia who had been admitted to the division of hematology were automatically transferred to Farber's service. But, as the new division chief, Nathan felt some responsibility for the patients his staff had been sending to Farber so he decided to take a look at how they were faring. He was shocked to find no long-term survivors. This was the late 1960s, a time when combination chemotherapy, which had so horrified Nathan during his training, had been adopted as standard treatment at the National Cancer Institute, St. Jude's Hospital, and a few other centers. These hospitals were reporting 20 to 30 percent long-term survivors. What was going on at the vaunted Jimmy Fund Clinic? Why were its results so dismal?

The reason lay in Farber's unshakeable belief that the debilitating side effects caused by giving combinations of drugs to children were unacceptable. He was sure that a single drug with manageable toxicities would be the solution—he would just have to find the right drug. And even if, in the worst case scenario, multiple drugs might be needed to cure leukemia, he thought they could be given sequentially rather than simultaneously in order to minimize side effects.

To Nathan, the data coming from the National Cancer Institute and St. Jude's showed that Farber was wrong. However, the ex-pathologist ruled the Jimmy Fund with an iron fist—if Nathan wanted to change the way childhood leukemia was being treated in Boston, he would need powerful allies. He started with Janeway. Nathan convinced him that Farber's approach led to poor outcomes and that his stubbornness was impeding progress. However, Janeway understood how politically perilous Nathan's position was. Farber had powerful friends in Congress who controlled appropriations for medical care and research. He had been a friend of Mary Lasker, the philanthropist and tireless advocate for medical research, and had won the eponymous Lasker Prize in 1966. Although Janeway was in favor of mandating combination chemotherapy for leukemia at Children's Hospital, he said that the only way he could do so would be if a panel of experts from the National Cancer Institute were to make such a recommendation to him.

Nathan grasped at this straw. He approached Nathaniel Berlin, his mentor from NCI and now the clinical director there, who agreed to bring a team to Boston. Berlin's colleagues reviewed Farber's data and concluded that the Jimmy Fund's clinical outcomes in childhood leukemia were indeed inferior to those at institutions where combination chemotherapy was being used. They presented their findings to Janeway who took in the highly confidential report in his typically impassive way. Janeway has been described by those who knew him well as aristocratic and reserved, a man of few words.[249] One wonders if he might also have been averse to confrontation. In this serious disagreement, in which the lives of children were at stake, it would have been appropriate for Janeway, as chief of medicine, to confront Farber directly. Instead, he asked Nathan to talk to him and see whether he could convince the "father of chemotherapy" of the error of his ways.

This was a dicey proposition for three reasons. First, Farber was chief of staff and one of the few full professors at Children's Hospital—he substantially outranked Nathan, who was chief of a small division and an assistant professor. Second, Farber already disliked Nathan because of his association with Dr. Diamond. And third, in another example of the tight-knit nature of Boston's Jewish community, Farber was a friend of the family. Nathan's maternal uncle Lou Gordon and his partner Arthur Lockwood had raised money for Farber's research and were founding trustees of Farber's Children's Cancer Research Fund which later became the Jimmy Fund.

Nonetheless, Nathan did as he was told. Farber had installed himself on the top floor of the Jimmy Fund Building in a cavernous office whose entrance was guarded by a Mrs. McGahee, his Cerberus. Once admitted, supplicants could approach the raised, altarlike platform that supported an enormous desk where Farber would be seated, waiting. Behind him was an expanse of white wall that, because he always wore an impeccable white lab coat buttoned to his neck, created the impression that his head was floating in space like that of the Wizard of Oz. The illusion gave Farber's dark eyes an even more penetrating menace than usual as he stared implacably downward at his sorry victims. Farber had placed a marble bird on the desktop—its red eyes seemed to float, too. He called it the Bird of Hope but it gave Nathan the creeps. Some swore the bird was Farber's familiar.

It was in this setting that Nathan informed Farber that his approach to the treatment of childhood leukemia was all wrong. The Wizard fumed.

"Fortunately, Dr. Nathan," he said evenly, "you are not in charge. I am in charge. For that reason, we will not torture these children. I will not kill seven children to preserve the lives of three."

This, of course, was precisely the stark trade-off that the pioneers of combination chemotherapy had accepted in order to cure those three children. Nathan himself had come to terms with this grim reality because, given current success rates, the other seven children would die of their leukemia anyway.

Nathan had to tell Janeway that he had gotten nowhere with Dr. Farber. The chief, in his laconic way, replied that Nathan would simply have to go back and try harder. While Nathan was busy marshalling fresh courage for the next encounter, his mother called. She began with "David, dear," an opening that Nathan knew meant trouble. She went on to say that her brother Lou had let her know that her son had been very rude to Dr. Farber. Nathan tried to tell her what the problem was and that he had not, in fact, been rude. In response, she said:

"Well, David, you know that Dr. Farber is a very great man."

"I know, Mother."

"He's a very great man and you've been rude to him. You must not be rude to Dr. Farber under any circumstances."

"Mother," said Nathan, "you've got to listen to me on this. This is my profession. I know what I'm talking about."

"I'm sure you do but you are never to be rude to Dr. Farber under any circumstances. Lou doesn't like it."[250]

Ruth's admonition did nothing to shake Nathan's resolve to convince Farber that he must adopt combination chemotherapy. Loins girded, he set off for the Jimmy Fund Building. His route ran through Prouty Garden, a bucolic space in the middle of the Children's Hospital campus. Walking toward him in the opposite direction was William Berenberg, the clinical director at Children's. Berenberg stopped and asked Nathan where he was going. When Nathan said that he was going to see Farber, Berenberg told him to "watch out for the match trick." Nathan asked what he meant but Berenberg simply said, "You'll see." As it happened, Berenberg knew what was going on because Farber had complained to him about Nathan.

Unsettled but determined to see things through, Nathan was ushered back into Farber's office. Once again, he approached the dais and made his pitch for the superiority of combination chemotherapy in childhood leukemia and, once again, Farber would have none of it. This time, though, Nathan was prepared. He said that if Farber refused to adopt what was manifestly the best approach to treat this disease, Nathan would no longer send children with leukemia to the Jimmy Fund. Instead, he would refer them to Massachusetts General Hospital where the pediatricians had agreed to give these children the latest combination of antileukemia drugs, a regimen that had been producing those 20 to 30 percent long-term survivals.

Farber turned red-faced but rapidly regained his composure. Without averting his blazing eyes from Nathan's, he reached into his desk to retrieve a large wooden kitchen match. He held it up, snapped it in half with one hand, and threw the pieces on the desk.

"I will break you like that," he whispered.

Nathan was so rattled that he jumped up and shouted, "That's the match trick!" which only made Farber angrier. He pointed to the door, telling him to leave and never return.[251]

Nathan had to trudge back to his boss to report Farber's continued intransigence. By now, though, Janeway had come to understand that Farber was not giving children with leukemia their best shot at survival. The situation was untenable. However, he also knew that these children needed intense, specialized medical care because they were so sick—both from their leukemia and their treatment. Over many years of practice, Farber's group, working on what was called Division 28 at Children's, had developed the skills and environment to care for them. If Nathan wanted the doctors in his division of hematology to give combination chemotherapy, Janeway insisted that they would have to do so in a setting where they could provide Farber-level medical oversight.

The Clinical Research Center emerged as an ideal solution. Janeway had created it to perform clinical research that required frequent, hands-on attention by the nursing staff. Subjects in these studies were not particularly sick but Janeway thought that the standards the Center had developed for paying constant and detailed attention to them could be adapted to the care of leukemia patients. He authorized Nathan to admit children with leukemia to the Center.

This was the very embodiment of the admonition to be careful what you wish for. Although Nathan had been given permission to create a new cancer service separate from the Jimmy Fund, Farber's position as chief of staff at Children's should have made this impossible. However, several events conspired to clear the path. The most stunning was Farber's sudden death in March 1973 while sitting at his elevated desk. The "match trick" fiasco turned out to be the last time Nathan saw him. While a tragic loss by any measure, Farber's death allowed Nathan, unopposed, to consolidate the clinical services into one cancer unit and hire new pediatric oncologists who were not beholden to Farber to staff it.

Another enabling event was Nixon's signing the National Cancer Act of 1971, which authorized the creation of fifteen regional comprehensive cancer centers across the United States.

Sidney Farber and Mary Lasker had been instrumental in corralling the Congressional votes needed to pass the Cancer Act, and Farber's Children's Cancer Research Foundation was designated as New England's comprehensive cancer center. In 1974, it was renamed the Sidney Farber Cancer Center in honor of its late founder.

Before Farber died, knowing that he would need someone to run the adult side of the cancer program, he recruited Emil Frei III to be physician-in-chief. This was the same Tom Frei who, with Emil Freireich, had pioneered combination chemotherapy at the National Cancer Institute and continued to proselytize for the approach after moving to MD Anderson Cancer Center in 1965. Frei's recruitment suggests that, at some level, Farber knew that combination chemotherapy was the right treatment for childhood leukemia after all. He just couldn't to do it himself.

As soon as Frei arrived in Boston in 1972, he began hiring oncologists to staff the adult service. After Farber's death the following year, he asked Nathan to do the same thing for the pediatric service. Nathan welcomed Frei's support knowing that he would need an ally if he wanted to revamp the Jimmy Fund Clinic. Farber had hired a cadre of pediatric oncologists who, in Nathan's opinion, were competent physicians and pleasant colleagues but were unlikely to do the cutting-edge clinical research needed to address the problem of childhood cancer. Farber had also not hired any physician scientists—doctors who also do laboratory research. They would be absolutely essential in a first-rate program.

One painful bit of housecleaning in this regard involved Norman Jaffe, who ran the Jimmy Fund's clinical program. Jaffe, a South African émigré, enjoyed a special status because he had treated Teddy Kennedy Jr. for osteosarcoma, a bone cancer, in his right leg. Kennedy's survival had been publicly touted as a triumph. Nonetheless, Nathan cast a gimlet eye on Jaffe and decided that he and some of his associates would have to go. In their place, he hired talented physicians who have stood the test of time. They included Steve Sallan, a six-foot, five-inch former submariner who trained as a pediatric psychiatrist before switching to oncology. Sallan had performed so well as a fellow at Children's and had such a deft touch with desperately sick children, that Nathan recruited him to the staff of the cancer center. Sallan would go on to have a distinguished career at Dana-Farber developing highly effective therapies for childhood leukemia, particularly acute lymphoblastic leukemia or ALL. Nathan hired another fellow, Howard Weinstein, to develop a similar program in the less common but more deadly acute myelogenous leukemia or AML.

Nathan had found his faculty, but where would he find their patients? A top-flight pediatric leukemia program, comparable to St. Jude's or MD Anderson's, needs a steady stream of children to hone its practice and participate in its clinical trials. However, childhood leukemia is, by any measure, a rare disease. One source might be the Children's Oncology Group, or COG, a large consortium of pediatric oncology centers across the country that recruits patients to its joint clinical trials. However, Nathan had watched in frustration as new clinical trial proposals were subjected to endless tweaking in an attempt to satisfy the priorities of the consortium members. He thought that the resulting compromises produced scientifically uninteresting trials that tested old questions. Instead, he wanted his service to be nimble and focused on the novel research questions it wanted to ask, not those being asked by others.

But again, a clinical research program that performs trials initiated by its own investigators only works if it can attract enough patients to enroll on them. Having spurned the Children's Oncology Group, Nathan turned to the graduates of the Children's Hospital pediatric oncology fellowship. Many had gone on to direct programs of their own and were happy to refer their leukemia patients to the new Children's/Sidney Farber Cancer Center program, helping the center fill its trials. By 1976, Nathan could boast that his program rivaled that of St. Jude's in the high quality of both its patient outcomes and its clinical research.

Meanwhile, Nathan raided other divisions at Children's for laboratory scientists. Among them were Herb Abelson, discoverer of a cancer virus that bears his name; Charles Scher, an expert in tumor viruses and growth factors; Ron McCaffrey who, while working with David Baltimore, discovered an unusual DNA synthesis enzyme in ALL cells; Robertson Parkman, who was interested in bone marrow transplantation for immune deficiencies; and Stephen Burakoff, an expert in T lymphocyte biology who had trained as internist and been a postdoctoral fellow with Baruj Benacerraf. Together with Nathan, they occupied laboratory space in the brand-new Dana Building, which also housed the clinics of the Sidney Farber Cancer Center.

Research was hardly Nathan's only priority. He was also deeply committed to giving patients and families the best clinical experience they could have at the worst times of their lives. To assess the care environment for himself, he spent several daytime and evening nursing shifts on Division 28. He was appalled by what he saw. While the nurses, social workers, and doctors were dedicated and compassionate, the facility provided nothing for the emotional support of patients and their families. There was no privacy: parents who were grief-stricken by the death of a child were reduced to weeping in the stairwells. Nathan decided to work every bit as hard to optimize support services for pediatric oncology as he would to enhance clinical and laboratory research.

For the next ten years, Nathan focused on managing the division of hematology and Oncology while devoting whatever time he could spare to his own research. But, as the 1980s began, Children's Hospital faced a leadership challenge that would profoundly impact him. Charles Janeway's retirement in 1972 after twenty-six years as the chair of the department of medicine had rattled Nathan because the former internist had played such an important role in recruiting him to Children's. Who would follow him? Would the next chief be his champion, too?

Nathan had a view into the process of replacing Janeway through his friend Fred Rosen, who was on the search committee. Rosen was enthusiastic about recruiting Mary Ellen Avery, chair of pediatrics at McGill University and physician-in-chief at Memorial Children's Hospital in Montreal. Mel, as she was known, was famous for discovering that the lungs of premature infants lack surfactant, a substance that keeps air sacs open. Deficiency of surfactant causes respiratory failure that was the most common cause of death in preemies. Avery's work led to treatments that have saved the lives of countless babies.

The search committee endorsed Rosen's recommendation and in 1974 Avery accepted its offer to be the first female physician-in-chief at Children's and the first female chair of a major clinical department, the department of pediatrics, at Harvard Medical School. This was both a substantive and symbolic triumph for Children's. Unfortunately, Avery's considerable talents in clinical medicine and research were not matched by her administrative skills and it soon became clear that she was not managing the department's finances well. Worse, at least to division chiefs like Nathan, was her limited capacity for identifying highly talented faculty and recruiting them to Children's. In the face of mounting criticism, she needed allies.

Unfortunately, Avery had a sarcastic side that did not sit well with Children's trustees; she gradually began to alienate them along with her senior faculty. This may bespeak sexism at Children's— plenty of men in leadership positions have sarcastic personalities that seem to be tolerated. Nonetheless, by 1984, between the poor financial state of the department and the mediocre performance of her recruits, Avery had lost the confidence of the board and the faculty and she was pushed out. The hospital began another search for a physician-in-chief.

The chaos at Children's became the subject of intense academic gossip in pediatrics circles, which made the job unattractive to outside candidates. Who would want to be known as the man who replaced Mel Avery? The search committee was forced to look inside. Nathan attracted its attention even though he was one of the disgruntled division chiefs who had contributed to Avery's ouster, raising questions of self-dealing. Baruj Benacerraf, who had succeeded Tom Frei as president of Dana-Farber, supported Nathan's candidacy because making him chief at Children's would move him out of the Farber allowing Benacerraf to consolidate his power—he had in mind one of his own trainees, Steven Burakoff, to replace Nathan. The dean of the medical school was also supportive because he thought, with the hubris that so often characterizes deans, he could control Nathan.

Finding these political considerations in alignment, the committee offered the job to Nathan. He said yes, becoming chair of the department of medicine and physician-in-chief at Children's in 1985.

RESEARCH, 1967–1985

Even as Nathan worked for nearly two decades to build a world-class pediatric oncology program, he pursued several lines of research. These fell into four categories: the antimicrobial properties of white blood cells, the molecular basis of red cell defects, erythrocyte development, and hemoglobin disorders. Crucially important during this period were two sabbaticals Nathan spent at the Massachusetts Institute of Technology. During the first, in 1970, he worked in a laboratory shared by David Baltimore, soon to receive the Nobel Prize, and Harvey Lodish, a skilled biochemist. That was where he met David Housman, Lodish's fellow and later an MIT faculty member, with whom he spent his second sabbatical in 1974. Nathan used these sabbaticals to learn about basic research techniques that he could apply to his patient-focused research. In fact, Nathan ascribed his extraordinary skill in recruiting talented researchers—his "good taste"—to being surrounded by the scientists at MIT.

Antimicrobial Properties of White Blood Cells

Nathan's interest in white blood cells began when his colleague Fred Rosen asked him to evaluate a patient with chronic granulomatous disease, a disorder in which children cannot fight infections because their white blood cells do not kill bacteria. They lead difficult and foreshortened lives, most dying in young adulthood. When Rosen made his request, the cause of white blood cell dysfunction in CGD was unknown. Nathan helped solve the riddle by connecting two seemingly disparate facts. First, he recalled that Manfred Karnovsky, a faculty member at Harvard Medical School, had discovered that a white blood cell's capacity to kill bacteria depended on its production of toxic molecules known as free radicals, a process that requires enzymes called oxidases. So, Nathan reasoned, if healthy white blood cells have active oxidases, perhaps those in CGD patients are defective. But how to prove it?

An answer came from the second fact. When Nathan was at the Brigham, he had tried to develop a simple test to identify patients with glucose-6-phosphate dehydrogenase (G6PD) deficiency, a common genetic abnormality described in Chapter 7. Cells constantly produce toxic free radicals during normal metabolism and the body fights a never-ending battle to prevent the damage they can cause. (Targeted generation of free radicals by white cells to kill bacteria is beneficial but general, widespread production causes harm.) G6PD provides protection by generating molecules that neutralize ambient free radicals. Hematologists like Nathan are interested in G6PD deficiency because the toxic free radicals that accumulate in the red cells of these individuals cause enough damage to produce anemia.

Nathan knew that a dye, nitro blue tetrazolium (NBT), turns deep blue when chemically modified by G6PD. Therefore, he thought, NBT should turn blue when added to a tube of blood from a normal person but remain colorless when the blood comes from someone with G6PD-deficiency. However, Nathan found that NBT turned the tubes blue in both cases. Trying to figure out what had gone wrong, he examined the blood under the microscope. To his surprise, it was only the liquid that had turned blue; the erythrocytes themselves remained colorless. Nathan had forgotten two things. First, the white cells in blood samples leak things that turn NBT blue even in the setting of G6PD deficiency. Second, NBT has a strong ionic charge and, like all charged molecules, it does not cross cell membranes. So, because NBT cannot get inside of erythrocytes, even those with normal G6PD did not turn blue. Nathan smacked himself on the forehead for what he called his "stupidity" and abandoned the project.

But now, years later, confronted with a CGD patient whose white blood cells could not kill bacteria, Nathan had an inspired idea—maybe he could show that the child's white blood cells were missing oxidases by mixing them with NBT. This time, the experiment would actually depend on white blood cells being leaky. He asked one of his fellows, Bob Baehner, to give it a try. In no time, Nathan saw Baehner running down the hall with a tube of white blood cells in each hand. One, from a normal volunteer, was deep blue due to the reaction of leaked oxidases with NBT but the other, from the CGD patient, was clear. He had proved that CGD is caused by a deficiency of oxidases in white blood cells.[252]

A coda to the CGD story involves William Castle, Nathan's hero from his student days. In 1968, the rules of retirement had forced Castle out of Boston City Hospital. However, sympathetic faculty gave him a home at the West Roxbury Veterans Administration Hospital where he served as a "distinguished physician." The medical service at the West Rox, as it was known, was staffed by interns and residents from the Brigham. Faculty from other Harvard hospitals often traveled to the West Rox to give them lectures and Nathan had been invited to talk about his work on CGD. When he finished his talk, Castle, who was in the audience, asked whether the anemia in G6PD deficiency might be caused by free radicals leaked into the blood by white cells. The white blood cells themselves would be protected because their mitochondria detoxify free radicals but red cells, which lack mitochondria, would be destroyed. Nathan was mortified that he had not thought of this. He and Baehner returned to the lab to test the idea, which turned out to be valid. The paper describing this phenomenon was Castle's last original research publication.[253]

Red Blood Cell Defects

Nathan maintained his interest in abnormalities that cause red blood cell destruction, known as hemolysis, and made important observations at opposite ends of a particular spectrum: red cells with too much water (hydrocytosis) and red cells with too little water (xerocytosis). Both conditions cause hemolysis and, characteristically, Nathan's interest arose from seeing patients with unexplained anemias.

The hydrocytosis story began when Frank Oski, Diamond's former fellow who was now at the University of Pennsylvania, met Bobby Yeagley. Yeagley was a three-and-a-half-year-old boy with severe hemolytic anemia. Under the microscope, his red blood cells looked hugely swollen with so much water that the hemoglobin had been diluted, turning them a pale pink. The amount of water in a cell is controlled by the concentrations of ions it contains, especially sodium and potassium. Nathan's team analyzed Yeagley's red cells and found that the amount of sodium in the cells was ten times its normal value and that of potassium was about half.

This had never been described before. Normal red cells have an intracellular ionic milieu quite different from surrounding plasma because, first, red cell membranes are intrinsically impermeable to ions and, second, the membranes have channels that actively control the passage of specific ions in and out of the cell. The ion concentrations on the inside of Yeagley's red cells were nearly the same as those in the plasma suggesting that his red cell membranes were overly permeable—they were letting too many ions move passively in and out of the cell and allowing too much water to seep in. The result was red cell destruction.[254] Later research by others showed that hydrocytosis is caused by mutations in proteins that regulate ion channels in the red cell membrane. Although no one else in Bobby Yeagley's family had his kind of anemia, Oski later found a family in which three generations were affected with a milder form attesting to its genetic basis.[255]

The xerocytosis story also begins with a single unusual patient, in this case a young woman with a lifelong history of hemolytic anemia. Under the microscope, her red blood cells could not have looked more different from Bobby Yeagley's. This woman's red cells appeared desiccated and crinkled with hemoglobin puddled at the cell periphery. The team showed that her red cells had selectively lost potassium ions while retaining sodium ions.[256] Nathan later came across a similar abnormality in a world-class competitive swimmer at Harvard who experienced hemolysis after strenuous exercise.[257] Others eventually showed that xerocytosis is the result of mutations in a gene encoding the protein PIEZO 1a, a membrane ion channel sensitive to mechanical stress.[258]

Erythrocyte Development

Just before moving his lab to the new Dana Building, Nathan completed his second sabbatical at MIT where he learned how to grow, or "culture," early red blood cell precursors in petri dishes. This was a powerful technique that allowed him to pursue several lines of research. One was an analysis of a rare congenital disorder called Diamond-Blackfan Anemia (DBA), first described by his predecessor. Using the culture technique, Nathan could show that red cell precursors in DBA patients are defective in transitioning from one early stage (known as CFU-S) to a later one (known as BFU-E). Further, the small number of BFU-E that these patients do produce are dysfunctional at their next stage of maturation (CFU-E). In particular, they do not respond to the hormone erythropoietin, which normally stimulates the production of red blood cells from CFU-E.[259]

Nathan and his colleagues also found that the normal development of red cell precursors such as BFU-E depends on other hormone-like proteins, or "factors," secreted by T lymphocytes, blood cells that are important in immunity.[260] They showed that T lymphocytes from DBA patients support the growth of normal red cell precursors but T lymphocytes from normal people do not support the growth of DBA precursors suggesting that the insensitivity to these factors in DBA is intrinsic to the precursors.[261] A biotechnology company called Genetics Institute, recently started in Cambridge, worked almost exclusively on identifying these kinds of factors and cloning the genes that produced them. By collaborating with the scientists at Genetics Institute, Nathan put himself in the thick of the biotechnology fever that gripped Cambridge in the late 1970s and early 1980s.

Hemoglobin Disorders

Nathan was fascinated by the idea that restoring the production of fetal hemoglobin, hemoglobin F (HbF), in patients with sickle cell disease might alleviate their symptoms. First, though, he would have to figure out how HbF synthesis is controlled. Because Nathan could measure the rate at which the different globin proteins are made, he already had a leg up. After his second sabbatical, he also knew how to isolate red blood cell precursors at various stages of maturity. By combining these tools, he thought he could identify the specific cells that make fetal hemoglobin and study them to discover how HbF synthesis is regulated.

In a series of papers from the early 1980s, Nathan and his fellows determined precisely when the gamma- to beta-globin switch occurs during red cell development.[262, 263, 264] Along the way, they discovered that a small but significant fraction of late precursor cells continues to make fetal hemoglobin even after most of the population had switched to making adult hemoglobin. Nathan called this the inherent "fetal hemoglobin program." Interestingly, the absolute amount of fetal hemoglobin made by late red cell precursors varies considerably among individuals.

At around this time, molecular biologists had discovered a correlation between the activity of a gene—how much protein encoded by that gene is being made—and the extent to which its DNA is chemically modified by the attachment of carbon compounds called methyl groups. In many cases, methylation of a gene's DNA is associated with inactivity. Conversely, loss of a gene's methyl groups often leads to reactivation. A cancer chemotherapy drug, 5-azacytidine, was known to remove methyl groups from DNA and scientists in Chicago showed that administering the drug to baboons increased the amount of fetal hemoglobin they made, presumably by removing methyl groups from gamma-globin's DNA.[265] Immediately thereafter, a thalassemia patient[266] and a sickle cell patient[267] were treated with 5-azacytidine. In both cases, the drug increased fetal hemoglobin synthesis, improving their anemias.

Nathan was excited by these results but he had a very different take on how 5-azacytidine worked. The drug had been designed as a standard chemotherapy agent with a three-dimensional structure similar to one of the building blocks of DNA but sufficiently different that its presence gums up the DNA synthesis machinery. That is how it works against cancer cells: it halts their growth during the DNA synthesis phase of the cell cycle. Nathan thought that, instead of demethylating gamma-globin DNA, 5-azacytdine caused growth arrest in red cell precursors leading to cellular stress that, in turn, stimulated gamma-globin synthesis. Fetal hemoglobin reactivation had been described in other settings in which red blood cell precursors are stressed and Nathan thought that 5-azacytidine treatment was just another example.

If Nathan were correct, then other drugs that arrest cell growth should have the same effect. His team tested a different DNA synthesis inhibitor, hydroxyurea, and found that it also turned on fetal hemoglobin synthesis in monkeys.[268] Because hydroxyurea does not cause demethylation, Nathan knew that his theory was correct. Based on these results, he gave hydroxyurea to two patients with sickle cell disease: fetal hemoglobin synthesis increased and their anemia improved.[269] A subsequent clinical trial showed that hydroxyurea lowered the frequency of sickle "crises"—the episodes of disabling pain caused by sickled cells getting stuck in blood vessels.[270] This has made hydroxyurea a standard treatment for sickle cell disease.

Prenatal Testing

Nathan's lab continued to hone its ability to measure different types of globins—both normal and abnormal—in red blood cells. In the back of Nathan's mind was the idea that using these techniques for prenatal testing might detect fetuses with severe thalassemia or sickle cell disease. Elective abortion might then lead to the eventual elimination or, at least, suppression of the mutated genes that cause those diseases. While the approach would be controversial, it had the potential to remake societies where thalassemia and sickle cell disease were endemic, like Sardinia or Cyprus.

Setting aside for a moment the ethical problems this work would entail, its technical hurdles seemed at the time nearly insurmountable. In the prenatal state, fetuses make fetal hemoglobin, which contains gamma-globin. However, sickle cell disease and many severe thalassemias are caused by abnormal *beta*-globin and, whether normal or abnormal, the fetus makes vanishingly small amounts. Nathan did not know if his techniques would be sensitive enough to detect it. So, his first goal was to optimize an assay for beta-globin in fetal blood.

This part of the story actually begins with Nathan's close friend David Weatherall, who, in 1968, described a method for physically separating different globin chains, which was an advance on Gabuzda's technique.[271] Yuet Wai (YW) Kan, a skilled biochemist, joined Nathan's lab and, using Weatherall's technique, he and Nathan were able to diagnose beta thalassemia in a newborn, in its "first day of life," using blood taken from the umbilical cord.[272] Later, they detected the abnormal globin of sickle cell disease in umbilical cord blood from fetuses aborted as early as fifteen weeks of gestation and in blood inadvertently drawn from the placenta during an amniocentesis in an eight-month pregnancy.[273] Both results indicated the feasibility of applying these techniques to widespread clinical prenatal testing.

A few years later, after leaving Nathan's lab to start his own, Kan reported the measurement of beta- and gamma-globin in placental blood obtained by ultrasound guidance. In this case, a Sicilian couple who had had two children with homozygous beta thalassemia came to him to request a prenatal diagnosis of their third pregnancy. Kan obliged and detected a normal ratio of beta- to gamma-globins suggesting that the fetus did not have beta thalassemia. He was correct.[274]

After Kan's departure, the prenatal diagnosis project was taken up by a new fellow, Blanche Alter. One of the thorniest problems the field faced was developing a safe and reliable method for obtaining fetal blood for globin measurements. Most obstetricians used ultrasound to guide a needle to the placenta which contains a mixture of fetal and maternal blood. Although this approach had a reasonably high success rate, it could also yield samples with inadequate amounts fetal blood and, worse, cause miscarriage.

Alter worked with obstetricians at the Brigham to analyze blood obtained by direct visualization of the placenta using a fetoscope rather than ultrasound. She and her team applied the technique to make a prenatal diagnosis of sickle cell disease.[275] In the same issue of the *New England Journal of Medicine* that announced Alter's results, Kan had a paper that reported using ultrasound to make a prenatal diagnosis of sickle cell disease.[276] Alter and Nathan then decided to perform a clinical trial to determine the reliability of ultrasound- and fetoscope-guided blood sampling for prenatal diagnosis. The results were worrisome. Not only was the diagnostic accuracy too low with either technique to be relied upon for clinical testing, nearly 10 percent of study participants lost their pregnancies as a result of the procedure. The prenatal test was not ready for clinical deployment.[277] The field was stuck.

This changed with the advent of molecular genetics. Stuart Orkin, who had been a fellow of Nathan's, was one of the first to apply its methods to human disease. One simple technique known as Southern blotting (named for its inventor) uses enzymes to cut DNA at specific locations. This generates a heterogeneous mix of DNA fragments that can be arrayed by size. Radioactive probes then identify which fragments contain genes of interest. Orkin used Southern blotting to analyze globin genes and make prenatal diagnoses of thalassemias.

His approach had two enormous benefits. First, the missing globin *genes* in thalassemia patients are absent from all cells, not just red blood cells, so the test would not have to be performed on fetal blood—no more placental needles and pregnancy loss. Instead, Southern blotting could be performed on DNA from cells obtained during amniocentesis, a more routine and much safer procedure. Second, because the radioactive probe can find globin genes in a sea of other DNA, there would be no need to chase after undetectable globin proteins.

Armed with this powerful tool, Orkin, Alter, and Nathan made prenatal diagnoses of thalassemia using DNA obtained from amniocenteses. They reported their success in the *New England Journal of Medicine* in July, 1978.[278] The significance of their accomplishment was quickly appreciated and reported on the front page of the *New York Times*.[279] Coincidentally, the same edition of the *Times* announced the birth of the first "test-tube baby." Louise Brown was above the fold; Orkin and Nathan were below. Far worse, the article's headline was "Doctors Isolate Human Gene," which is not at all what Orkin had done. He had merely detected the presence of globin genes. The overstatement elicited an angry backlash from medical geneticists around the world who castigated the Children's team and the *New England Journal of Medicine* for "rushing [the] report into print" ahead of others who really were isolating the gene.[280] Although no lasting harm was done to anyone's reputation, the incident helped make Nathan wary of the popular press and its propensity to distort scientific findings.

Of course, the real controversy around this work was the ethical one. If the rationale for prenatal testing is the elimination of mutated genes from the population, the only way to do so is by therapeutic abortion. Nathan recognized how provocative this would be, especially in Boston's conservative Catholic milieu. Harvard University, Children's Hospital, and the Peter Bent Brigham Hospital, where the obstetrical procedures were being performed, were nervous. Further, this was all happening at the same time as the infamous case of Dr. Kenneth Edelin who had been convicted by a Boston jury in 1976 of manslaughter for having performed a second trimester abortion at Boston City Hospital. In response to his conviction, and prior to its reversal on appeal, the Massachusetts legislature passed laws restricting fetal research. Nathan and his team were forced to do much of their work in collaboration with colleagues at Yale because of Connecticut's more accommodating legal climate.

Nathan respected the local abortion opponents but he was convinced of the moral and ethical rectitude of his work. He wrote thought pieces,[281, 282] including one for the *Villanova Law Review*, which offered his take on the ethics of fetal research. The essays are remarkable for their explicit acknowledgment that, in the opinion of abortion opponents, beneficial results from research using aborted fetuses might encourage public acceptance of abortion. But Nathan's defense is convoluted. He begins by asserting that many parents who are heterozygous for thalassemia or sickle cell genes choose to terminate all of their pregnancies rather than accept the 25 percent risk of giving birth to a homozygous, fully affected child. Thus, by perfecting prenatal testing through fetal research,

75 percent of those pregnancies could come to term. He suggests, therefore, that the "aim" of this research is to *preserve* pregnancies rather than terminate them.

This is a strained argument that seems very much of its time. It is unclear how many doubly heterozygous couples were really ending their pregnancies rather than rolling the dice and hoping for the best. It seems unlikely that the number would have been impressively large. Further, the "aim" of this research was clearly not preservation of pregnancies—it was to discover how to identify which pregnancies could be terminated to rid the population of mutated globin genes. The birth of children with normal globin genes or only one copy of an abnormal gene would be a happy but incidental outcome. Still, it was typical of Nathan to incorporate humanistic considerations into his work and it eaarned him the respect of his philosophical opponents.

Chapter 9

LEADERSHIP

Before taking the reins as department chair, Nathan went on a trip to India and Nepal with Jean. They visited Dal Lake in Kashmir, then Nathan challenged himself to the Annapurna trek, reaching the base camp at an elevation of fifteen thousand feet. This strenuous, high-altitude forced march was excellent preparation for the rigors Nathan would face when he returned to Boston.

A decade of indifferent leadership had left the department of medicine ill-equipped to meet the challenges that threatened its ability to provide optimal care for children and to train the next generation of pediatricians. The problems fell into four broad categories: poor performance of some of the subspecialty divisions within the department of medicine; external pressures undermining traditional models of residency training; declining financial support for research; and, a deteriorating physical plant. As chair, Nathan had to address all of these.

Fortunately, he had strong support within the department. Most important was Fred Lovejoy, the associate physician-in-chief. Lovejoy had grown up in Concord, Massachusetts; after graduating from Yale, he went to medical school at the University of Virginia and then did his internship and residency at Bellevue, New York's legendary city hospital. This was an unusual trajectory for the scion of an old New England family but it appealed to Charles Janeway, another old New Englander, who recruited Lovejoy to be chief resident at Children's. The Lovejoys and the Janeways had summer homes near each other in Annisquam, a small waterfront town near Gloucester, north of Boston. After his chief residency, Lovejoy ran the residency program at Children's from 1978 to 2005 and developed a reputation as a brilliant recruiter of young talent. Janeway also appointed him associate physician-in-chief, a position he retained under Avery and one he would now hold under Nathan.

Lovejoy's value to Nathan cannot be overstated. In his previous job as division chief, Nathan had been responsible for a handful of fellows who were doing subspecialty training in hematology and oncology after completing their residencies. But, as chair of the department of pediatrics, Nathan was now responsible for thirty to forty interns fresh out of medical school as well as another sixty to eighty residents in their second and third years. He needed to make sure that these young physicians received the best possible training in pediatrics and he wanted the residency program at Children's to be known as the best in the world. Nathan was confident that if he accomplished the former, the latter would follow.

Even though the residency program was a core interest, Nathan would be far too busy to give it the personal attention it needed. This is where Lovejoy shone. He figured out how to organize the best possible teaching experiences for the interns and residents— where they would spend their time, what their responsibilities would be, and how hard they would need to work. Lovejoy did it all with a caring touch that included a yearly Christmas party at his home for all of the interns, residents, and their families. Most important, Lovejoy also ran the intern selection process that identified the best candidates each year and fed them into the residency pipeline.

The success of Children's residency program can be judged, in part, by the careers of its graduates. Lovejoy and Nathan reviewed this metric for residents who had trained at Children's from 1974 through 1986.[283] The program was explicitly designed to train future leaders in pediatrics, which meant that trainees were expected to embark on careers in academic medicine rather than become full-time private practitioners of pediatrics. By this narrow definition, the program was a success: 66 percent of its graduates were in academic positions compared to 20 percent of graduates from other U.S. pediatrics programs. All was not rosy, however. The proportion of women in the program had barely budged during those twelve years from 30 percent to 39 percent, and significantly more men than women had entered academic positions (75 percent of the men versus 25 percent of the women). Only 5 percent of the graduates were African-American. Correcting these deficiencies became a priority.

Nathan was also concerned about ways in which the resident experience was changing. His own fondest memory of residency was the autonomy he enjoyed in managing his patients—being thrown in the deep end starting on day one. He thought that this was the best way to attain true clinical mastery. Now, however, external forces had conspired to severely limit opportunities for interns and residents to have direct responsibility for patient care. The sea change began in 1984 when Libby Zion died in New York Hospital after her intern and resident gave her sedatives that interacted lethally with an antidepressant she had been taking. The ensuing high-profile malpractice case led to reforms in residency training including a legislatively mandated reduction in the number of consecutive hours that interns or residents could work. Also, because Zion's intern had been unsupervised during much of the night of Zion's death, another reform compelled training programs to limit the autonomy of interns and residents. Major medical decisions would now have to be reviewed and approved by senior staff physicians. These reforms were reinforced by insurers who would not reimburse hospitals unless a senior staff physician had signed off on the patient's management plan.

Nathan wanted to put more authority in the hands of residents in a way that would not jeopardize patient safety or hospital reimbursement. His first intervention was to change the organizational structure of the medical service. He decentralized care by creating three clinical units: infants, children, and young adults, and named them for legendary pediatricians. Each was led by a service chief, chosen because he or she was an outstanding clinician and someone with a track record in clinical research. The service chief was responsible for identifying the staff physicians who would oversee the interns and residents and have ultimate legal responsibility for patient care. The service chiefs were also on the lookout for opportunities to provide increased patient care responsibilities, especially for the senior, third-year residents. Nathan hoped that chiefs who shared his vision might be able to restore to the residency some of the confidence-building authority he had enjoyed during his own training.

Lovejoy analyzed the new model after it had been in place for six years.[284] He identified several positive outcomes including improved continuity of patient care, better tracking of intern and resident performance, and enhanced supervision and counseling of those trainees. Referring physicians reported increased satisfaction with their interactions with Children's. However, Lovejoy also found that the model paid too much attention to formal lines of accountability and demanded excessive documentation of clinical activities. While the latter generated increased revenue for the hospital—the more detailed the documentation, the better the reimbursement from insurers—residents complained that caring for patients had turned into a bookkeeping exercise. To be fair, this was not the fault of the service chief model. Rather it was the hospital's administrative response to strong financial incentives set up by insurance companies. Meanwhile, opportunities for intern and resident autonomy—Nathan's rationale for the creating the model—failed to materialize.

As Nathan thought about other ways to give residents more responsibility, it occurred to him that some routine aspects of pediatric care do not require supervision by senior physicians and their value is so well established that insurers might pay without supervisor sign-off. However, he also knew that those activities occur more commonly in community-based or primary care practices than in subspecialty hospitals like Children's. So, he wondered if there might be other settings in which Children's residents could directly manage routine pediatric cases with more autonomy than they had at Children's. Such a setting did exist—at Boston City Hospital, which had been rebranded as Boston Medical Center (BMC).

Nathan and Lovejoy floated a novel idea: Why not combine the residency programs at Children's and BMC? Each hospital would gain something from the other: Children's residents would be exposed to community-based pediatrics with its greater opportunity for autonomy; BMC's residents would be exposed to more subspecialties. The latter would be something of a godsend for BMC since its pediatric residency program was being threatened with loss of national accreditation because it offered so few opportunities for subspecialty training.

The chair of pediatrics at BMC, Barry Zuckerman, saw the potential benefits of the merger, so he asked Bob Vinci, an emergency care specialist who was in charge of the residency program, to work with Lovejoy to assess the feasibility of the proposed arrangement. The challenges were daunting: the residency program at Children's was more than twice as large as BMC's; the tangible resources at Children's, a private hospital, were far greater than those at BMC, a public hospital; the cultures at the two institutions were markedly different—specialty-focused versus community-focused—and a longstanding source of pride for each.

Nonetheless, Lovejoy and Vinci persisted, and the result was the Boston Combined Residency Program (BCRP), which has been a resounding success.[285] Because the two hospitals are physically separate, each retained its own residency director who reports to his or her respective chief. However, the program is fully integrated in the sense that residents consider themselves to be in the BCRP rather than one hospital or the other. The goal of the merger—to give more autonomy to residents while also providing subspecialty training—has been realized, making BCRP one of the most sought-after pediatric residencies in the world. A marker of its success is that, unlike many combined programs created during the medical merger mania of the 1990s, the BCRP is still alive and well decades after its inception.

Revamping the pediatric residency program was just one of the changes that Nathan wanted to bring to Children's. Another was an upgrade of the hospital's physical plant. More patient rooms were needed and the existing ones were outdated; the operating rooms were crowded and overbooked; an expanding research enterprise had outgrown its laboratories. Because Children's had no empty land it could expand into, a new hospital, in effect, had to be built on the site of the old one.

Nathan would need an ally for this daunting project. The two largest clinical services and, therefore, the main sources of revenue for the hospital were surgery and medicine. The surgeon-in-chief, counterpart to Nathan's physician-in-chief, was Aldo Castaneda, a pioneer in the correction of congenital heart defects. He and Nathan were like-minded and developed a superb working relationship. They knew they would be more likely to get what they wanted if they could present a united front to administrators and the board of trustees, so they met every Friday to coordinate their requests. This was a powerful strategy: the two chiefs could legitimately claim to represent the interests of most of the patients and faculty at Children's, making disagreement with them perilous.

What did they want? Nathan believed that hospitals should be places where technologically sophisticated interventions are used for the benefit of patients. To him, then, the main beneficiaries of the renovation would be technology-heavy specialties like surgery, cardiology, or radiology. Between his longstanding and unsubtle hero-worship of surgeons and his prioritization of complex specialties, Nathan's recommendations smacked of deference to the department of surgery, at least so it seemed to the faculty in the department of medicine. Even within medicine, his decision to allocate generous space and funding to the division of cardiology was resented by other divisions, including hematology/oncology, his recent academic home. Nathan stuck to his guns but the criticism was unpleasant.

Meanwhile, the hospital also needed a new emergency room. The ER is a portal through which many patients first enter a hospital, and Nathan thought of it as Children's front door. He wanted to build an appealing new ER and to see it managed in a way that would provide an exceptional experience for patients. The construction of a new, state-of-the-art ER was enabled by a gift from Richard and Susan Smith, the Dana-Farber trustees who Nathan had known since childhood and who would play an important role in the next phase of his career. The Smiths were motivated by the death of their son, who had suffered brain damage when a throat infection closed off his airway and the emergency procedure to reopen it was delayed.

For years, the ER had been jointly managed by the departments of medicine and surgery. Castaneda had appointed a general surgeon named W. Hardy Hendren III to oversee the surgical side of the ER. Hendren was highly accomplished, famous for being the first in Boston to separate conjoined twins. He had also been a carrier-qualified naval aviator in World War II and he brought that toughness with him into the hospital—one of Hardy Hendren's nicknames was Hardly Human. Not surprisingly, he and Nathan butted heads. Nathan eventually concluded that his plans for updating the ER would get nowhere with Hendren in charge, so he convinced Castaneda to remove him and let Nathan's department of medicine run the show. Nathan recruited a superb new ER director named Gary Fleisher, who did an outstanding job and later became chair of the department of medicine.

Next, Nathan turned his attention to the general pediatric outpatient clinic, the other portal of entry into Children's Hospital.

The facility had become too small to accommodate its growing volume and its poor management was contributing to the discomfort of sick children and their families. The clinic was overseen by the division of general pediatrics, which was led by Mel Levine, a well-known specialist in learning disabilities. Nathan asked two outside experts to review the situation and make recommendations for improving the division and its clinic. One of the reviewers was Anne Dyson, a pediatrician and philanthropist whom Nathan knew well. Because her professional interests included educating pediatricians about community-based care, she was eminently qualified. The other was Julius Richmond, chair of the department of psychiatry at Children's, a former U.S. surgeon general, and the co-founder and first national director of Head Start.

Dyson and Richmond acknowledged Levine's expertise and vision in the area of learning disabilities but criticized his leadership of the division. They recommended that he be replaced by Judith Palfrey, an expert in community-based pediatric care and advocacy, especially for disabled children. Nathan made the switch and the division of general medicine went on to thrive. Palfrey also successfully reorganized the outpatient clinics.

Nathan's strategy for elevating the status of general pediatrics at Children's Hospital included a push for T. Berry Brazelton to be granted tenure as a Harvard Medical School professor. Brazelton was a renowned pediatrician interested in the behavior of neonates and very young children. He was also an inveterate popularizer of the science of childhood behavior and, for a time, a ubiquitous presence in magazines and on television. To some of the stodgier gatekeepers at Harvard, this kind of celebrity did not comport with scholarly achievement and Brazelton's promotion was stalled. Nathan forcefully presented the case for Brazelton's scholarship to the promotions committee while disingenuously nodding to his notoriety by relating that one of Nathan's daughters once asked him why nobody knew who her father was while everyone knew Dr. Brazelton. Nathan's arguments and charm swayed the committee. He later raised funds from donors in Brazelton's native Texas to create an endowed chair in his name to support a professor of general pediatrics. Palfrey was the first incumbent.

A tragic coda to this story involves the ousted director of general pediatrics, Mel Levine, who left Children's in 1987 to become a professor of pediatrics at the University of North Carolina at Chapel Hill. In 2008, a lawsuit was filed in Boston alleging that Levine had abused seven male patients at Children's Hospital between 1967 and 1984.[286] One of the victims had filed a complaint with the Massachusetts Board of Registration in Medicine in 1993 that was dismissed. Children's claimed that it had received no complaints about Levine while he was employed there. Although Levine maintained his innocence, he voluntarily surrendered his North Carolina medical license in 2009 when the state medical board said it was prepared to show evidence that Levine had performed genital examinations on patients at U.N.C. that "were not medically indicated or properly documented."[287] In early 2011, a class action suit in Boston claimed that Levine had abused forty boys and offered disturbing details.[288] One day later, Levine committed suicide, shooting himself in the head.

It is difficult to know whether hints or rumors of Levine's alleged sexual abuse had been circulating at Children's when Nathan removed him as director of general pediatrics and whether they may have contributed—consciously or not—to his decision. Regardless, the change in leadership was one of the earliest and best examples of an intervention Nathan made to reshape one of his divisions.

Other divisions in the department of medicine were also in need of attention. Nathan's old hematology/oncology division was on the easier end of the spectrum. He had appointed two chiefs to replace him as division head, one to oversee the program at Dana-Farber and the other to run things at Children's. The arrangement worked well at first because the inaugural co-chiefs cooperated with each other. However, this structure—two chiefs trying to run a single division spread between two hospitals—would lead to conflict in later years. Nonetheless, the patients were well cared for, the division produced outstanding research, and the fellowship program attracted some of the most talented young pediatric oncologists in the world.

In contrast, the division of gastroenterology was a mess. Its chief was Alan Walker, who had been given the task of running the division of pediatric gastroenterology at Massachusetts General Hospital as well as the one at Children's. By all accounts he was not a skilled manager and both divisions were suffering—no substantive research was being performed and some of the best clinicians had left. To make matters worse, two former Children's residents had gone into private practice in pediatric gastroenterology and were using their clinical privileges at Children's to siphon patients from the hospital practice into theirs. Angry about this direct competition, Nathan offered full-time positions at Children's to both physicians. When they demurred, intent on holding onto their private practice, Nathan convinced the hospital to restrict their privileges. This was a tricky maneuver because one of them happened to be a friend and fellow countryman of Castaneda's—both were Guatemalan. Nonetheless, the hospital supported Nathan. The two physicians sued but the Superior Court of Massachusetts entered a summary judgement for the hospital. The physicians lost again on appeal.[289]

Nathan's handling of the gastroenterology problem shaped the future of his leadership. Early in his tenure, Nathan had made it clear that he wanted the clinics in his department to be staffed by full-time physicians employed by the hospital. The dustup with the division of gastroenterology came shortly after he became chief, so the way he handled it would set the tone for later conflicts. By sticking to his principles—even in the face of a lawsuit brought by a buddy of Castaneda's—Nathan sent an unambiguous message that he meant what he said and would follow through on his promises. In the end, the chief of the division of gastroenterology resigned from Children's to devote his full attention to the group at Mass General. To replace him, Nathan lured back one of the clinicians who had left the division earlier and he, in turn, attracted a stable of first-rate physicians.

The division of immunology presented a more personal challenge. Its leader was Fred Rosen, one of Nathan's first professional colleagues and a strong advocate for his appointment as physician-in-chief. Rosen was an infinitely entertaining raconteur and a first-rate researcher. However, his scientific interests were narrow and the division's research output was disappointing. On the clinical side, the division oversaw treatment for allergies and asthma, common pediatric problems, which meant that Nathan would have to take a careful, objective look at the service. When he did, he saw that it was being managed poorly. Among other things, Rosen's sarcastic and nakedly elitist attitude had alienated many of his co-workers.

Nathan reluctantly concluded that Rosen would have to step down. He convinced his friend to do so by arranging a swap: in exchange for giving up leadership of the division of immunology, Rosen could run the newly created Center for Blood Research (CBR). The CBR was what was left of the Protein Foundation, a laboratory started by Edwin Cohn in the 1940s for purifying the protein components of blood. It also housed the Blood Grouping Lab, which had been started by Dr. Diamond to perform blood typing for transfusions. Rosen accepted the trade and within a few years, made a great success of CBR by recruiting several outstanding scientists.

Neonatology was another high-profile problem for Nathan, one made more difficult by politics. The subspecialty of caring of newborns was essentially invented by a Children's Hospital physician named Clement A. Smith. Mary Ellen Avery, Nathan's predecessor as department chair, had trained with Smith in the 1950s and was the discipline's leader when she was recruited to Children's. Smith, who was still a presence at the hospital, never forgave Nathan for the role he played in displacing his protégé and, so, from day one of Nathan's chairmanship, the neonatologists did not trust him.

Newborn care at that time was provided by the Joint Program in Neonatology, which Avery had created to unite the services of Children's, The Boston Hospital for Women, and Beth Israel Hospital. One of her former fellows, H. William Taeusch, Jr., was chief. Although its physicians were superb, the Joint Program never functioned well and by the time Nathan was chair, its faculty were complaining about its awkward structure. Also concerning was the fact that the Joint Program's research did not match the high caliber of its clinical care. In particular, no one was working on fetal development, one of the hottest areas of study in neonatology. To remedy this, Nathan recruited Merton Bernfield, a neonatologist and developmental biologist at Stanford, to become the new chief. Bernfield was a mixed blessing. The clinicians did not like him but he accomplished what Nathan asked of him—he elevated the quality of the division's research and attracted external funding. An added benefit of Bernfield's recruitment, from Nathan's point of view, was that it removed a Mel Avery loyalist from the ranks of the division chiefs.

Nathan made more leadership changes in pulmonary, endocrinology, and genetics. The outcomes were mixed but each continued the process of exchanging Avery holdovers for Nathan appointees—this would make his job easier.

Finally, Nathan turned his attention to cardiology, a division that offered unique challenges, some structural, others frankly criminal. The former arose from a tradition at Children's in which some departments had established nonprofit foundations to manage their clinical practices. The faculty who provided patient care were employees of their foundations rather than the hospital and the foundations billed patients for services. Children's administrators were enamored of this model because it spared them the miseries of negotiating with physicians and paying their salaries and benefits—those onerous tasks were left to the foundations.

Nearly every department at Children's had its own foundation, but Nathan refused to form one for his. He acknowledged that the foundation model could work for departments like surgery, which had a cadre of physicians performing expensive clinical interventions reimbursed at high rates. The foundation could use that money to subsidize the salaries of other members of the department whose activities generated lower revenues. This was impossible in the department of medicine, where the vast majority of faculty were engaged in clinical activities that resulted in low reimbursement. Many also cared for patients who were uninsured or on Medicaid. With much less opportunity for cross-subsidization, it made more sense for Nathan's faculty to be employed by the hospital and to negotiate their salaries in a uniform way.

The exception was cardiology. In particular, interventional cardiologists—physicians who thread narrow catheters into the hearts of patients to visualize structures or repair defects—generate substantial revenue. With money comes power: The cardiologists had convinced Avery and the hospital to allow their division to create a foundation similar to those of the departments. The Boston Children's Heart Foundation was established in 1983, two years before Nathan became chief.

The Heart Foundation prevented Nathan from using a powerful tool that other chairs of medicine had at their disposal. Everywhere else, a chair could use some of the large financial margin generated by a division of cardiology to allocate resources to underfunded areas of the department or to subsidize research. That option was not available to Nathan because of the self-contained nature of the Boston Children's Heart Foundation—the cardiologists kept the margins they generated. This made the job of department chair at Children's less attractive than it might have otherwise been and may have contributed to the difficulty the hospital experienced in recruiting outside candidates to replace Avery.

The Heart Foundation was annoying, but Nathan could live with it; less tolerable was the criminal activity of its chief. Bernardo

Nadal-Ginard was a Catalan who had been recruited with great fanfare to run the division of cardiology at Children's in 1982. A medical scientist with a PhD in addition to his MD, Nadal-Ginard was an accomplished laboratory researcher who had made a name for himself by using techniques of molecular biology to understand heart disease. The dean of Harvard Medical School was an enthusiastic supporter of Nadal-Ginard and put him in charge of the school's MD-PhD Program.

With the benefit of hindsight, the first hint of trouble might have been an announcement in the society pages of the *Boston Globe* that Nadal-Ginard and his wife, a researcher at Children's, had purchased the Hunnewell Mansion in Back Bay for $1.6 million because their vast collection of modern art "needed a larger house for proper hanging."[290] Not many academic cardiologists have this concern.

Scarcely a week later, the *Globe* reported on its front page that Children's had placed Nadal-Ginard on administrative leave after a routine audit of the Heart Foundation's finances uncovered serious irregularities.[291] As chief of cardiology, Nadal-Ginard was also president of the Heart Foundation and oversaw its books. The audit revealed that he had used foundation funds for personal expenses and a subsequent investigation by the attorney general resulted in an indictment on twenty-two counts of embezzlement. A jury found Nadal-Ginard guilty on twelve counts and he was sentenced to a year's imprisonment followed by two years of community service.[292] The conviction was upheld on appeal.

There was more. Like other foundations at Children's, the Heart Foundation had been providing its highly paid physicians with much of their total compensation as retirement benefits. The audit found that Nadal-Ginard had altered the terms of those benefits in his favor without notifying the Heart Foundation's board. When he and a few other board members cashed out their retirement funds, Nadal-Ginard pocketed $4.2 million, a sum far greater than the others got. The foundation, now led by its other board members, filed a civil suit claiming, first, that Nadal-Ginard was not entitled to the amount he had received and, second, that the payout had resulted in a total salary package that far exceeded the caps for faculty at Children's Hospital and Harvard Medical School. The latter claim was laughably disingenuous since most of the other faculty members employed by the Foundation also enjoyed total compensation packages that exceeded those loosely enforced salary caps. Regardless, a federal judge found for the plaintiffs and ordered repayment of the payout along with interest and costs—a total of $6.5 million.[293] To raise the money, Nadal-Ginard's art collection was auctioned by Sotheby's.

Had he thought of it, Nathan might have cited the potential for embezzlement as one of the reasons for opposing foundations. However, his critique had been based on what he considered to be their problematic structure which, because of its independence from hospital oversight, led to maldistribution of clinical revenues and underfunding of efforts that were part of the hospital's mission. Of course, this same lack of central monitoring had enabled Nadal-Ginard's theft. Now, Nathan could use the risk of criminal activity to bolster his argument that the department of medicine should not have foundations. Predictably, physicians who benefited from the foundation model thought Nathan was being overly conservative and condemned his attitude as a throwback to outmoded notions of departmental centralization. Ironically, their stance was crystallized by Nadal-Ginard, who proudly told an interviewer from the *Boston Globe* that, as division chief, he had resisted David Nathan's attempts to "take over" cardiology.[294]

Nathan's low opinion of the foundation model was further validated five years later when the chief of the department of radiology at Children's was charged with embezzling funds from the Radiology Foundation.[295] The amount was small—$70,000—and the loss was detected precisely because of the careful monitoring Children's put in place after the Nadal-Ginard affair. However, it was another example of foundation-related malfeasance and fueled

Nathan's opposition. All to no avail, however, since the foundation model continues to thrive at Children's Hospital and in the department of medicine.

Nathan believed that his struggles with the divisions were necessary for him to create an ideal department of medicine. However, these confrontations were annoying and they were wearing him down. Fortunately, balanced against this administrative drudgery was a major accomplishment that would change the face of research at Children's: attracting support from the Howard Hughes Medical Institute (HHMI).

Hughes had created HHMI in 1953 primarily as a tax dodge to protect the profits of Hughes Aircraft. But HHMI was technically a medical philanthropy, so Hughes assembled an elite group of advisors to help him direct HHMI money to scientists who were doing basic biomedical research and education. However, HHMI's governance was utterly opaque as was its process for selecting the beneficiaries of its largesse. For one thing, Hughes himself was the HHMI's sole trustee.

Things changed after Hughes died. A board was formed to assume responsibility for the institute and one of its first actions was to sell Hughes Aircraft to General Motors for $5.2 billion. The board used the proceeds to create an endowment to support HHMI's medical research mission. But rather than building its own bricks-and-mortar laboratories, the trustees crafted a model in which HHMI would hire outstanding scientists who continued to work at their home institutions. At first, HHMI focused on a limited number of specific research areas and only a few elite institutions. Importantly, grants to these institutions included funds for building research space and recruiting faculty. This model of providing money both for research and infrastructure made HHMI a highly prized source of funding.

Among the new trustees at HHMI were George Thorn, Nathan's old boss, and Donald Frederickson, ex-director of the National Institutes of Health and, more remotely, a resident at the Peter Bent Brigham when Nathan was a medical student. One of the research areas HHMI supported was genetics and Nathan thought that the geneticists at Children's, including his protégé Stu Orkin, might attract HHMI's interest. After some intense lobbying, HHMI agreed to make Children's one of its external research sites. It not only provided money to support the research of Children's geneticists but it also financed an expansion of the hospital's main research building. Additional HHMI funds allowed Nathan to recruit superstar scientists like Fred Alt, who was using genetics to understand immunology, and two of the world's foremost structural biologists, Don Wiley and Steve Harrison.

Landing the HHMI agreement was a coup. The generous funding and the prestige that came with it gave Nathan the means to recruit and retain high-profile scientists who solidified Children's reputation as a home for serious, cutting-edge research. That kind of reputation builds on itself and explains why, to this day, scientific research at Children's thrives—in part, because of HHMI's early investment. At the same time, one of the most daunting tasks for a research hospital is finding money for its facilities. Nathan's procurement of external funds for new construction made him a hero to the academic and administrative leadership of the hospital. Forging the relationship between HHMI and Children's is one of Nathan's major legacies.

As 1994 began, Nathan was at a crossroads. He was about to turn 65 and mark his tenth year as department chair. His friend and ally, Aldo Castaneda, had warned Nathan not to overstay his time as chair and to leave the position no later than his sixty-sixth birthday. Castaneda had taken his own advice earlier in the year, stepping down as chair of surgery. It was a development Nathan had dreaded—Castaneda's absence would make his job much harder.

In thinking back on his time as chair, Nathan realized how tired he had become of the job's endless administrative hassles. Every day seemed to bring a new struggle with the cardiologists and the Nadal-Ginard affair had been exhausting. He was ready to hand the chiefship to someone else, return to his small lab, and teach students and residents. Jean Nathan could not have endorsed his plan more exuberantly.

Nathan informed hospital executives of his intention. Everything was put in place to transition out of leadership. Nathan could almost smell the Nantucket air.

Then came the phone call.

RESEARCH, 1985–1995

Although Nathan was much busier as department chair than he had been as division chief, he nonetheless maintained an active research program pursuing, for the most part, projects he had already been working on. For example, his group continued to investigate what Nathan had called the fetal hemoglobin program, the switch in the fetus from fetal hemoglobin, HbF, to adult hemoglobin, HbA. His other main area of interest was finding better ways to treat iron overload in thalassemia patients.

The Fetal Hemoglobin Program

As late as 1985, surprisingly little was known about how the fetus transitions from making HbF to HbA as it nears birth. A simple unanswered question was whether individual red blood cell precursors make a sudden all-or-none switch from fetal to adult hemoglobin or, instead, gradually shut down HbF synthesis as they ramp up HbA. Thanks to advances his group had made in the previous ten years, Nathan could isolate red cell precursors, grow them in petri dishes, and measure how much of the different hemoglobins they made. Nathan reasoned that if precursor cells flipped a binary switch randomly during the transition period, then in a large population of precursors, some cells would be making only fetal hemoglobin and others only adult hemoglobin. In other words, there should be two discrete subpopulations. If he were to make a histogram showing how frequently cells making specific amounts of, say, adult hemoglobin appeared in the overall population, it ought to reveal the presence of two subpopulations of cells—those making lots of adult hemoglobin and those making almost none. The overall population in this example is described by statisticians as "skewed" because it is biased toward the ends of the histogram. If, however, all precursors gradually ramp up adult hemoglobin, then the histogram would show a more uniformly distributed population—a bell-shaped curve with the top of the bell corresponding to the mean amount of adult hemoglobin made by all of the cells. This kind of population is referred to as "normal" or Gaussian, the opposite of skewed.

When Nathan's group measured the amount of adult hemoglobin made by red cell precursors from rhesus monkeys at the midpoint of the fetal-to-adult hemoglobin transition, they found a skewed distribution.[296] Thus, the fetal hemoglobin program is controlled by a binary switch that shuts off fetal hemoglobin production in any particular red cell precursor at random. This known as a "stochastic" process. Blanche Alter did most of the work on these experiments and her observations provided the basis for research done by others over the next ten years to understand exactly how the switch happens. The mechanism, which was eventually described by Stu Orkin and his student Vijay Sankaran, involves suppression of gamma-globin synthesis by a protein called BCL11A that is lifted as the fetus matures.[297]

The fetal-to-adult hemoglobin switch continued to be interesting to Nathan because of his earlier demonstration that hydroxyurea enhances HbF production in patients with sickle cell disease. As described in Chapter 8, Nathan's group showed that this was not the result of DNA demethylation, as others had thought, but a response to inhibiting cell proliferation although the mechanism was still unknown. Now, Nathan could investigate this phenomenon in more detail using his red cell precursor system. Surprisingly, treating the precursors in petri dishes with the same amount of hydroxyurea that worked in patients produced no increase in HbF production. In other words, the effect of hydroxyurea in patients was not a direct one on red cell precursors—it required the whole person. Nathan's group discovered that hydroxyurea and similar agents exert their effects on HbF production by killing red cell precursors—that stimulates the bone marrow to recruit their replacements from a pool of early progenitors, and it is these early progenitors that make high amounts of HbF.[298] This important insight helped explain the clinical efficacy of these drugs in sickle cell disease.

In a related project, Nathan's team studied a cohort of sickle cell patients from the Eastern Province of Saudi Arabia whose levels of HbF were three-to-five times higher than those seen in American sickle cell patients.[299, 300] With help from Stu Orkin, the group showed that a single DNA change in the region of the genome that controls gamma-globin production tracked with high HbF expression in the Saudis with sickle cell.[301] However, family members who had the DNA change but did not have sickle cell disease made normal, low levels of HbF. Thus, the effect of the DNA change was apparent only in the setting of anemia, which recruits large numbers of red cell precursors, reminiscent of the effects of hydroxyurea on HbF production.

Also related to this work was Nathan's ongoing study of the impact of hormonelike factors on the growth and maturation of red cell precursors, work that continued to be enabled by his collaboration with Genetics Institute. The company, known colloquially as GI, had perfected ways to clone genes encoding proteins that stimulate blood cell growth and maturation. Nathan's group used its colony forming assays to examine the effects of these proteins on red cell precursors and found that some of GI's molecularly cloned growth factors could stimulate human red cell progenitors.[302, 303] Nathan's lab also made the important discovery that one of these growth factors, GM--CSF (granulocyte/macrophage colony-stimulating factor), which had been assumed to be specific for white blood cell precursors, also enhanced the growth of red cell precursors.[304] Finally, with colleagues at NIH, Nathan's group showed that GM-CSF helped mice recover their white blood cells more rapidly after bone marrow transplantation.[305] This observation led to its use in transplant patients.

Treating Iron Overload in Thalassemia

The most serious threat to the well-being of thalassemia patients continued to be the iron their organs accumulate as a result of frequent blood transfusions. A year's worth of red cells provides more iron than the total amount present in a normal adult and there is no efficient way to remove the excess. To make matters worse, thalassemia patients absorb more dietary iron than normal individuals. The direst effect of all of this iron is heart failure. In the mid-1960s, the average age at which cardiac toxicity first appeared in thalassemia patients was sixteen; half of them would die within three months.[306]

These patients desperately needed something to help them excrete their excess iron in urine or feces. Chelators were a possibility. These are molecules that bind tightly to metal ions and are used in a variety of industrial applications. An attempt to adapt chelators to human use began in the early 1960s with the synthesis of an iron-specific chelator called deferoxamine (DFO). Because DFO cannot be absorbed orally and lasts only a short time in the bloodstream, it had to be administered by intravenous or intramuscular injection. Therefore, DFO was first tested by giving it to children while they were receiving their blood transfusions.[307] The drug did promote excretion of iron in the urine but insufficient amounts were available to test whether it could improve clinical outcomes.

A few years later, when Nathan was chief of the division of hematology/oncology, he took up the challenge of optimizing chelation therapy. He was fortunate to have two outstanding hematology fellows to drive this work. One was Sue Shurin, who had trained at Johns Hopkins and Tufts and later became director of pediatric hematology/oncology at Case Western Reserve. The other was Richard Propper, who had come from Stanford. Together, they changed the way thalassemia patients are treated.

In their first study, Nathan and his fellows reasoned that the longer a thalassemia patient could be "exposed" to DFO, the more iron he or she would excrete. As expected, a twenty-four-hour intravenous infusion of high-dose DFO produced an impressive amount of excreted iron.[308] In those days, however, continuous intravenous infusion of a drug outside of the hospital setting was utterly impractical. That motivated Propper to contact inventor Dean Kamen, who had developed a portable pump for continuous insulin injection under the skin. Kamen's company provided the pumps and Nathan's team set up a trial to determine if continuous subcutaneous infusion of DFO might be effective in thalassemia patients.

The trial demanded a lot from its participants: every morning they would have to insert a needle into the skin of their abdomen and strap the pump—about the size of a cigarette carton—to their waist. Every night, they would place the pump on a bedside table and in the morning start the process all over again with a fresh needle. Somehow, the team got twenty-six patients to comply with this awkward regimen and it was fortunate they did because the results were stunning. Subcutaneous DFO was 90 percent as effective as intravenous DFO in stimulating iron excretion.[309] The team had proven that there was a practical way to prolong the exposure of thalassemia patients to the chelator. Nathan's old friend David Weatherall wrote an enthusiastic editorial to accompany the article in the *New England Journal of Medicine* that reported the findings.[310] He mentioned that a twelve-hour infusion was nearly as effective as the twenty-four-hour infusion tested in the trial, and that became standard therapy.

DFO's ability to enhance iron excretion was one thing, but could it prevent cardiac toxicity and prolong the lives of thalassemia patients? This was an extraordinarily difficult question to answer. Iron overload develops slowly in thalassemia, often taking two decades to become clinically severe; testing DFO for its impact on disease would be a prolonged and expensive proposition. Nonetheless, Nathan and his group made an attempt. Nearly ten years after demonstrating the feasibility of continuous subcutaneous DFO, they collaborated with pediatricians at the Hospital for Sick Children in Toronto to analyze the clinical outcomes of patients treated at both sites. They analyzed the data in a clever way: about half of the kids who were supposed to be on the DFO pump for twelve hours every day simply would not do it. In medical jargon they would be called noncompliant. Among the nineteen noncompliant patients, twelve developed cardiac disease and seven died. In contrast, of seventeen patients who were compliant, only one developed fatal cardiac disease.[311] This was a strong indication that DFO might prolong survival in thalassemia patients.

The team did the best they could with the available data, but the study had shortcomings. First, it was not a randomized trial so there might have been something else about the compliant children that protected them from cardiac disease. Second, it could not evaluate the group of patients who might have derived the greatest benefit from DFO—those who started treatment in early childhood. Since DFO had been standard therapy for only nine years, kids who had been treated since they were little were not yet old enough to be at risk for heart disease—the team had no choice but to look at older patients. Still, the suspicion was that DFO's efficacy would, if anything, have been underestimated in the older children. That left room for hope.

It took ten more years for the proper study to be done. In 1994, another collaboration, this time involving Boston Children's Hospital, the Hospital for Sick Children in Toronto, and the Children's Hospital of Philadelphia, reported on ninety-seven thalassemia patients who had been on twelve hour infusions of DFO for a median of twelve years. Ordinarily, cardiac failure would have occurred in 63 percent of these patients by age sixteen but, in this study, only 39 percent had cardiac disease and their average age was twenty-three.[312] Although the analysis did not have the cachet of a randomized control trial—which might have been unethical given the strong hints of DFO's efficacy—the difference from historical outcomes was striking enough to ascribe the clinical improvement to DFO. A similar study from another group was published in the same issue of the *New England Journal of Medicine*.[313]

Despite the positive results, many of the subjects in the study were still noncompliant. Presumably, they would have followed instructions more closely—and might have had even better outcomes—if the treatment had been easier to take. The hunt was on, then, for an oral chelator. One candidate was deferiprone (DFP), which had been developed by Apotex Research, a Canadian drug company. Dr. Nancy Olivieri, a lead investigator on the DFO trial, began testing it in thalassemia patients at the Hospital for Sick Children. DFP is an inefficient chelator—it takes three DFP molecules to bind an iron atom *versus* only one DFO—and its affinity for iron falls as the amount of iron in the blood falls. But it can be taken by mouth and even though it is a less effective chelator than DFO, better compliance might lead to better clinical outcomes. In fact, in one of Olivieri's early studies, she gave DFP to patients who had failed DFO and saw reductions in iron levels in their livers[314] thanks, presumably, to better compliance.

That study described only a few patients who were treated for a short period of time, so in Olivieri's next trial, she enrolled more patients and gave them a longer course of DFP. But during routine monitoring for side effects, she began to see something alarming: trial participants were developing liver damage. When she informed the hospital's clinical trial oversight committee and Apotex about DFP's toxicity, all hell broke loose. Apotex, which had sponsored the trial, accused Olivieri of running it poorly and misinterpreting the results. The company terminated the trial and tried to keep Olivieri from publishing her results by invoking the nondisclosure agreement she had signed. The University of Toronto and the Hospital for Sick Children provided little support for Olivieri.

Eventually, Olivieri did publish her findings.[315] But, because of the controversy, no one was willing to undertake a definitive trial of DFP and even now, its toxicity profile is uncertain. Other investigators have not seen the liver damage Olivieri reported[316] and at least one study suggests that its protective effects are comparable to, if not better than, DFO.[317] Unfortunately, patients on DFP tend to develop arthritis that can be severe enough for them to discontinue it.

Without clear-cut evidence for DFP's safety and efficacy, regulators in the U.S. and Canada would not approve its use. Meanwhile, another company, Novartis, developed a competing oral chelator called deferasirox (DFX), which is well absorbed and persists for a long time in the bloodstream. Nathan was involved in some of the initial studies of the drug.[318] Although no trials indicate that DFX is superior DFO and its potential for long-term toxicity is unknown,[319] its pharmacology made it a popular choice in the U.S.

The history of iron chelation in thalassemia had particular resonance for Nathan because of the long medical journey he took with one of his patients, Khaled Al-Hegelan. Nathan first saw the six-year-old in 1968 when his parents—his father was a Saudi diplomat and his mother a Syrian attorney—brought him to Children's Hospital. Khaled was the archetype of a beta thalassemia patient: a small boy with a prominent forehead, stick-like limbs, multiple healed fractures, and a large, rapidly beating heart. Nathan bonded with Khaled and his family, as did generations of hematology fellows who helped care for him over the ensuing decades. As each new chelation strategy emerged, Nathan would try it on Khaled. The effects were variable, sometimes because of the treatments themselves but more often because of Khaled's intermittent compliance, most notably when, as an adolescent and young adult, he rebelled against the strictures of a continuous infusion pump. During those episodes, his body would accumulate enough iron to cause heart failure accompanied by fluid accumulation in his lungs and shortness of breath. Khaled's symptoms could be so severe that Nathan would have to admit him to the hospital for prolonged infusions of high-dose DFO, which reduced his iron levels long enough to give his heart a chance to heal. Khaled's medical management was further complicated by HIV and hepatitis C, which he contracted from contaminated blood transfusions. For over five decades, Nathan and his team suppressed the infections and managed the iron overload. Khaled is now thriving in his fifties on deferasirox.[320]

In 1990, Nathan decided to write a book about Khaled. He wanted to use the story of a brave child and his family to frame the advances that had been made in the treatment of thalassemia. Nathan was excited by the idea, but the demands of his chairmanship left no time for writing. His friends Derek Bok, a former president of Harvard, and his wife Sissela, an eminent philosopher and daughter of Gunnar Myrdal, urged him to apply for a mini sabbatical at the Bellagio Center, the Rockefeller Foundation's property on Lake Como (Figure 14). With their sponsorship, Nathan was accepted and spent several uninterrupted weeks writing the book that came to be called *Genes, Blood, and Courage: A Boy Called Immortal Sword* in which Khaled was identified by a pseudonym. It was well-received but the accolade most meaningful to Nathan was a favorable review in the journal *Nature* by Max Perutz, the Nobel laureate who had determined the structure of hemoglobin.

Figure 14. Jean and David Nathan at the Bellagio Center. (Courtesy of David G. Nathan.)

Chapter 10

RUNNING THE PLACE

Nathan was keenly aware of the crisis unfolding at Dana-Farber in the wake of Betsy Lehman's death. Like everyone in Boston, he had read the daily articles in the *Globe* excoriating the institute and its leadership. But, unlike everyone else, Nathan knew the objects of the *Globe's* scorn—he had grown up with some of them, had worked for years with others, and had trained many of the younger ones. His experience told him that they were well-meaning, highly dedicated professionals. So, while Nathan could not help but respond viscerally to the human tragedy of the overdose, he also had sympathy for Dana-Farber's faculty and staff. He urged the members of his department of medicine at Children's to support their colleagues across the street, reminding them that "there, but for the grace of God, go we."

But that sentiment, with its implication that tragic events occur by chance or the absence of God's grace, did not apply here and Nathan knew it. His compassion for the professionals at Dana-Farber did not blind him to the systemic problems that had created an environment in which serious medical errors like the overdose could occur. Nathan could see that his own dedication to the primacy of patient well-being was not shared by leadership at Dana-Farber.

How could this have been allowed to happen at an institution founded by Sidney Farber, someone so anxious about the welfare of his patients that he could not give them combination chemotherapy?

Part of the answer was that ever since Tom Frei had stepped down as president in 1980, Dana-Farber had been led by laboratory scientists. First was Baruj Benacerraf, a brilliant, Nobel Prizewinning immunologist who, although trained as a physician, had not touched a patient since his internship. He was followed in 1990 by Christopher Walsh, another superb scientist, but one even more removed from medicine—Walsh was a PhD with no medical training whatsoever. Although a skilled and compassionate academic leader, Walsh did not have the instincts needed to run a cancer hospital. He compounded his deficiency by appointing as physician-in-chief someone with limited clinical experience and interest.

Just as people reveal their biases through their actions, institutions make decisions that reveal their preferences. Dana-Farber's leadership choices fairly screamed that it had lower regard for clinical care than scientific research. A stark indicator of the institute's priorities was the fact that the director of nursing position had been vacant for over a year when the overdose occurred. Another was the very existence of inpatient beds at Dana-Farber. Cancer patients with the potential to become deathly ill were being treated on the upper floors of a research building with no immediate access to surgery, intensive care, or emergency interventions—they had to undergo a risky transfer to the Brigham to access these services. For years, whenever Nathan thought about those beds, he told himself and anyone who would listen that they were a disaster waiting to happen.

To be fair, Dana-Farber's attitude toward clinical care in the 1980s and early 1990s was shared by other leading academic medical centers although it differed in degree. For most of the twentieth century, American medicine oscillated between being patient-focused and science-focused. The Flexner Report, published in 1911, had swept aside the chaotic and poorly regulated practice of nineteenth-century medicine through its emphasis on scientifically based medical training. While beneficial for the medical enterprise, the approach was criticized in the 1950s for its potential to dehumanize patients; medical education responded by returning its attention to clinical training and de-emphasizing science. Then the biomedical research explosion, which began in the 1970s, provided unprecedented insight into the way biological systems work. The relevance of some of these findings to medicine—particularly to cancer—were compelling even if they could not yet be translated into practical interventions. Nonetheless, the mere promise elevated scientists who were most eloquent about the potential of basic research into positions of leadership in clinical institutions—thus the presidencies of Benacerraf and Walsh. Nathan and his ilk were considered passé.

This dichotomy framed much of the newspaper coverage of the tragedy at Dana-Farber. After the overdose, a *Boston Globe* columnist wrote that, "[q]uite simply, Lehman was the victim of the vast differences in ambition and tradition between doctors and scientists, differences between the MDs and PhDs who today are about equally involved in medicine at its highest levels."[321] And, "It was not that cancer researchers at Dana-Farber did not care about Lehman and all their other patients; it was that scientific research—not patient care—was their first priority." While this may have been overly reductionist—the Farber did have full-time clinicians who cared deeply about patients—it captured the public's sense that the institute's lackadaisical attitude to clinical care had caused Betsy Lehman's death.

Dana-Farber's trustees understood that the overdose jeopardized the institute's very survival and that any rescue plan had to start with installing strong clinical leadership. Initially, they considered asking Nathan to move to Dana-Farber to help Walsh run clinical operations. But when Walsh resigned a few months later, the idea of appointing Nathan as president became an attractive alternative—it would be a way to rebalance Dana-Farber's focus.[322] But the trustees also knew that, beyond clinical leadership, they needed a president who was determined and nimble enough to deal with the multiple existential threats facing the institute. Accrediting agencies and the Massachusetts Department of Public

Health had issued highly critical reports. Loss of accreditation or disqualification for Medicare funding—which might happen if the Department of Public Health could not be satisfied—would blow up Dana-Farber's business model. The gravity of these threats was compounded by their timing. Massachusetts General Hospital and Brigham and Women's Hospital had just merged to form Partners HealthCare, creating a medical behemoth—the largest private employer in the state—which would have liked nothing more than to absorb the Farber and its oncology business, ending Sidney Farber's dream of a freestanding cancer hospital and research center. Thus, the new president faced challenges on three fronts: overseeing the response to investigations about the overdose, defending the Institution from a Partners takeover, and making fundamental structural changes to prevent another clinical catastrophe.

For all of this attention to clinical care, scientific research was still a core component of Dana-Farber's mission. The trustees knew that letting research wither while the institute focused on its clinical enterprise would also imperil Dana-Farber's existence. They needed to be sure that, along with everything else, a new president would protect research and have the support of the science faculty .

In Nathan, the trustees thought they had found the rare person whose experience had given him the tools needed to meet Dana-Farber's multiple threats. In the research domain, Nathan had spent his professional life exploiting basic science findings for the benefit of patients. But critically important in the current crisis, he had always placed the patient, not the science, front and center. He believed that there was no other morally justifiable way to deal with sick and worried people, and he had created structures at Children's to support his belief. The trustees understood that this was exactly the balance the Dana-Farber required in its leader. They made their choice and asked Dick Smith, the former chair of the board and Nathan's childhood friend, to sound him out about becoming Dana-Farber's next president.

Nathan was tempted to accept the offer even though he had two very good reasons for not doing so. First, after twenty-eight years in academic leadership, he had dealt with enough administrative headaches to last a lifetime. His stint as department chair had been particularly trying. Professionally, he was ready to return to research and teaching; personally, he was looking forward to spending more time with his family. Jean had patiently waited for this transition and, now that Nathan was sixty-five years old, she expected him to fulfill his promise to be more present with her and the grandchildren. When Nathan told her about his interest in the position, she made her displeasure clear. But she also understood the vital role that her husband could play in saving an important medical institution. She also knew about the personal connection that made Dick Smith's offer resonate with him: Nathan had grown up near Dick Smith and their parents knew each other well. Jean eventually conceded. In return, Nathan promised that his presidency would only last for five years and that he would spend every summer on Nantucket. He made this a condition of accepting the offer (Figure 15).

Figure 15. David Nathan with Dick Smith (left) and Susan Smith (center). (Courtesy of David G. Nathan.)

The second reason for Nathan's hesitancy was his inexperience in hospital operations. It was one thing to be a department chair with primary responsibility for the academic performance of the faculty and the financial performance of the practice plan. It was quite another to be in charge of the much more complex finances of a hospital with its departments of nursing, facilities, government relations, and so on. Here, Nathan was saved by his instincts. He had a keen sense for what did and did not work in patient care. He had demonstrated some of that aptitude at Children's and was confident that he could make decisions that would be in the best interest of patients at Dana-Farber. But he was also honest with himself about what he did not know and had no compunction about turning to others with more knowledge and skill. In particular, he would be helped by Dorothy Puhy, the utterly competent and dedicated chief financial officer who had been recruited by Walsh, and by Jim Conway, a Children's administrator who Nathan persuaded to move to the Farber as chief operating officer. They formed the core of a talented management team that would help Nathan realize his vision for a reborn Dana-Farber.

Before formally accepting the offer, Nathan did some diligence. He met with Benacerraf, the former DFCI president, who encouraged him to take the job. As a gesture of deep respect, he also met with Walsh, the outgoing president, who endorsed his appointment. Most importantly, Nathan met with Eugene Braunwald, the powerful chair of the department of medicine at Brigham and Women's Hospital. Nathan's vision for the adult oncology service would have two components: first, move Dana-Farber's inpatient beds to the Brigham while keeping them under Dana-Farber's license and, second, have all outpatient oncology visits happen at Dana-Farber. This would mean the end of the Brigham's competing oncology service. Both steps could only happen with Braunwald's approval and cooperation. Fortunately, he saw the promise of the model and gave Nathan his support.

Nathan also met with Gary Countryman, who had only recently been named chair of the board of trustees. Countryman enthusiastically supported Nathan's appointment and his plans to move the inpatient beds. In fact, Nathan's proposal was not a surprise to Countryman since the idea had already been broached during early negotiations with Partners HealthCare.[323] The trustees sensed, however, that Walsh was having trouble making up his mind about moving the beds. He knew that some at the institute believed that, despite their risk, the inpatient beds were an integral part of Dana-Farber's identity. Nathan provided welcome clarity on this point—to him, the risks unquestionably outweighed the benefits—and it was one of the reasons Countryman was so enthusiastic about offering him the presidency.[324]

The executive committee of the board met a few days later and, after an hour of deliberation, invited Nathan into the meeting to make its official offer. Nathan accepted and, true to his sense of social responsibility, asked that his salary be no greater than that of a Harvard Medical School professor rather than the seven figures typical of Boston hospital CEOs. Nathan then informed Children's of his decision; Fred Lovejoy was appointed interim chair of medicine and physician-in-chief. Reaction at Children's was generally positive, given that Nathan was already near the end of his term. His close academic friend, Fred Rosen, seemed bemused by the idea that Nathan had ever really intended to retire. Rosen said of Nathan that "[h]e's a man who sustains causes in a very vigorous way, and when he doesn't have one, he's at loose ends."[325] Fixing the Farber was a cause worthy of sustaining.

Walsh officially stepped down on September 13, 1995, and Nathan's appointment was announced a few days later. Dana-Farber's press release took pains to emphasize Nathan's clinical bona fides and they were dutifully picked up in news coverage. In one article, Countryman was quoted describing Nathan as "a clinician's clinician who understands the needs of patients and the business of patient care."[326] Nathan himself, while complimenting

Chris Walsh, told reporters, "I want to be sure the clinical care is absolutely tops. It's hard to do that as a chief executive officer if you haven't done clinical care yourself. It's not Chris's métier."[327] Some of harshest critics of the Farber's history of scientifically inclined leadership were enthusiastic about the appointment of a chief with clinical sensibilities.[328] In addition to welcoming the new emphasis on clinical care, there was a sense of relief that a tough leader was now in charge of a troubled institution: one reporter later called Nathan "hard-nosed."[329]

On October 17, 1995, David Nathan became the fourth president of Dana-Farber Cancer Institute. The overwhelming consensus was that he was the right person for the job. However, an irony must be acknowledged. Nathan, the man who had gladly turned over all childhood cancer to Sidney Farber thirty years earlier and then fought him tooth and nail about how best to treat it—the man who Sidney Farber promised to "break" like a matchstick—was now running the cancer center bearing Dr. Farber's name. Nathan was not the only one who assumed that Farber was spinning in his grave.

A set of daunting problems awaited Nathan as he started his new job. Heading the list was the fallout from the overdose which continued to cast a pall over the institute. Swift, decisive action would be needed to restore morale and to let the world know that Dana-Farber was still a viable, independent, and safe hospital. Politically, Nathan would have to do something right away to demonstrate his effectiveness and highlight his commitment to patient safety. He began by assembling a leadership team that reflected his patient-focused values. One key position, physician-in-chief, had been addressed by Walsh a few months earlier when he replaced David Livingston with Steve Sallan, the pediatric oncologist who had worked with Nathan on reshaping the pediatric leukemia service ten years earlier. Aware of Livingston's strengths as a scientist, Nathan asked him to chair a committee that would help oversee Dana-Farber's research activities. Wisely, Nathan gave the position no line authority.

To fill the position of chief operating officer, Nathan recruited Jim Conway from Children's. He told Conway that, in addition to overseeing clinical operations and the transfer of the inpatient beds to the Brigham, he would be in charge of patient safety, emphasizing that this must be Conway's highest priority. Nathan then enticed a tough, no-nonsense oncologist from Brigham and Women's named Larry Shulman to be chief medical officer, the person in charge of patient care. This was a deft maneuver that sent a strong message to Dana-Farber's clinical faculty. Shulman had run the Brigham's medical oncology fellowship which, for years, competed fiercely and unpleasantly with Dana-Farber's. Hiring Shulman told everyone that those days were over—the Brigham was to be Dana-Farber's partner. Finally, to shore up nursing, Nathan reorganized its structure. Walsh, rather than filling the director of nursing position, had instead designated a staff nurse named Susan Grant as "head nurse," reporting to an administrator for clinical services. This structure was completely unacceptable to Nathan, who thought that the president of a hospital must be accountable for nursing. After consulting with nursing leaders elsewhere, he elevated Grant to the position of vice president for nursing, which reported directly to the president.

With this strong operational team in place, Conway could turn his attention to the high-priority task Nathan had assigned him: to make Dana-Farber a model of patient safety. Conway and his partners—Shulman, Grant, and, later, Saul Weingart, the vice president for quality improvement and patient safety—were extraordinarily successful. They embraced the new insights that were emerging from contemporary analyses of medical errors, the most important of which is that errors occur because of system failures. Humans will always make mistakes but in high-risk settings, robust systems can lower the likelihood that errors will occur and mitigate their consequences when they do. Airline pilots are not perfect—they make mistakes—but with preflight and inflight checklists and with copilots and other team members empowered to question the pilot, airline accidents have been on a steady decline.

Conway hammered home the idea that everyone at Dana-Farber shares responsibility for preventing medical errors. It was the foundation of his effort to create a culture of patient safety that had not existed before. He and his team reinforced that culture by implementing new systems including rules mandating closer supervision of fellows, policies requiring nurses to be trained on new treatment protocols, and interdisciplinary teams to review new protocols and report toxicities.[330] A board-level quality committee was reorganized to enhance oversight of patient safety; its existence sent a message about how highly the institute prioritizes safety.

Conway and his team promulgated the principle that safety is part of everyone's daily work rather than a special project that draws attention today but perhaps not so much next year. Instead of creating a separate office to oversee patient safety, they made it an explicit responsibility of leadership at all levels; safety issues were reported to the board committee rather than to a staff-level committee. The team created systems for detecting errors and introduced the routine use of root cause analyses of errors and near misses. They developed an electronic chemotherapy order entry system that required a substantial initial investment of almost $2 million, which the institute readily made. Finally, to emphasize the importance of transparency in restoring patient confidence, the institute created patient and family advisory councils that formally contributed to decision-making.

These changes were as much cultural as they were operational. Their rapid acceptance by Dana-Farber's rank and file reflected the demoralized staff's hunger for practical steps that would restore confidence. The turnaround was impressive. Within a year, the hospital accreditation agency that had placed Dana-Farber on probation—a humiliating reprimand for a major teaching hospital—re-examined the institute and changed its assessment to "accreditation with commendation," its highest score.[331] Success built on success, and within ten years of Betsy Lehman's death and the *Boston Globe*'s flaying of Dana-Farber, the newspaper could describe the institute as "one of the most safety-conscious hospitals in America, with computers that trigger alarms at potential over-doses, a hypervigilant error-reporting system, and a top executive who pushes measures in pursuit of the old physician's promise to 'first do no harm.'"[332]

Even as the safety work was advancing, other problems stem-ming from the tragedy competed for Nathan's attention. Two weeks after he became president, the institute released a six-page summary of the findings of the internal and external investigations into the overdoses. The original reports ran to sixty-five pages. The summary's brevity plus the fact that the full reports were kept confidential led to concerns in some quarters that the institute was hiding something. This suspicion was stoked by a *Globe* reporter named Richard Knox who was informed of the contents of the original reports by a "confidential source" and wrote an article about what he had learned.[333] Among other things, according to Knox, the confidential report said that the clinical performance of James Foran, the fellow who had written the incorrect chemo-therapy order, had been deteriorating prior to his error, but insti-tute leadership had taken no action. In addition, while the sum-mary released by Dana-Farber acknowledged that the physician in charge of the protocol had neglected to check the medication orders in Lehman's medical record after her death—which was one reason the overdose had not been discovered for two months—it did not name that person. Knox did: she was Lois Ayash. Further, the confidential report stated that Ayash had been reprimanded for her oversight and held responsible for ambiguities in the proto-col plan that contributed to Foran's incorrect order. Again, Ayash was unnamed in the public summary, but Knox identified her. He also reported that both Ayash and Foran were being investigated by the Board of Registration in Medicine, information that was supposed to be confidential. These multiple breaches of confidentiality contributed to Ayash's decision to take legal action taken (described below).

The public summary went on to say that the investigative committees had not thought it sufficient simply to assign responsibility for the overdose to the physicians involved in the trial. A root cause of the tragedy, it said, was the paucity of patient care expertise among Dana-Farber's leaders. The committees had identified "an apparent lack of emphasis upon formal quality assurance procedures" and recommended strengthening clinical leadership at the institute. While the release of the summary and its coverage by the media shined an unflattering light on Dana-Farber, its effect on the public was mitigated by a description released at the same time of thirty-nine steps the institute had taken to correct clinical deficiencies, including better oversight of fellows in training. Dana-Farber also pointed to the fact that, since the overdose, it had replaced all of its top managers, several of its middle managers, its president, its physician-in-chief, and its pharmacy chief, and had named a vice president of nursing who reported directly to the president.

Despite the reports' emphasis on systems failures that had contributed to the overdoses, the state's professional licensing boards were indeed investigating individuals who may have been at fault. The pharmacy board reprimanded three Dana-Farber pharmacists for relying solely on the protocol schema and the doctor's orders when they prepared the chemotherapy rather than using their professional judgment to anticipate the effects of such high doses of Cytoxan. This is an odd rebuke considering that the protocol was designed to administer unusually high doses of Cytoxan and that the practice at Dana-Farber had been for pharmacists to follow the protocol schema and the physician's orders. These mitigating factors may explain why the pharmacy board issued a reprimand rather than suspending or revoking the pharmacists' licenses. Still, the board made its point that pharmacists have a duty to the patient that is not superseded by their employers' faulty policies or practices.[334]

For its part, the Board of Registration in Medicine determined that Foran had "negligently practiced medicine...committed misconduct...and was guilty of malpractice."[335] The Board suspended his license for three years retroactive to October 31, 1995, a relatively mild rebuke given that the suspension had expired by the time it was imposed in November 1998. The board decided against a more severe sanction because Foran had had no prior experience with high-dose chemotherapy when he committed his errors and had given the correct dose to two other patients. The practical impact on Foran was minimal since he had left for a fellowship at St. Bartholomew's Hospital in London shortly after the overdoses were discovered. The board also investigated Ayash and issued her a warning letter that, technically, was not a disciplinary action.[336]

The responsibility nurses might have borne for the overdoses was a more complex and controversial issue. On one hand, there was general agreement that Dana-Farber's systems for detecting, reporting, and reducing medical errors had been grossly inadequate. And the idea of critiquing systems rather than blaming individuals was becoming instrumental in guiding institutions toward developing an infrastructure that protects patients. In the case of the nurses, for example, Dana-Farber had no policy at the time of the overdoses requiring them to doublecheck a physician's chemotherapy orders against the treatment scheme in the protocol. Had such a policy been in place, and had the nurses complied with it, the mistaken order would have been caught and canceled. There was a sense within the institute that the nurses should not be blamed because they failed to do something that was not required of them at the time.

On the other hand, nurses are licensed health care professionals who have a fiduciary responsibility to their patients. Some might argue that this duty extends to taking actions that, although not explicitly required by policy, are nonetheless in their patients' best interests. To suggest otherwise might indicate a patronizing view of nurses that accords them a lower standard of professional responsibility than other members of the clinical team.

This, at any rate, is what the Board of Registration in Nursing thought. In 1999, nearly five years after the overdoses, the board took action against eighteen Dana-Farber nurses.[337] Specifically, it cited two nurses for "signing off" on the order and sixteen for either continuing to administer the incorrect dose or not verifying the dose during their care of the patients. Two of the nurses accepted the board's reprimand and agreed to two years of probation and retraining. The other sixteen disagreed with the reprimand, causing the board to initiate disciplinary hearings against them. Both Nathan and his new vice president for nursing called the board's action "inappropriate and unwarranted" and noted that neither the institute's internal investigators, the outside accreditors, nor the Department of Public Health had found fault with the nurses. This was a spirited defense but not strictly true: the Department of Public Health had cited problems in the nursing program at Dana-Farber and explicitly referred the case to the Board of Nursing to determine if any individual nurses had engaged in misconduct.[338]

In the end, the board dropped its charges against two nurses and reprimanded sixteen.[339] It insisted that the latter be held individually accountable for not checking the chemotherapy doses even in the absence of a hospital policy requiring them to do so. Nathan again railed against the board. He was not alone. Lucian Leape, a prominent architect of patient safety systems, wrote an opinion piece in the *Boston Globe* stating that the board's actions were "misguided, inappropriate, and harmful."[340]

Throughout Nathan's career in academic leadership, he had shown profound respect for nurses. His loyalty to Dana-Farber's nurses in the face of the board's disciplinary actions, and the pugnacious way he expressed it, was a huge morale booster for everyone at the institute, not just the nurses. Nathan's approach also helped keep Dana-Farber's focus on developing systems that would improve patient safety and creating a culture of shared account-ability rather than blame. While his attitude elided the question of personal responsibility for the nurses, a question that had guided the decisions of the state boards of registration in medicine and pharmacy, it helped rally the institute in a time of crisis.

LOIS J. AYASH V. DANA-FARBER CANCER INSTITUTE AND OTHERS

As Nathan's presidency continued, the multitude of issues arising from the overdoses were being resolved. Dana-Farber expeditiously settled the malpractice claims made by the families of Lehman and Bateman, the patient who had survived her overdose.[341, 342, 343, 344] Professional boards took their actions against the doctors, pharmacists, and nurses. Conway and his team reengineered the institute's safety infrastructure. But one complication continued to fester and would not be resolved until 2005, long after Nathan had stepped down.

It started with Dana-Farber's internal investigation. The investigative panel was charged with identifying the physi-cians who had been involved in the tragedy and assessing their culpability. The panel quickly decided that Foran, the fellow in training who wrote the incorrect orders, bore substantial responsibility. Livingston, Dana-Farber's physi-cian-in-chief, had met one-on-one with Foran soon after the overdoses were discovered and had come to the same conclusion. Livingston referred Foran's case to an inter-nal disciplinary committee, which suspended his clinical privileges.

The panel also assigned some responsibility to Lois Ayash, the author of the high-dose chemotherapy pro-tocol and the physician in charge of its implementation.

The panel thought Ayash was culpable in two ways. First, she had written the dosing section of the protocol in an ambiguous manner which had contributed to the fatal misinterpretation by Foran, the pharmacists, and the nurses. Second, she had failed to review the medication orders in the medical records of Lehman and Bateman after their toxic events, thereby missing an opportunity to discover that they had been overdosed. Panel members were particularly critical of her for not checking the orders even after she had seen data indicating that the blood levels of Cytoxan in these two patients were three times what they had been in their previous treatment cycles or in other patients on the protocol.

For her role in the overdoses, Ayash was referred to the internal disciplinary committee and her clinical privileges were also suspended. While the committee criticized her for not checking the physician orders, it conceded that this had not been standard practice. The committee also found no evidence that Ayash had engaged in a cover-up of the facts or any willful misconduct and recommended that she be given a written reprimand.[345] However, ultimate authority for issuing corrective actions at Dana-Farber was invested in the hospital's Clinical Executive Committee, which reviewed the disciplinary committee's recommendation and decided to downgrade Ayash's punishment to a less serious oral reprimand. Livingston and Ayash were then invited to respond to the Clinical Executive Committee's decision. Livingston wrote a letter indicating his belief that Ayash bore significant responsibility—he suggested that Lehman's life might have been saved had Ayash discovered the overdose by reviewing the orders in a timely fashion— and urged the disciplinary panel to give her a written reprimand. His suggestion was not acted upon. Whether or not an early intervention could have saved Lehman remains a controversial and unanswerable question.

Unlike Livingston, Ayash did not respond to the executive committee's invitation to comment. Rather she wrote directly to Walsh, who was still president, arguing against the finding that she had any direct responsibility for the overdoses and maintaining that an earlier discovery of the incorrect order would not have changed the fatal outcome for Lehman.[346] In August of 1995, Dana-Farber's board of trustees unanimously recommended an oral reprimand for Ayash and her clinical privileges were restored.

Dana-Farber was obligated by law to report its earlier suspension of Ayash's clinical privileges to the Board of Registration in Medicine. The board, after conducting its own investigation, issued a warning letter to Ayash that focused on her failure to check the orders in the medical record. The referral of Ayash's case to the Board of Registration, its investigation, and its final determination were all required to be confidential.

The actions of the Board of Registration in Medicine, as well as those of Dana-Farber, were acceptable to all parties—Ayash thought Dana-Farber's oral reprimand was "incredibly fair"[347]—and this is where things might have quietly settled. But it was not to be.

When Dana-Farber first disclosed the overdoses in March 1995, the *Boston Globe* reporter Richard Knox broke the news in a front-page article stating that Ayash—the only physician he identified by name—had countersigned the fatal chemotherapy order.[348] Seeing her name in the newspaper was upsetting enough but Ayash was more disturbed by the assertion that she had signed off on the order. She had not. Although Knox was informed of his error within four days of the article's publication,[349] the *Globe* waited two and a half months before it published a correction and did so in a small box labeled "For the record" on page 2.[350] Dana-Farber also made no effort to correct the mistake.

Knox then wrote a series of articles in which he revealed highly confidential information about the activities of Dana-Farber's inquiry and disciplinary panels, attributing his information to unnamed sources. In one piece, he reported that two Dana-Farber physicians were the subjects of disciplinary proceedings.[351] Although Knox did not identify Ayash, he had mentioned her name in his first, front-page article and she worried that readers would assume that she was one of the doctors he was writing about. In fact, she was but, surprisingly, no one at Dana-Farber had told her that she had been referred to the disciplinary panel until the *Globe* article appeared—Livingston had not spoken to her as he had to Foran. Ayash said she had been "blindsided" by Knox and the *Globe*.[352] She felt ambushed again a month later by another front page article in which Knox did identify her and Foran as the only physicians to be "singled out in an internal disciplinary process."[353] She had been assured in writing by the disciplinary panel that its deliberations would be secret.[354]

Knox began another line of attack in an article describing an interview he had conducted with Livingston. Knox had pointed out to the physician-in-chief that, after Lehman's and Bateman's overdoses, two other patients on the research protocol had received the proper doses of chemotherapy.[355] He asked whether someone on the team might have "quietly corrected" the errors in Lehman's and Bateman's records before the next two patients were treated. In other words, Knox was asking whether the mistake might have been covered up. In reply, Livingston said that Knox's question was "smack in the bull's eye of the investigation....It's right in the target range." Ayash took this to mean that Livingston was accusing her of covering up the error. She was appalled.

Finally, Knox wrote an article about the results of Dana-Farber's investigations into the overdoses in which he identified Ayash as the physician who had been in charge of the protocol and who had neglected to examine the medical record to determine if Lehman and Bateman had been overdosed.[356] He also reported that she had been "formally reprimanded by a Dana-Farber disciplinary panel" and was "under investigation by the Massachusetts Board of Registration in Medicine." Again, all of this information was supposed to be confidential.

On February 1, 1996, Ayash sued Dana-Farber, David Livingston, the *Boston Globe*, and Richard Knox.[357] She accused Dana-Farber and Livingston of scapegoating her. She alleged that the institute and its physician-in-chief had issued press releases containing "peer review" material—primarily the deliberations of the disciplinary panel—which is considered confidential under state law. She also alleged that they leaked other confidential information to Knox. As for the *Globe* and Knox, Ayash accused them of invading her privacy, of publishing inaccurate articles describing a cover-up, and of "erroneously attributing culpability to [her] thereby destroying her reputation and well-being."[358]

The day after Ayash filed her lawsuit, she met with Stephen Sallan—who had replaced Livingston as physician-in-chief—and another senior medical leader. They informed her that she would not be allowed to resume her research on high-dose chemotherapy because members of the clinical team thought she was too difficult to work with and that her return would be awkward. Sallan suggested that Ayash try to finish her scientific manuscripts from home. A few months later, she was called to another meeting in which she was informed that the institute would be eliminating ten percent of its clinical positions due to its tenuous finances. Unfortunately, hers was on the list and her employment would end in ten months. She was urged to find another job.

Ayash added a claim of employer retaliation to her lawsuit.

Then things got complicated. Ayash's legal strategy hinged on showing that Dana-Farber and Livingston had harmed her by leaking confidential information to the press. Ayash and her lawyer insisted that the only way they could prove this would be for the *Globe* and Knox to reveal their sources so that they—the sources—could be compelled to testify about leaking material to Knox.

Knox and the *Globe* adamantly refused to identify their sources, arguing that doing so would undermine freedom of the press. However, the Superior Court judge hearing the case sided with Ayash and ordered the *Globe* and Knox to divulge their sources.[359] When they refused again, Ayash's lawyer asked that Knox be held in contempt and jailed until he complied. The judge demurred saying, "It's a waste of a good jail cell."[360] Instead he imposed fines: Knox would pay one hundred dollars per day until he named his sources and the fine would increase by one hundred dollars for every week he remained silent. The *Globe* would have the same fine schedule but starting at $1,000 per day with $1,000 added for every week of recalcitrance.[361] An appeals court judge agreed to delay the fines while Knox and the *Globe* appealed.

After reviewing the case, the appeals court set aside the lower court's order for the *Globe* and Knox to reveal their sources, saying that it presented a "danger to the free flow of information."[362] But the court also acknowledged the merits of Ayash's contention that she needed this information to make her case. So, rather than settling the question, the appeals court sent the case back to the same lower court judge who had first heard it, instructing him to perform a balancing test to weigh the public's "right to know"—defined here as reporting something newsworthy based on a guarantee of confidentiality—against Ayash's right to obtain evidence that would help her lawsuit. Not surprisingly, given his original ruling, the lower court judge reinstated the order for the *Globe* and Knox to reveal their sources writing that "Ayash's need for this information is tangible and substantial and outweighs 'the public's interest in protecting the free flow of information'...Ayash's claims against the DFCI and Knox are absolutely dependent on confirmation that the source(s) was an agent or employee of DFCI."[363]

Faced with the *Globe*'s and Knox's continued intransigence, the judge made an unusual ruling.[364] Ayash had brought three counts against the paper and its reporter: libeling her for overstating her role in the overdose, infliction of emotional distress, and interfering with her business relationship with her Dana-Farber employers. But rather than hearing their defense, the judge summarily found the *Globe* and Knox liable on all three counts. He intended his judgment to be a sanction against the paper and Knox for not revealing their sources thereby hindering Ayash's ability to prove her case. As a result, during the trial, the *Globe* and Knox would not be allowed to defend themselves against Ayash's allegations; they could only argue the damages. This ruling had actually been suggested by Ayash's attorney several months earlier.[365]

With the liability of the *Globe* and Knox established, Ayash's case against Dana-Farber and Livingston could proceed. The trial was brutal. On the stand, Livingston said that Foran's error was due to his "abject stupidity" and another senior hospital official called Foran one of the worst fellows at the institute.[366] In response to questions about why Ayash's contract had not been renewed, witnesses described her as stubborn and as a doctor who showed a lack of compassion for her patients.[367] Ayash's own testimony was remarkable for its tone deafness: she claimed that her research protocols—including the one on which Lehman died and Bateman was rendered an invalid—were suspended because of "hospital politics." She cited the same reason for the Board of Registration's sanction letter, claiming that its chastisement for not checking whether Lehman and Bateman had been overdosed was "way out-[side] of the jurisdiction of the licensing board." It was not. And she revealed a touch of paranoia by suggesting that the wording in the Board of Registration's letter was too close to that of Livingston's, implying collusion between Dana-Farber and the board.[368] Then, there was Ayash's reluctance to take any responsibility for the overdoses. Referring to the malpractice settlement, she said , "I don't believe I deserve blame in this case but I am willing to accept it."[369] A crisis counsellor hired by Dana-Farber in the wake of Lehman's death said that Ayash had told her she "didn't understand what all the fuss was about" since Lehman had advanced breast cancer—implying that she was going to die anyway.[370]

After twenty days of testimony involving thirty witnesses and 163 documents, the case went to the jury.[371] In her closing argument, Ayash's lawyer suggested that, when the overdoses were disclosed, Dana-Farber and Livingston were plunged into a public relations nightmare and decided that the only way out was to feed a victim to the press.

They chose Ayash because she was a woman without a powerbase in a "male-dominated bastion."[372] After two and a half days, the jury found that Dana-Farber had violated Ayash's right to privacy by disclosing confidential details of its investigation, that it had violated her contract, and that it had retaliated against her. The jury rejected her claim of gender discrimination. She was awarded $2.1 million from Dana-Farber and Livingston for lost wages ($600,000) and emotional distress ($1.5 million). She was awarded an additional $2.1 million from the *Globe* and Knox for the claims already upheld by the judge before the trial. The jurors apportioned $840,000 of the overall award to Livingston and $420,000 to Knox.[373]

Dana-Farber and *Globe* appealed. In 2005, the state supreme judicial court upheld the $2.1 million award against the *Globe* and Knox. However, it overturned two of the findings against Dana-Farber: it said that the hospital had not violated Ayash's privacy by releasing confidential material and that Livingston had not unfairly terminated Ayash's position. However, the court did uphold the finding that Dana-Farber and Livingston had retaliated against her for filing her lawsuit. The court vacated the $2.1 million verdict and ordered a new trial to determine damages related to the retaliation finding.[374] Dana-Farber chose to settle for an undisclosed amount. The *Globe*, still upset because it never had an opportunity to defend itself against the libel claim, appealed to the U.S. Supreme Court, which, despite the interesting freedom-of-the-press question, refused to hear the case.

Knox never did reveal his sources—to this day, the faculty and staff at Dana-Farber refer to his source or sources as "Deep Throat"—and their identity remains one of the institute's enduring mysteries.[375, 376]

Critically important issues besides the overdose and its aftermath were clamoring for Nathan's attention. Most immediate was the transfer of Dana-Farber's inpatient beds to the Brigham. The salutary effects on patient safety were so obvious to Nathan that he expected all of the interested parties to be aligned. This was not the case. Political, financial, and regulatory considerations turned the move into a multidimensional problem.

Political challenges arose from the behavior of individuals who believed they had a stake in the location of Dana-Farber's inpatient beds. Internally, for example, some Dana-Farber trustees believed that the beds were integral to the institute's mission and that moving them to another hospital heralded the beginning of the end of an independent Dana-Farber Cancer Institute. However, Nathan had the support of the board chair, Gary Countryman. He and other like-minded trustees played an essential role in wrangling consensus from the board.

Countryman also helped Nathan by streamlining the way the board made decisions. Like other nonprofits, Dana-Farber had assembled its board with a few goals in mind. One was governance but another was philanthropy. Over the years, the institute had tilted too far toward the latter, ending up with an eighty-five-member board that struggled with an awkward governance structure. Nathan convinced Countryman to assemble a small group of senior trustees who could make rapid decisions and authorize the CEO to act as needed. They were Countryman, Dick Smith, Richard Morse (another childhood friend of Nathan's), and Richard Lubin, an investor who was chair of the finance committee. Nathan called them the Four Horsemen. They helped smooth the way for Nathan's interactions with the executive committee of the board whenever he needed approval for controversial or expensive plans.

Another internal political constituency was the clinical faculty. Their professional identities had been rooted in being Dana-Farber doctors who took care of Dana-Farber patients in Dana-Farber beds. Despite the overdose, the physicians believed that the care they delivered was special and uniquely beneficial to cancer patients. They worried that moving the beds to the Brigham would undercut their autonomy and render them helpless bystanders as they watched the quality of cancer care decline toward mediocrity. The fact that no such thing had happened to inpatient pediatric cancer care at Children's Hospital made no difference.

Nathan took a two-pronged approach to the parochial attitude of the medical oncologists. First, he assured them that the only acceptable outcome of his negotiations with the Brigham would be a model in which Dana-Farber oncologists controlled the care given to Dana-Farber patients. He convinced the physicians, as well as the trustees, that this would be an absolute condition for moving the beds.

Second, he changed the leadership of the department of medical oncology, the academic home of the physicians. When the Sidney Farber Cancer Center was getting started, its new president, Tom Frei, recruited George Canellos, a lymphoma expert he knew from the National Cancer Institute, to be chair of medical oncology. Canellos arrived in 1975 and was still in his position when Nathan became president in 1995. Although Canellos had somehow emerged unscathed from the overdose and was not opposed to moving the beds, Nathan thought that a new chair could help engender enthusiasm for the move. So, while the negotiations with the Brigham were getting underway, he began an international search for a new chair.

A much trickier entity, with its own political interests, was Partners HealthCare, the newly created corporate parent of Brigham and Women's and Massachusetts General Hospitals. Prior to the existence of Partners, Nathan would have negotiated solely with the Brigham about the beds. Now, he had to include Partners, which meant that Mass General would be indirectly involved. Mass General's presence would make the negotiations considerably more difficult because the hospital competed head-to-head with

Dana-Farber for oncology patients and would hardly view a strong Dana-Farber/Brigham oncology alliance as a positive development.

The idea of moving Dana-Farber's inpatient service to the Brigham had actually been floated soon after Partners was formed—Partners' vision was to absorb Dana-Farber rather than compete with it. The principles had even retained The Boston Consulting Group to evaluate the concept. Meetings had been suspended while Dana-Farber dealt with the overdose but they restarted once Nathan was on board. The parties were making progress although it was not smooth sailing. In advance of one critically important meeting with the consultants, Nathan was called to a small preparatory session with Samuel O. Thier, president of Partners; Jack Connors, chair of Partners' board; and Gary Countryman. Although Partners was touted as a "merger of equals," Mass General was dominant—it was larger than the Brigham and had much more money. The Brigham still suffered from its legacy as a threadbare academic hospital with lousy amenities. Thier was also presumed to be biased toward Mass General, having moved to Partners from his previous position as president of the hospital.

Mass General is known for catering to its surgeons. They do an impressive number of operations—about twenty thousand per year—which makes money for the hospital. That gives them a very powerful voice. Mass General has always considered the Brigham to be its main competitor for surgical cases and the structure of the Partners merger did nothing to change that since the surgery departments retained their separate bottom lines. Cancer surgery makes up a significant proportion of surgical volume and these patients are often referred to surgeons by oncologists. Thus, a strong alliance between Dana-Farber, with its large patient population, and the Brigham, with its own surgical practice, was perceived by Mass General as a threat.

Samuel Thier had been sensitized to this issue by Mass General's surgeons. So, at the meeting with Nathan, Connors, and Countryman, he demanded a guarantee that, if Dana-Farber moved its beds to the Brigham, all surgical referrals from Dana-Farber's outpatient clinics would go in precisely equal measure to Mass General and the Brigham. Nathan told Thier that such an arrangement would be impossible. Oncologists refer patients to surgeons they know and trust and will not stand for being forced to make referrals they do not want to make. Furthermore, Thier's demand ran counter to the new model of multidisciplinary clinics that Nathan was setting up at the Farber. He wanted patients to be seen by medical oncologists, radiation oncologists, and surgeons all in a single visit. That would make life much easier for the patients and would likely produce better outcomes. Forcing oncologists to send half of their patients across town to Mass General would undercut the model.

But Nathan was a canny negotiator. He knew that getting his way on surgical referrals would require giving something to Mass General in return, so he focused on their medical oncology service. For years, the hospital had neglected medical oncology—it had a small clinical group that provided the kind of care typically found in a community practice. They did very few bone marrow transplants and their fellowship training program was tiny and unpopular. Nathan offered to create a joint oncology fellowship for Dana-Farber, the Brigham, and Mass General. Because Dana-Farber's fellowship was the most competitive in the country, Nathan's proposal would give Mass General instant credibility for oncology training and provide it with a pipeline of first-rate oncologists for its faculty.

Thier was outraged. His surgery proposal had been about real money while Nathan's counterproposal was about academics and research—both major money losers—plus a vague promise of future faculty enhancement. Thier, whose temper was legendary, raised his voice, pounded the table, and stormed out of the room. The other three sat in silence until Connors, board chair at Partners, turned to Countryman and said, "Well, Gary, your guy is a lot nicer than my guy."[377] In the full meeting with the consultants that followed,

Nathan refused to give in to the surgical referral demand and, instead, got an agreement to create Dana-Farber/Partners Cancer Care which, among other things, oversaw a combined fellowship. Within ten years, the fellowship program helped put Mass General oncology on the map.

After that, negotiations on the beds moved quickly. Dana-Farber would have thirty oncology beds under its own license at Brigham and Women's. Physicians and nurses caring for patients in those beds would come from and be overseen by Dana-Farber. Housekeeping and dietary services would be provided by the Brigham. The Massachusetts Department of Public Health approved the proposal and Medicare said that it fell within one of its provisions known as a "hospital-within-a-hospital." That was a critically important determination because it meant that Dana-Farber's inpatient activities would continue to qualify for Medicare reimbursement. One of the arguments against moving the beds had been the possibility that Dana-Farber would lose the revenue associated with inpatient care. Medicare's ruling helped allay that fear as did a complex agreement on sharing other patient care-related revenues. Dorothy Puhy, Dana-Farber's CFO, played a central role in negotiating an agreement that helped keep Dana-Farber financially healthy.

On the outpatient side, the Brigham merged its small oncology service with Dana-Farber's to form a single service that would see patients in renovated space at the Farber. The structure and management of the clinic would be dictated by the new chair of the department of medical oncology. Both Nathan and Eugene Braunwald, chair of department of medicine at the Brigham, had their eye on Jim Griffin, a young hematologist at Dana-Farber, but Griffin said he was not yet ready to take on such a huge administrative task.

This meant that Nathan would have to perform a formal search for a chair, something he was not keen to do. He was worried that top talent outside of Dana-Farber might not be attracted to the institute at this moment in its history. The overdose had been in the news for over a year, generating the kind of publicity that could make someone hesitate. Smart candidates might want to see a few years of stability before committing to a leadership job at the Farber. Nathan also knew that even before the overdose, Dana-Farber's clinical program had a reputational problem. When Tom Frei was forced to step down as president 1980, he still wanted a leadership role in clinical research. So, a department of medicine was created for him. This gave Dana-Farber both a department of medical oncology and a department of medicine, a confusing enough structure for faculty within the institute, but one that seemed pointlessly muddled to those outside.

Even worse, it was dangerous. Faculty in the department of medicine were instructed to pursue Frei's interest in high-dose chemotherapy—they wrote and ran the clinical trial involved in the overdoses. And although they were medical oncologists, they had shockingly little integration with the department of medical oncology, which nominally oversaw clinical care. It is difficult to know if this isolating structure might have fostered a culture that could generate an ambiguously worded protocol and consider it acceptable not to search for an error in medication orders after the overdoses. At the very least, it could not have helped.

So, Nathan got rid of the department of medicine and announced that he was recruiting the leader of a single, unified department of medical oncology. Although his move made the job more rational, it did not make the search any easier. Nathan spent nearly a year screening and interviewing applicants only to be disappointed with all of them. In desperation, he turned to an internal candidate, Lee Nadler. This was a controversial choice. Nadler was an accomplished scientist and active clinician who had been at the Farber since his fellowship in the 1970s. However, many faculty and staff thought he had an abrasive personality, and Braunwald was opposed to his appointment. But, by promising to take full responsibility for whatever problems Nadler might cause, Nathan convinced Braunwald to set aside his objections.

Nadler became chair of the department of medical oncology and established the multidisciplinary subspecialty specialty clinics that Nathan was so eager to see. To run them, he appointed outstanding leaders who either already had or were developing international reputations in their fields. He also recruited a cadre of first-rate cancer scientists who helped re-establish the department's research reputation. Nadler was an effective chair but he was still difficult to deal with. When Nathan stepped down from the presidency, he made sure that Nadler left his position, too, so that the next president could appoint his or her own choice.

Nathan had settled the medical oncology leadership question just in time. Soon after appointing Nadler, Nathan discovered that he would need his help, along with that of a small army of other institute leaders, to deal with a curveball thrown by the National Cancer Institute. Dana-Farber had been one of the fifteen original Comprehensive Cancer Centers created by Nixon's National Cancer Act in 1971. The NCI funded these regional centers of clinical and research excellence through grants that had to be renewed every five years. Renewals were huge efforts requiring hundreds of pages of documentation that the center was meeting the mission of a Comprehensive Cancer Center as defined by NCI. The renewal application culminated in a high-stakes site visit by a team of outside experts. Dana-Farber had successfully renewed its Cancer Center grant every time it had been evaluated.

The president of Dana-Farber is the leader of its Comprehensive Cancer Center grant and Nathan was just gearing up for the next renewal application when he got a call from Richard Klausner, the director of the NCI. Apparently, the Massachusetts General Hospital had decided that it, too, wanted to be a Comprehensive Cancer Center. Harvard Medical School and the Harvard School of Public Health had also inquired about becoming an NCI-designated basic science cancer center. Klausner's patience was wearing thin.

Comprehensive Cancer Centers were meant to be regional vehicles for promoting cancer care and research. The notion that Boston would house multiple centers was anathema. Nathan sympathized with Klausner and felt embarrassed—it was silly for Harvard institutions to compete with each other for Cancer Center designations.

Klausner flew up from Washington to meet with leaders from the Harvard hospitals, the medical school, and the school of public health. He told the group, which was assembled in Nathan's office, that the NCI would accept only one Comprehensive Cancer Center application from Harvard in the upcoming renewal cycle and that the various supplicants would have to consolidate themselves into a single cancer center. Thus was born the Dana-Farber/Harvard Cancer Center or DF/HCC.

Although Klausner had preached a simple message, creating DF/HCC would be anything but. Seven institutions were involved: five hospitals (Dana-Farber, the Brigham, Children's, Beth Israel Deaconess, and Mass General) and two schools (Harvard Medical School and Harvard School of Public Health). Some of the entities—particularly the Brigham and Mass General—had been actively competing for decades; others had little or no experience working together. Nathan understood that consolidation would require strong central planning so he tapped David Livingston to ride herd on the consortium. Livingston developed several close partnerships, especially with scientists at the medical school, as he oversaw the compilation of a single grant application that could convince reviewers that former sworn enemies were working together in perfect harmony. Livingston and his team succeeded. The renewal application was approved and Dana-Farber's Comprehensive Cancer Center grant now supported DF/HCC.

Of course, not all rivalries can be suppressed by fiat. One of the most contentious arguments around DF/HCC—and one that continued to threaten its very existence for years—was its name. Leadership at Mass General was livid that it still included the words "Dana-Farber." Why couldn't it just be called the Harvard

Cancer Center? In fact, Nathan had worked to keep "Dana-Farber" in the cancer center's name. He knew that everyone at the institute, including the trustees, was worried that Dana-Farber was losing its independence. It was still reeling from the overdoses and the sanctions imposed by accrediting agencies and its beds had just been transferred to the Brigham. There was a feeling that the universe was systematically chipping away at Dana-Farber's identity.

Nathan was afraid that removing Dana-Farber's name from the new Comprehensive Cancer Center would decimate morale. He convinced the dean of Harvard Medical School, Joseph Martin, that a name change would be too high a price to demand for Dana-Farber's participation. The institute had been the recipient of the original center grant in 1971 and had kept it going for twenty-five years. Even the NCI recognized the institute's position as first among equals—it had already designated the new cancer center as the Dana-Farber Comprehensive Cancer Center and it awarded the grant to Dana-Farber, which then disbursed funds to the member institutions. NCI's position was an acknowledgment that the cancer program at Dana-Farber was more comprehensive and larger than the programs at the other entities. So, the consortium continues to be called the Dana-Farber/Harvard Cancer Center and Mass General continues to be unhappy.

Nathan, though, was proud of what the consolidation had accomplished. Through DF/HCC, the five hospitals share all cancer-related clinical trials—the consortium is now a clinical research powerhouse running hundreds of trials that enroll thousands of patients every year. On the laboratory research side, the enforced camaraderie nurtured a slew of highly productive scientific collaborations that might not have otherwise happened.

Nathan next turned his attention to beefing up Dana-Farber's research faculty. Recruiting outstanding scientific talent would be another way to restore luster to the institute's reputation and boost morale, but Nathan was also responding to a financial imperative. The institute had just opened a new research building named for

Dick and Susan Smith, the largest donors to the construction fund. Nathan understood that the only way to recover operating costs for this kind of building would be through the research activities it housed; research grants and contracts provide funds for those costs. Like all newly opened buildings, the Smith Building was underpopulated. Nathan knew that he would have to recruit new faculty as quickly as possible to get the dollars flowing.

This was the kind of project that Nathan loved. He had been enamored of smart, aggressive scientists since doing his sabbaticals at MIT. The brilliance of the faculty who surrounded him there had left an indelible mark. He was also uniquely tolerant of the challenging personality traits that occasionally accompany such talent. He said that his forbearance was something he had learned from his mother who had taught him "to see the best in people," even narcissistic scientists. Nathan would apply a rubric for evaluating faculty that he called the "pain-in-the-ass to genius" ratio, occasionally using more colorful terms. He could abide someone with a fairly high ratio as long as that person was doing good science and not completely disruptive. But even Nathan had limits. He once described the way his response to a truly impossible faculty member might evolve:

> I sometimes compare it to our dog, Topsy. My father loved Topsy, buy Topsy kept biting people. He bit the mailman. He bit a woman who came to see my mother, and my father's excuse was he didn't like her hat. My father just tolerated Topsy. Finally Topsy bit somebody important and he had to be sent to a farm. My father called almost every day about Topsy and one day, one of the farmers said, "We had to put him down." Some faculty are like that.[378]

Only rarely was Nathan vexed enough to put down a faculty member.

What he was really excited about was the chase: the process of luring a brilliant new talent and giving that person resources and room to shine. Nathan put together an external advisory board chaired by Phil Sharp, a Nobel laureate from MIT, to advise him on identifying the most promising targets—the scientists who might be enticed to come to Dana-Farber. The committee helped Nathan and the department chairs go on a recruiting binge that brought a number of exciting new faculty to the institute.

Nathan's most successful recruitment by far, and one he roped in without the help of Sharp's committee, was Stan Korsmeyer. Korsmeyer was a brilliant scientist who had made a name for himself by identifying genetically determined pathways that control cell death. He found that some cancers occur when mutations in these pathways subvert the process of normally scheduled cell death, leading to an uncontrolled accumulation of cells—the hallmark of cancer. Korsmeyer's discoveries had earned him a Howard Hughes Medical Institute Investigatorship at Washington University in St. Louis.

Nathan had known about Korsmeyer for years. Paul Heller, chief of hematology at the University of Illinois at Chicago and, incidentally, a survivor of Buchenwald and Auschwitz, told Nathan about an amazingly talented medical student whom he ought to meet. That student was Stan. Nathan did run into him a few years later at NIH, where Korsmeyer was doing his cell death work with a classmate of Nathan's from medical school, Thomas Waldmann. Later, when Nathan was chief at Children's, he was so impressed with Korsmeyer's progress at Wash U that he made Korsmeyer promise to let him know if he ever wanted to leave his hometown of St. Louis—Nathan promised he would do whatever it took to get him to Boston.

Soon after Nathan started at the Farber, he heard through the academic grapevine that Korsmeyer was looking at opportunities on the West Coast. After chiding Stan for not letting him know about his itchy feet, Nathan went into high recruiting gear. He obtained assurances from the Howard Hughes Medical Institute that, should Korsmeyer decide to come to Harvard, his investigatorship could move with him. He then charmed Korsmeyer's wife and children. Finally, he dangled a very generous offer that Stan accepted.

Korsmeyer's recruitment accomplished several things. First, most scientists were betting that Stan would win a Nobel prize, so his recruitment put the research world on notice that Dana-Farber was still home to serious scientific talent. Second, Nathan's willingness to marshal the resources needed to recruit someone of Korsmeyer's status boosted the morale of basic researchers. They had been feeling neglected, watching from the sidelines, as so much attention was focused on the clinical side of the institute after the overdose. Finally, in its early years, Dana-Farber had been infamous for nasty interactions among its research faculty. Although the environment had improved, some residual ill-feeling and bad behavior persisted. As a prominent outsider and a true gentleman, Stan could pour oil on troubled waters. The conduct of Dana-Farber's scientists improved along with their morale.

Seven years after Stanley Korsmeyer arrived at Dana-Farber, he died of lung cancer at age fifty-four. This was a terrible blow to the institute and to cancer research. Nathan, who had left the presidency by then, felt the loss personally. To honor Stan's memory, he urged everyone at Dana-Farber to "work much harder, become even better as trainers, and love each other as a family." He asked the researchers to pick up Stan's "fallen lance" and continue his mission to "defeat cancer."[379]

The tragedy of Korsmeyer's death still lay in the future when Nathan, keeping his promise to Jean, relinquished Dana-Farber's presidency in 2000. In five short years, he had made an unprecedented impact. He had guided the institute through its rebirth after the overdose and implemented what would become an international model for patient safety. He had moved the inpatient beds to the Brigham without undercutting Dana-Farber's identity as an independent cancer hospital and negotiated a reasonable *modus vivendi* with the much larger and more powerful Partners HealthCare. He had spearheaded the creation of the Dana-Farber/Harvard Cancer Center, which continues to be the largest and, by several measures, most successful comprehensive cancer center in the country, keeping it intact despite the centrifugal forces exerted by some of its members. And, through skillful recruitment, he had rebuilt the clinical and research reputation of the institute, making it a top destination for talented faculty. Clinic visits were growing as was inpatient activity. Fundraising was exploding. Nathan had put Dana-Farber in an extraordinarily advantageous position for its next president, Nathan's former student Ed Benz (Figure 16).

Figure 16. David Nathan cutting a cake at the celebration of Dana-Farber's fiftieth anniversary. Tom Frei is third from the left. (Courtesy of David G. Nathan.)

CODA

The great twentieth-century pediatrician, Béla Schick, once said,

> Every chief of service should have a pet dog, like Ulysses had. When he retires from the hospital he should leave his dog on the floor of the department he served, because when he returns the only one who will recognize him will be his dog.[380]

While this rings true for most presidents and chiefs emeriti, it does not for Nathan. After retiring from the presidency, he continued to make substantive, well-recognized contributions to Dana-Farber. The development office regularly called on him to cultivate donors with whom he had a relationship and cajoled him into meeting new friends of the institute to inspire them. Not surprisingly, he was adept at attracting a number of gifts. Nathan also served on Dana-Farber's board of trustees and was a reliable participant at the board's science committee meetings. He was aware, from personal experience, that former presidents are sorely tempted to give unsolicited advice to new presidents and was particularly sensitive about this because he knew his successor so well. Keeping this in mind, he executed his tasks at Dana-Farber with a deft touch and maintained a familiar but not overbearing presence.

Nathan also used this time to indulge his passion for teaching and mentoring. He taught principles of hematology to medical students and imparted his skill in the morphological analysis of blood cells to new generations of residents and fellows. He identified trainees who he thought had tremendous promise—individuals who are or who are likely to be stars in Pediatric Hematology/Oncology—and took them under his wing, personally counselling them about career choices and advocating for their advancement.[381] He continued to display his remarkable skill for matching individuals to jobs that exploit their skills, adding to the already impressive number of people who owe their professional success to his insights.

Nathan participated in projects outside of Dana-Farber as well. One of the most important started in 1995 with a call from Harold Varmus, who was then the director of the National Institutes of Health. Varmus was worried about two things: a decline in patient-oriented clinical research being supported by NIH and underutilization of NIH's clinical center where Nathan had trained forty years earlier. Varmus thought that the latter problem might be a consequence of the former. He assembled a group of outside advisors that he called the Director's Panel on Clinical Research and asked Nathan to chair it. The panel's goals were to evaluate the state of clinical research and to develop recommendations for its enhancement. Members of the panel included some of the most eminent clinical researchers in the country including, ironically enough, Samuel Thier who, as board chair of Partners HealthCare, was making life so difficult for Nathan in the negotiations around the inpatient beds.

Not only was Varmus's request to chair the panel a great honor for Nathan but the work was in his sweet spot. Nathan had devoted his professional life to patient-oriented research and was acutely aware of how its stature had been eclipsed by the ascendancy of basic research. He was keen to lead a project that might preserve the kind research he had long championed.

The panel worked for two years and reported its findings and recommendations in 1998.[382] The sorry state of clinical research had been easy to document. The panel found that the proportion of NIH funds supporting clinical research had declined from 40 percent of the total in 1972 to 25 percent in 1995. Fewer grant applications were coming from MDs, and academic medical centers were making little effort to provide salary support for physicians so that they could do research. Rather, they expected MDs to generate their total salaries through clinical work, leaving no time for science. The data confirmed that the MD investigator was a vanishing breed.

Nathan's panel made concrete recommendations starting with its insistence that the NIH must, at the very least, maintain its current level of funding for clinical research. Other practical suggestions included new kinds of grants for fellows and recent graduates of specialty training programs who needed support for mentored training in clinical research. These could be paired with salary grants for the mentors. The panel also urged the review committees evaluating clinical research grant applications to appoint MD members who understand and perform that kind of research.

Many of the panel's recommendations were accepted and some, such as the grants for training clinical investigators, have become standard components of NIH's portfolio. The panel wisely avoided addressing Varmus's question about underutilization of the clinical research center. While the decline in clinical researchers may have contributed in a small way to the problem, it was really an unintended consequence of fifty years' worth of NIH funds being distributed around the country to enhance clinical research infrastructure. As high quality research institutions sprang up nationwide, NIH's clinical center lost its unique appeal; there were fewer and fewer reasons to send patients there.

Although the report of the Director's Panel was well received, the lives of clinical researchers remained precarious. Their plight motivated Nathan to continue his advocacy in other settings, such as the Howard Hughes Medical Institute, where he served on the scientific advisory council. HHMI had traditionally awarded its investigatorships to scientists doing very basic research. Nathan successfully lobbied Hughes to support physicians engaged in clinically relevant science. He did the same while on the scientific advisory board of the Doris Duke Charitable Foundation. That organization is now known for the generous funding it provides for clinically oriented researchers.

The post-presidency gig Nathan enjoyed most was trustee of Rockefeller University. One reason was the staggering quality of its basic science research: its current small faculty boasts five Nobel laureates and, since its founding, there have been twenty-five. Interactions with faculty at Rockefeller reminded Nathan of his experience at MIT but multiplied several-fold. The other reason he loved Rockefeller was its small experimental hospital. To Nathan, this clinical unit was a physical manifestation of the kind of research he had practiced and loved. His years chairing the Hospital Committee and serving on the Scientific Advisory Committee of the board were among his most gratifying.

One of retirement's welcome gifts was time to write. The vestiges of Nathan's English major occasionally peaked through his technical writing but, to a would-be author, that was unsatisfying. Now, at last, he could fully indulge his literary tendencies. Bursting with ideas for a new book, Nathan arranged another five week residency at the Bellagio Center in 2003. There, he produced *The Cancer Treatment Revolution*, a popular work published in 2007 which chronicled the new age of cancer therapies. In typical Nathan style, he presented the information through the experiences of three cancer patients.

Throughout his life, Nathan had been a magnet for honors and awards. He received some prior to retirement including his election in 1983 to the American Academy of Arts and Sciences, an honorific society founded by John Adams and John Hancock among others, whose members are leaders in the humanities, science, and public affairs. William Castle was one of his nominators. In 1999, Nathan was elected to the American Philosophical Society, another learned order, this one founded by Benjamin Franklin. He was nominated by a Society member, an expert in genetics, who had been impressed by *Genes, Blood, and Courage*, Nathan's first book. In 1990, President George Bush presented Nathan with the National Medal of Science for his work on thalassemia and the pathophysiology of red cells.

More honors accrued after retirement. In 2003, Nathan received the John Howland Award, the highest tribute of the American Pediatric Society. This tickled him because Janeway and Diamond had been previous recipients. (As had Béla Schick, whose epigraphs begin this book and this chapter.) In 2006, he was awarded the Kober Medal, the lifetime achievement award of the Association of American Physicians, one of the first scientifically oriented physician's organizations in the United States. Nathan is one of only four individuals to receive both the Howland Prize and the Kober Medal,[383] which is distinction enough, but he also received the Coulter Award from the American Society of Hematology, possibly making him the only recipient of top honors in pediatrics, internal medicine, and a subspecialty.

Nathan's proudest tribute by far was the honorary doctor of science degree he received from Harvard University on graduation day in June 2010. He shared the stage with Meryl Streep and Richard Serra (Figure 17).

Figure 17. David Nathan and Meryl Streep receiving their honorary degrees from Harvard at commencement 2010. (Image © President and Fellows of Harvard College, credit Kris Snibbe/Harvard University.)

These accolades were vehicles for Nathan's peers and trainees to acknowledge the immense contributions he made to American medicine. But American medicine also made contributions to Nathan—the events of the first half of the twentieth century that shaped American medicine also shaped Nathan's life. His education was rooted in the didactic model promulgated by the Flexner Report; he was introduced to research at Boston City Hospital and the Thorndike Laboratory, placing him in the lineage of clinical scientists that began with Minot and Castle; he was present at the dawn of NIH's explosive expansion.

While influenced by the forces that dominated medicine in the first half of the twentieth century, Nathan's own influence extended over the second half. His research had a profound effect on patients who suffer from diseases of red blood cells and, in the course of his long career, he trained three generations of hematologists who continue to improve those lives. Nathan's leadership kept Boston Children's Hospital at the forefront of pediatrics and it rescued Dana-Farber. His is a remarkable legacy, one that continues to impact the next century of American medicine.

ENDNOTES

1   Bianco Nogrady, "Nature Index Annual Tables 2023: First Health-Science Ranking Reveals Big US Lead," *Nature Index* (June 15, 2023), https://doi.org/10.1038/d41586-023-01867-4.

2   Facts surrounding the overdose and its investigation were gathered from several sources, including: Lois J. Ayash v. Dana-Farber Cancer Institute and Others, 367 (443 Mass. 2005); Richard M.J. Bohmer and Ann Winslow, "Dana-Farber Cancer Institute, The," Harvard Business School, Case 699-025 (revised July 1999); and Richard A. Knox, "Hospital Eyes Patterns in Overdoses," *Boston Globe*, March 26, 1995, 1.

3   Adam Pertman, "Betsy A. Lehman 39; Globe Columnist on Personal Health," *Boston Globe*, December 4, 1994, 56.

4   Emil Frei III and G.P. Canellos, "Dose: A Critical Factor in Cancer Chemotherapy," *American Journal of Medicine* 69, no. 4 (1980), 585–594.

5   Frei et al., "Bone Marrow Autotransplantation for Solid Tumors—Prospects," *Journal of Clinical Oncology* 7, no. 4 (April 1989), 515–526.

6   Knox, "Doctor's Orders Killed Cancer Patient," *Boston Globe*, March 23, 1995, 1.

7   *Ayash v. Dana-Farber Cancer Institute and Others.*

8   Alice Dembner, "Doctor Testifies on Role in Patient Death," *Boston Globe*, January 31, 2002, 25.

9   Knox, "Doctor's Orders Killed Cancer Patient."

10 *Ayash v. Dana-Farber Cancer Institute and Others.*

11 Bohmer and Winslow, "Dana-Farber Cancer Institute, The."

12 Lois J. Ayesh et al., "Cyclophosphamide Pharmacokinetics: Correlation with Cardiac Toxicity and Tumor Response," *Journal of Clinical Oncology* 10 (1992), 995–1000.

13 Although this patient, Maureen Bateman, had enrolled on 94-060 prior to Betsy Lehman (Bateman was the second patient enrolled on the protocol, Lehman was the third), delays in treatment schedules led to her receiving this course of therapy two days after Lehman.

14 Knox, "Maureen Bateman, Cancer Patient Injured by Treatment Overdose; at 55," *Boston Globe*, May 30, 1997, 35.

15 Knox, "Doctor's Orders Killed Cancer Patient."

16 Knox, "Anguish, Inquiry at Dana-Farber," *Boston Globe*, March 23, 1995, 17.

17 Knox, "State Faults Dana-Farber," *Boston Globe*, March 24, 1995, 1.

18 Knox, "Doctor's Orders Killed Cancer Patient."

19 *Ayash v. Dana-Farber Cancer Institute and Others.*

20 Bella English, "A Lesson Learned Too Late for Betsy," *Boston Globe*, March 25, 1995, 17.

21 Lawrence K. Altman, "Committees Find Signs of Weak Leadership at Dana-Farber," *New York Times*, October 31, 1995.

22 Knox, "State Probe Cites Lax Management at Dana-Farber," *Boston Globe*, May 25, 1995, 1.

23 Knox, "Dana-Farber on Probation," *Boston Globe*, April 15, 1995, 17.

24 Knox, "Dana-Farber Head Quits 2nd Post, Vows Changes," *Boston Globe*, May 26, 1995, 1.

25 Knox, "President of Troubled Dana-Farber Steps Down," *Boston Globe*, September 13, 1995, 1.

26 Knox, "President of Troubled Dana-Farber Steps Down," *Boston Globe*, September 13, 1995, 1.

27 Knox, "Dana-Farber Puts Focus on Mistakes in Overdoses," *Boston Globe*, October 31, 1995, 1.

28 English, "A Lesson Learned Too Late for Betsy."

29 David Gordon Nathan, personal communication.

30 Nathan, personal communication.

31 Gary Countryman, personal communication.

32 Nathan, personal communication.

33 Joseph F. Dinneen, "John Nathan Living Sermon on Tolerance," *Boston Globe*, August 27, 1940.

34 The address is most often given as 71 Prentiss Street, but sometimes also as 590 Parker Street.

35 "City Document No. 8," in *Report of the Joint Special Committee in the Matter of the Roxbury Color and Chemical Company* (Norfolk County Journal Press: Roxbury, MA, 1856).

36 "Real Estate Transfers. Suffolk County," *Boston Post*, January 31, 1876.

37 Henry Gardner, "Address of His Excellency Henry J. Gardner, to the Two Branches of the Legislature of Massachusetts," January 9, 1855, https://archive.org/details/addressofhisexce00mass_0.

38 Gardner, "Address of His Excellency Henry J. Gardner."

39 Dinneen, "John Nathan Living Sermon on Tolerance."

40 Nathan, personal communication.

41 Dinneen, "John Nathan Living Sermon on Tolerance."

42 Nathan, personal communication.

43 "Widow's Rights," *Boston Post*, February 10, 1897.

44 "Widow's Rights."

45 "Mrs. Nathan Loses," *Boston Post*, February 16, 1897.

46 "Widow's Rights."

47 Dinneen, "John Nathan Living Sermon on Tolerance."

48 Nathan, personal communication.

49 Dinneen, "John Nathan Living Sermon on Tolerance."

50 *Fibre and Fabric* 69, no. 1900 (July 1921).

51 "Kodikon Is Wonderful," *Boston Globe*, December 9, 1937. Kodicon Products was located at 5 Bromfield Street, Boston, MA. Kodicon itself was a mixture of aspirin and vanishingly small amounts of colchicine.

52 "In The Matter of Bernard M. Wolf Trading as Kodicon Products Company," *Federal Trade Commission Decisions, Volume 25*, (1939), 1037–1044.

53 "Corporations Card File," Office of the Secretary of the Commonwealth of Massachusetts, chrome-extension:// efaidnbmnnnibpcajpcglclefindmkaj/https://corp.sec.state. ma.us/CorpWeb/CardSearch/ViewPDF.aspx.

54 Nathan, personal communication.

55 "Honors of Latin School," *Boston Globe*, June 2, 1911.

56 "Young Orators in a Prize Contest," *Boston Globe*, June 5, 1914.

57 "Boston Latin Graduation," The Boston Globe, June 22, 1916.

58 Ibid.

59 "Young Orators in a Prize Contest."

60 "Harvard Has One of the Huskiest Freshman Crews Seen on Charles River in Years," *Boston Globe*, April 9, 1915.

61 "Harvard's Husky Freshman Crew," *Boston Globe*, May 16, 1915.

62 Corydon Ireland, "The Choicest of Their Kind," *Harvard Gazette*, July 25, 2014.

63 "Emanuel Geoffrey Nathan," in *Harvard 1920 Class Album* (Cambridge, Massachusetts: Harvard University, 1920).

64 Marcia Graham Synnott, *The Half-Opened Door: Discrimination and Admissions at Harvard, Yale, and Princeton* (New Brunswick, New Jersey: Transaction Publishers, 2010), xxv.

65 Synnott, 93.

66 Synnott, 29.

67 Synnott, 36.

68 Synnott, 36.

69 Synnott, Table 4.1, 97.

70 Synnott, Table 4.1, 97.

71 Synnott, Table 1.1, 15.

72 *Harvard 1920 Class Album.*

73 Synnott, 22.

74 Synnott, 96.

75 Nathan, personal communication.

76 ssterns (username), "Hey, I have some more information..." December 31, 2007, 10:45 p.m., comment on blog post, Cinema Treasures, http://cinematreasures.org/blog/2007/7/31/nathan-gordons-olympia-circuit.

77 While the story may be apocryphal, Napoleon's supposed appellation has been cited repeatedly: "Napoleon Named Vilnius 'Jerusalem of the North,'" VilNews, January 9, 2011, https://vilnews.com/2011-01-napoleon-named-vilnius-%E2%80%98jerusalem-of-the-north%E2%80%99#:~:text=Napoleon%20was%20the%20one%20who,an%20exception%20to%20the%20rule.

78 Joshua D. Zimmerman, *Poles, Jews, and the Politics of Nationality,* (University of Wisconsin Press, 2003).

79 "Death of Jacob Gordon," *Rochester Democrat and Chronicle,* September 14, 1919.

80 "Bartlett Street Butcher Sued," *Rochester Democrat and Chronicle,* January 6, 1900.

81 *Shoe and Leather Reporter* 136, no. 1 (October 2, 1919).

82 Bosley Crother, Hollywood Rajah: The Life and Times of Louis B. Mayer (New York: Holt, Rinehart, and Winston, 1960).

83 "Men Behind Theater Plan Saying Little," *Rochester Democrat and Chronicle,* May 28, 1908, 17.

84 "New Playhouse for Vaudeville?" *Rochester Democrat and Chronicle*, June 11, 1908.

85 "Picture Shows Profitable," *Rochester Democrat and Chronicle*, February 4, 1914.

86 "Photoplay Company's Officers," *Rochester Democrat and Chronicle*, February 13, 1914.

87 *Showmen's Trade Review*, April–June, 1949.

88 "Jacob Gordon Left Estate of $102,500," *Rochester Democrat and Chronicle*, July 15, 1922.

89 *Spotlight* (East High School: Rochester New York, 1919).

90 "Ruth Nathan, 90, Retired Social Worker," *Boston Globe*, October 31, 1991.

91 "Miss Ruth Gordon Bride of Emanuel G. Nathan," *Boston Globe*, April 1, 1925.

92 Entman, JF, *Searching for the Mandls*. Almond Tree, St. Augustine FL, 2022. Pp. 88-94. (Although it has been difficult to find any documentary evidence about the Winter family, Nathan family lore suggests that Charlie and Marianne's father, Friedrich Winter was the founder of the Austrian equivalent of America's Railway Express.)

93 "Immigration to the United States, 1933-1941; Documents Required to Obtain a Visa." Holocaust Encyclopedia, United States Holocaust Museum, https://encyclopedia.ushmm.org/content/en/article/documents-required-to-obtain-a-visa.

94 College Art Association (CAA) Newsletter 14, no. 2, 1989, 14.

95 DGN memoir, 63.

96 Scott Eyman, *Lion of Hollywood: The Life and Legend of Louis B. Mayer* (New York: Simon and Schust, 2008).

97 Jacob and John Nathan each contributed ten dollars to the American Jewish Committee in 1916. "The American Jewish Committee, Ninth Annual Report, 356 Second Avenue, New

York, NY, 1916," *Lord Baltimore Press*. Other names on the list: A. Lincoln Filene, Samuel Gryzmish, Louis E. Kirstein, Jacob R. Morse, Moses M. Morse, Julius C. Morse, Harris Poorvu, and David Stoneman—all prominent Boston philanthropists.

98 "Benefit Pop Concert," *Boston Globe*, May 7, 1940.

99 "To Feed Jewish Soldiers," *Rochester Democrat and Chronicle*, March 22, 1918.

100 "Married Together," *Boston Globe*, April 9, 1894.

101 Formally known as the Frances Stern Nursery School and Kindergarten, Inc, at 178 Mason Terrace, Brookline, MA. In "The Boston Symphony Orchestra Program," fifty-third season, 1933–1934, fourth program, 1933.

102 "Institute for Policy Studies," Heritage Foundation, April 19, 1977, https://www.heritage.org/conservatism/report/institute-policy-studies.

103 It seems uncharitable not to list them: Miss Daley in first grade, Miss Saunders in second, Miss Spargo in third, Miss Lamb in fourth, Miss Armitage in fifth, and Miss Taylor in sixth. Miss Taylor was his favorite. DGN memoir, 20.

104 *Journal of the National Education Association* 10 (1921): 131.

105 DGN memoir, p. 20.

106 "Thomas Bell's Bequest to Roxbury Latin School and Forest Hills," Jamaica Plain Historical Society, April 14, 2005, https://www.jphs.org/people/2005/4/14/forest-hills-and-the-bell-bequest-to-roxbury-latin-school.html.

107 F. Washington Jarvis, *Schola Illustris: The Roxbury Latin School 1645-1995* (David R. Godine: Boston, 1995).

108 *A Handbook of American Private Schools: An Annual Survey*, 7th ed. (Boston: Porter Sargent, 1922), 77.

109 "Rooted in History," the Roxbury Latin School, https://www.roxburylatin.org/about/history/.

110 Francis Russell, "The Coming of the Jews," *The Antioch Review* 15, no. 1 (1955), 19–38.

111 Russell, 32.

112 Russell, 33.

113 Russell, 33

114 This is something at which the Nathan cousins excelled. See Chapter 2.

115 Russell, 33.

116 "George Northrop, Headmaster, Dies," *New York Times*, August 1, 1964, 21.

117 "Jewish Fund Drive Planner Meet Here, Hear Nazi Victim," *Boston Globe*, September 10, 1946, 1.

118 "About," History, Andover, https://www.andover.edu/about/history.

119 Claude Fuess, *An Old New England School: A History of Phillips Academy Andover* (Houghton Mifflin Company: Boston and New York, 1917).

120 Janine Ko, "Andover Community Embraces Changing of the Guard," *Phillipian*, January 12, 2012, https://phillipian.net/2012/01/12/andover-community-embraces-changing-of-the-guard/.

121 Ko.

122 Frederick S. Allis, *Youth from Every Quarter: A Bicentennial History of Phillips Academy, Andover* (Lebanon, New Hampshire: University Press of New England, 1979).

123 Allis.

124 Allis.

125 "Aaron Family Papers," Manuscript Collection No. 621, American Jewish Archives, http://collections.americanjewish archives.org/ms/ms0621/ms0621.html.

126 https://www.historic-structures.com/pa/pittsburgh/eberhardt_and_ober_brewery.php; retrieved February 7, 2024.

127 Rachel Weaver, "China Maker Counts Generations of Loyal Buyers," Trib Total Media, June 4, 2012, https://triblive.com/home/1914652-74/company-china-fiesta-laughlin-homer-color-loyal-buyers- commercial-dinnerware.

128 "Our History," Fiesta Tableware Company, https://fiesta factorydirect.com/pages/our-history.

129 Née Mina M. Lippman, according to "Guide to the Aaron Family Papers, 1848—1978, Bulk 1920–1970," https://historicpittsburgh.org/islandora/object/pitt%3 AUS-QQS-MSS248/viewer.

130 "Aaron Family Papers."http://collections.americanjewish archives.org/ms/ms0621/ms0621.html

131 Née Maxine Goldmark according to "Guide to the Aaron Family Papers, 1848—1978, Bulk 1920–1970," https://historicpittsburgh.org/islandora/object/pitt%3AUS-QQS-MSS248/viewer.

132 "Maxine G. and Marcus Lester Aaron Fund," Pittsburgh Foundation, https://pittsburghfoundation.org/node/25073.

133 "Our History," Fiesta Tableware Company.

134 Née Stella Hamburger according to "Guide to the Aaron Family Papers, 1848—1978, Bulk 1920–1970," https://historicpittsburgh.org/islandora/object/pitt%3AUS-QQS-MSS248/viewer.

135 Fannie's letters to her parents while at college are archived at https://digitallibrary.vassar.edu/collections/other-collections/vassar-college-student-letters/beea484a-70c1-41e1-82ea-91f4807f76aa. They provide an intimate view of a young Jewish girl's college experience away from home in the early 1920s.

136 "Mrs. Nina Friedman," *Pittsburgh Press*, December 1, 1919, 23.

137 J. D. Salinger ascribes a similar memory to Buddy Glass in *Raise High the Roofbeam, Carpenters*: "All sit-up coaches on trains in 1942 were only nominally ventilated, as I remember." J. D. Salinger, *Raise High the Roofbeam, Carpenters and Seymour: An Introduction* (Boston: Little, Brown, 1955, 1959), 11.

138 Bainbridge Bunting, *Harvard: An Architectural History*, ed. Margaret Henderson Floyd (Cambridge, Massachusetts: Belknap Press, 1985), 184.

139 "Large Percentage of Claverly Hall Students Will Not Move to Houses," *Harvard Crimson*, March 30, 1955, https://www.thecrimson.com/article/1955/3/30/large-percentage-of-claverly-hall-students/.

140 "Emil Drvaric," 1947 Football, Harvard, https://gocrimson.com/sports/football/roster/emil-drvaric/13558.

141 "Drvaric Named to All-Ivy League First Eleven as Yale Places Four," *Harvard Crimson*, December 11, 1946, https://www.thecrimson.com/article/1946/12/11/drvaric-named-to-all-ivy-league-first/.

142 "Emil Drvaric & the 1943 Great Lakes Bluejackets," National Museum of the American Sailor, July 27, 2015, https://sailorsattic.wordpress.com/2015/07/27/emil-drvaric-the-1943-great-lakes-bluejackets/.

143 DGN memoirs, 16.

144 DGN memoirs, 65.

145 "David G. Nathan," American Society of Hematology, https://www.hematology.org/about/history/legends/david-nathan-bio.

146 E. J. Evans, "Platoon Leaders Class," *Leatherneck* 31, issue. Platoon Leaders Class. *Leatherneck* 31, issue 11 (November 1948).

147 Evans, "Platoon Leaders Class."

148 Evans, "Platoon Leaders Class."

149 Likely Major General Lemuel C. Shepard at that time.

150 DGN memoirs, 65.

151 Ray Monk, *Robert Oppenheimer: A Life Inside the Center* (New York: Anchor Books, 2012).

152 "John Vincent Kelleher," *Harvard Gazette*, April 28, 2005, https://news.harvard.edu/gazette/story/2005/04/john-vincent-kelleher/.

153 DGN, personal communication.

154 DGN memoirs, 7.

155 Primus V, "How to Cook a Thesis," *Harvard Magazine* (January-February, 2005), 88.

156 Abraham Flexner, *Medical Education in the United States and Canada: A Report to the Carnegie Foundation for the Advancement of Teaching* (New York: The Carnegie Foundation for the Advancement of Teaching, 1910).

157 Thomas P. Duffy, "The Flexner Report—100 Years Later," *Yale Journal of Biology and Medicine* 84, no. 3 (2011): 269–276.

158 Thomas N. Bonner, *Iconoclast: Abraham Flexner and a Life in Learning* (Baltimore and London: Johns Hopkins University Press, 2002), 61.

159 *Announcement 1954–55, Harvard Medical School and School of Dental Medicine* (Cambridge, Massachusetts: Official Registrar of Harvard University, 1954), https://archive.org/stream/announcementofme5455harv/announcementofme545. The assignment of grades and class rank was frighteningly rigorous in that era. This document describes, in detail, how grades were determined:
- Final grades in each course will be based upon such examinations or other tests as are determined by each

department. Grading is on the scale of A, B, C, D, and E (denoting failure).

- Grades are averaged on the basis that A =1, B = 2, C = 3, D = 5 and E = 8, and since the time devoted to courses varies, grade averages will take into account the time assigned to courses, giving them computation values as follows:

  o First Year: Anatomy 5; Histology 5; Physiology 5; Biological Chemistry 5.

  o Second Year: Pathology 6; Bacteriology 4; Pharmacology 4; Physical Diagnosis 2; Laboratory Diagnosis 2; Surgery 2.

  o Third Year: Medicine 6; Surgery 6; Pediatrics 3; Obstetrics 3; Preventive Medicine 2

  o Fourth Year: Proportional to month's work. Each student in the fourth year must secure credit for eight one-month courses of 144 hours or their equivalent. Required courses fill seven months' time, leaving one month free for elective work. In the following statements whole courses have a value of 144 hours and half-courses of 72 hours.

160 *Announcement 1954–55, Harvard Medical School and School of Dental Medicine,*

"An estimate of total yearly expenses shows that the average cost of the school year is $2,300 for each academic year. This estimate includes tuition, medical health fee, board and room, books, laundry and incidentals.

The fees are: — For matriculation, $5; for medical health fee, $50 for each year; for instruction (including laboratory charges except microscope rental, breakage, damage and loss of apparatus), $800 for each year. In September 1954 the tuition was increased to $1,000."

161 DGN memoirs, 11.

162 Ann B. Barnet, "What Do Women Want, or the Couch in Building A," *Harvard Medical Alumni Bulletin* 54, no. 5 (August 1980): 16–18.

163 "History of Women at HMS: Matriculation of Women at Harvard Medical School," Joint Committee on the Status of Women, https://jcsw.hms.harvard.edu/history.

164 *Subversive Influences in the Educational Process: United States Senate, Subcommittee to Investigate the Administration of the Internal Security Act and Other Internal Security Laws, of the Committee on the Judiciary* (Washington, DC: US Government Printing Office, 1953), 1166–1168.

165 "D.A. Probes Infractions of Teachers Oath Here," *Harvard Crimson*, November 18, 1953.

166 "State Major Target for Probers of Reds," *Boston Globe*, December 22, 1953.

167 "Anti-Communist Hysteria Strikes in All Directions," *Freedom— The Anarchist Weekly* 14, no. 31 (1953): 1.

168 "John Harvard's Journal: Yesterday's News, 1953," *Harvard Magazine* (July-August, 2018).

169 "Anti-Communist Hysteria Strikes in All Directions."

170 Jeffrey M. Elrod and Anand B. Karnand, "Boston City Hospital and the Thorndike Memorial Laboratory: The Birth of Modern Haematology," *British Journal of Haematology* 121, no. 3 (2003): 383–389.

171 *A History of the Boston City Hospital from Its Foundation Until 1904*, eds. David W. Cheever, George W. Gay, and J.B. Blake (Boston: Municipal Printing Office, 1906).

172 Count D. Gibson Jr., "A Visiting Physician Looks at the Tufts Medical Service at the Boston City Hospital," *Tufts Medical Alumni Bulletin*, November 1964, 17–18.

173 Ephraim Friedman, "Annual Discourse—The Boston City Hospital: A Tale of Three 'Cities,'" *New England Journal of Medicine* 289 (1973): 503–506.

174 W.B. Castle, "George Richards Minot, 1885-1950," National Academy of Sciences, Washington, DC, 1974.

175 Castle, "George Richards Minot, 1885-1950."

176 Elrod and Karnand, "Boston City Hospital and the Thorndike Memorial Laboratory."

177 E.J. Conway and E. O'Malley, "Microdiffusion Methods. Ammonia and Urea Using Buffered Absorbents (Revised Methods for Ranges Greater than 10µg. N)," *Biochemical Journal* 36, nos. 7–9 (1942): 655-661.

178 The solution involved inactivating adenosine deaminase in red blood cells by washing the blood with trichloroacetic acid.

179 Nathan, F.L. Rodkey, "A Colorimetric Procedure for the Determination of Blood Ammonia," *Journal of Laboratory Clinical Medicine* 49, no. 5 (1957): 779–785.

180 W. Saxon, "Dana Lyda Farnsworth, 81: Led Harvard Health Service," *New York Times*, August 5, 1986, 22.

181 Flexner, 240.

182 J.A. Greene and S.H. Podalsky, "The Teaching Hospital," in *The Teaching Hospital: Brigham and Women's Hospital and the Evolution of Academic Medicine*, P.V. Tishler, C. Wenc, J. Loscalzo, eds. (New York: McGraw-Hill Education, 2014), 2.

183 Greene and Podalsky, 29. The surgeon was Francis D. Moore, MD.

184 Greene and Podalsky, 31.

185 Paul A. Offit, *The Cutter Incident: How America's First Polio Vaccine Led to the Growing Vaccine Crisis* (New Haven, Connecticut, and London: Yale University Press, 2005), 89.

186 "The Polio Outbreak of 1955: Lessons from an Epidemic," https://answers.childrenshospital.org/polio-outbreak-1955/

187 M.K. Klein, *The Legacy of the "Yellow Berets": The Vietnam War, the Doctor Draft, and the NIH Associate Training Program,* unpublished manuscript (Bethesda, Maryland: NIH History Office, 1998).

188 80th Congress, 2nd Session, House of Representatives Report No. 2438, "Selective Service Act of 1948. Conference Report," June 19, 1948.

189 Public Laws, Chapter 939, Sept 9, 1950, "An Act To Amend the Selective Service Act of 1948, as amended, so as to provide for special registration, classification, and induction of certain medical, dental, and allied specialist categories, and for other purposes," 826–828.

190 "Beacon of Hope: The Clinical Center Through Forty Years of Growth and Change in Biomedicine," U.S. Department of Health and Human Services, Public Health Service, National Institutes of Health, 1993.

191 Sandeep Khot, Buhm Soon Park, W.T. Longstreth Jr, "The Vietnam War and Medical Research: Untold Legacy of the U.S. Doctor Draft and the NIH 'Yellow Berets,'" *Academic Medicine* 96, no. 4 (2011): 502–508.

192 Klein, *The Legacy of the Yellow Berets.*

193 They included Thomas Waldmann (who became chief of the metabolism branch at NIH), Sherman Weissman (Sterling professor of genetics, Yale University), Kenneth Warren (director of health services, Rockefeller Foundation), John Laszlo (president, American Cancer Society), and DeWitt

Goodman (director, Arteriosclerosis Research Center, Columbia University).

194 Other PHS stations included PHS headquarters, PHS hospitals throughout the country, Indian Health Service hospitals, the National Center for Urban and Industrial Health, the National Communicable Disease Center (the precursor to the Centers for Disease Control), and the Arctic Health Research Center.

195 Klein, *The Legacy of the Yellow Berets*.

196 Klein, *The Legacy of the Yellow Berets*.

197 Khot S, Park BS, Longstreth WTJr, "The Vietnam War and Medical Research: Untold Legacy of the U.S. Doctor Draft and the NIH Yellow Berets." Acad Med **86**:502-8 (2011).

198 Khot, Park, and Longstreth, "The Vietnam War and Medical Research."

199 Klein, *The Legacy of the Yellow Berets*.

200 Klein, *The Legacy of the Yellow Berets*.

201 J. Kelly, "Is It Hot Here or Is It Just Answer Man?" *Washington Post*, August 31, 2008.

202 Nathan used a moving company owned by an African-American man whose son was in the crew. That young man, Henry Owen, Jr., later became a trustee of Dana-Farber Cancer Institute during Nathan's presidency.

203 "Beacon of Hope: The Clinical Center Through Forty Years of Growth and Change in Biomedicine."

204 L. Wills, P.W. Clutterbuck, and B.D.F. Evans, "A New Factor in the Production and Cure of certain Macrocytic Anaemias," *Lancet 229* (1937): 311–314.

205 S. Farbert et al., "Temporary Remissions in Acute Leukemia in Children Produced by Folic Acid Antagonist 4-Aminopteroyl-Glutamic Acid (Aminopterin)," *New England Journal of Medicine 238* (1948): 787–793.

206 Farber et al., "Temporary Remissions."

207 Farber et al., "Temporary Remissions."

208 NCI Oral History Project, interviews with C. Gordon Zubrod, MD, History Associates, Incorporated. Rockville, Maryland, 1997.

209 NCI Oral History Project, interviews with Nathaniel Berlin, MD, PhD, History Associates, Incorporated. Rockville, Maryland, 1997.

210 NCI Oral History Project, interviews with Zubrod.

211 NCI Oral History Project, interviews with Berlin.

212 DGN memoirs, 36.

213 DGN memoirs, 36.

214 In fact, clinical associates were given the rank of lieutenant commander, which carried the entitlement of two half-inch stripes with a quarter-inch stripe in between, but Nathan's response of "two" was close enough.

215 Berlin, J.H. Lawrence, and H.C. Lee, "The Pathogenesis of the Anemia of Chronic Leukemia: Measurement of the Life Span of the Red Blood Cell with Glycine-2-C14," *Journal of Laboratory and Clinical Medicine* 44, no. 6 (1954): 860–874.

216 Nathan and Berlin, "Studies of the Production and Life Span of Erythrocytes in Myeloid Metaplasia," *Blood* 14 (1959): 668–682.

217 Nathan and Berlin, "Studies of the Production and Life Span."

218 These included Bernard Landau, professor of biochemistry and medicine at Case Western Reserve University; Herbert Levine (the son of cardiologist Samuel A. Levine), chief of cardiology at Tufts University; Saul Rosenberg, professor of medicine at Stanford where, with Henry Kaplan, he contributed to the development of effective treatments for Hodgkin disease.

219 George W. Thorn, "A Department of Medicine in 1963–1973," *New England Journal of Medicine* 270 (1964): 281–286.

220 G.H. Whipple and W.L. Bradford, "Racial or Familial Anemia of Children Associated with Fundamental Disturbances of Bone and Pigment Metabolism (Cooley-Von Jaksch)," *American Journal of Diseases of Children* 44, no 2 (1932): 336–365. "The terminology for this disease is unsatisfactory.... Cooley had described a clinical entity, and it may be wise to use his name to distinguish this disease. We do not like the term "erythroblastic anemia" used by Cooley, as there is nothing especially characteristic about this feature of the blood. The disease is limited almost wholly to Italians, Greeks and Syrians, i.e., to the people originating about the Mediterranean Sea. For this reason the term "thalassemia," derived from the Greek θαλασσα, meaning the great sea and used to designate the Mediterranean, may have an appeal. Mediterranean disease or anemia likewise might be appropriate. As the anemia is only one of several factors in this disease, the term Mediterranean disease might be most accurate and comprehensive."

221 The original address was 11 Elmwood Street.

222 Max Perutz et al., "Structure of Haemoglobin: A Three-Dimensional Fourier Synthesis at 5.5-Å. Resolution, Obtained by X-Ray Analysis," *Nature* 185 (1960):416–422.

223 R.S. Rhinesmith, W.A. Schroeder, and L. Pauling, "A Quantitative Study of the Hydrolysis of Human Dinitrophenyl (DNP) Globin: The Number and Kind of Polypeptide Chains in Normal Adult Human Hemoglobin," *Journal of the American Chemical Society* 79: (1957): 4082–4086.

224 V.M. Ingram, "Gene Mutations in Human Haemoglobin: The Chemical Difference Between Normal and Sickle Cell Haemoglobin," *Nature* 180 (1957): 326–328.

225 D.J. Weatherall and J.B. Clegg, *The Thalassaemia Syndromes*, 4th ed. (Oxford: Blackwell Sciences, 2001), 14.

226 Weatherall and Clegg, 39.

227 Deborah Charness, personal communication.

228 T.G. Gabuzda, Nathan, and F.H. Gardner, "Comparative Metabolism of Haemoglobins A and F in Thalassaemia," *Nature* 196 (1962): 781–782.

229 Gabuzda, Nathan, and Gardner, "The Turnover of Hemoglobins A, F, and A2 in the Peripheral Blood of Three Patients with Thalassemia," *Journal of Clinical Investigation* 42 (1963): 1678–1688.

230 Gabuzda, Nathan, and Gardner, "The Metabolism of the Individual C14-Labeled Hemoglobins in Patients with H-Thalassemia, with Observations on Radiochromate Binding to the Hemoglobins During Red Cell Survival," *Journal of Clinical Investigation* 44 (1965): 314–325.

231 Phaedon Fessas, "Inclusions of Hemoglobin in Erythroblasts and Erythrocytes of Thalassemia," *Blood* 21 (1963): 21–32.

232 Nathan and R.B. Gunn, "Thalassemia: The Consequences of Unbalanced Hemoglobin Synthesis," *American Journal of Medicine* 41 (1966): 815–830.

233 W.N. Valentine, K.R. Tanaka, and A. Miwa, "A Specific Erythrocyte Enzyme Defect (Pyruvate Kinase) in Three Subjects with Congenital Nonspherocytic Hemolytic Anemia," *Transactions of the Association of American Physicians* 74 (1961).

234 Tanaka, Valentine, and Miwa, "S. Pyruvate kinase (Pk) Deficiency Hereditary Nonspherocytic Hemolytic Anemia," *Blood* 19 (1962): 267-95.

235 F.A. Oski and L.K. Diamond, "Erythrocyte Pyruvate Kinase Deficiency Resulting in Congenital Nonspherocytic

Hemolytic Anemia," *New England Journal of Medicine* 269 (1963): 763–770.

236 F.A. Oski et al., "Extreme Hemolysis and Red-Cell Distortion in Erythrocyte Pyruvate Kinase Deficiency. I. Morphology, Erythrokinetics and Family Enzyme Studies," *New England Journal of Medicine* 270 (1964): 1023–1030.

237 Nathan et al., "Life-Span and Organ Sequestration of the Red Cells in Pyruvate Kinase Deficiency," *New England Journal of Medicine* 178 (1967): 73–81.

238 Nathan et al., "Life-Span and Organ Sequestration."

239 DGN memoirs, 67.

240 The lecturer was Philip Noel-Baker, a British Quaker who had been an advocate for banning aerial bombardment in World War II and became a strong voice for nuclear disarmament. Noel-Baker was awarded the Nobel Peace Prize for his disarmament work in 1959. He was also an outstanding athlete and won a silver medal in the fifteen-hundred-meter race in the 1920 Summer Olympics. He may be the only person to have won both a Nobel Prize and an Olympic medal.

241 Sidel had come to Lown's attention because of an article he wrote condemning the release of confidential information about a patient, including his homosexuality, by a psychiatrist after the patient's defection to the Soviet Union (V.W. Sidel, "Confidential Information and the Physician," *New England Journal of Medicine* 264 [1961]: 1133–1137.) Some of the others invited by Lown included Roy Menninger (a Brigham psychiatry resident and son of Karl Menninger, founder of the Menninger Clinic); Sidney Alexander (a cardiologist who later became president of Physicians for Social Responsibility); H. Jack Geiger (a graduate of Western Reserve University School of Medicine who trained at Boston City Hospital

and the Harvard School of Public Health; he also served as president of Physicians for Social Responsibility and founder and president of Physicians for Human Rights; he was one of the earliest developers of the idea of a community health center); Alexander Leaf; George Saxton; Robert Goldwyn; and Bernard Leon Winter.

242 "Editor's Note. The Medical Consequences of Thermonuclear War," *New England Journal of Medicine* 266 (1962): 1126–1127.

243 F.R. Ervin et al., "Human and Ecologic Effects in Massachusetts of an Assumed Thermonuclear Attack on the United States," *New England Journal of Medicine* 266 (1962): 1137–1145.

244 V.W. Sidel, H.J. Geiger, and B. Lown, "The Physician's Role in the Postattack Period," *New England Journal of Medicine* 266 (1962): 1137–1145.

245 DGN, personal communication.

246 H.H. Fudenberg, "Dialysable Lymphocyte Extract (DLyE) in Infantile Onset Autism: A Pilot Study," *Biotherapy* 9 (1996): 143–147 (1996); and Russell Schierling, "According to the Media, It's Flu Season Again. Alzheimer's Anyone?" Doctor Schierling, September 20, 2011, https://www.doctorschierling.com/blog/its-flu-season-again-alzheimers-anyone.

247 DGN memoirs, 55.

248 DGN memoirs, 68.

249 R.S. Geha, Charles A. Janeway and Fred S. Rosen, "The Discovery of Gama Globulin Therapy and Primary Immunodeficiency Diseases at Boston Children's Hospital," *Journal of Allergy and Clinical Immunology* 166 (2005): 937–940.

250 DGN, personal communication.

251 Nathan, *The Cancer Treatment Revolution* (Hoboken, New Jersey: John Wiley & Sons, 2007), 63–64.

252 R.L. Baehner and Nathan, "Leukocyte Oxidase, Defective Activity in Chronic Granulomatous Disease," *Science* 155 (1967): 836–836.

253 Baehner, Nathan, and W.B. Castle, "Oxidant Injury of Caucasian Glucose-6-Phosphate Dehydrogenase-Deficient Red Blood Cells by Phagocytosing Leukocytes During Infection," *Journal of Clinical Investigation* 50 (1971): 2466–2473.

254 H.S. Zarkowsky et al., "Congenital Hemolytic Anemia with High Sodium, Low Potassium Red Cells. I. Studies of Membrane Permeability," *New England Journal of Medicine* 278 (1968): 573–581.

255 F.A. Oski et al., "Congenital Hemolytic Anemia with High-Sodium, Low-Potassium Red Cells. Studies of Three Generations of a Family with a New Variant," *New England Journal of Medicine* 280 (1969): 909–916.

256 B.E. Glader et al., "Congenital Hemolytic Anemia Associated with Dehydrated Erythrocytes and Increased Potassium Loss," *New England Journal of Medicine* 291 (1974): 491–496.

257 O.S. Platt and Nathan, "Exercise-Induced Hemolysis in Xerocytosis. Erythrocyte Dehydration and Shear Sensitivity, *Journal of Clinical Investigation* 68 (1981): 631–638.

258 R. Zarychanski et al., "Mutations in the Mechanotransduction Protein PIEZO1 Are Associated with Hereditary Xerocytosis," *Blood* 120 (2012): 1908–1915.

259 Nathan et al., "Erythroid Precursors in Congenital Hypoplastic (Diamond-Blackfan) Anemia," *Journal of Clinical Investigation* 61 (1978): 489–498.

260 Nathan et al., "Human Erythroid Burst-Forming Unit: T-cell Requirement for Proliferation in Vitro," *Journal of Experimental Medicine* 147 (1978): 324–339.

261 Nathan et al., "Normal Erythropoietic Helper T Cells in Congenital Hypoplastic (Diamond-Blackfan) Anemia," *New England Journal of Medicine* 298 (1978): 1049–1051.

262 B.P. Alter et al., "Control of the Simian Fetal Hemoglobin Switch at the Progenitor Cell Level," *Journal of Clinical Investigation* 67 (1981): 458–466.

263 R.M. Macklis et al., "Synthesis of Hemoglobin F in Adult Simian Erythroid Progenitor-Derived Colonies, *Journal of Clinical Investigation* 70 (1982): 752–761.

264 A.D. Friedman et al., "Determination of the Hemoglobin F Program in Human Progenitor-Derived Erythroid Cells," *Journal of Clinical Investigation* 75 (1985): 1359–1368.

265 J. DeSimone et al., "5-Azacytidine stimulates Fetal Hemoglobin Synthesis in Anemic Baboons," *Proceedings of the National Academy of Sciences* 79 (1982) 4428–2231.

266 T.J. Ley et al., "5-Azacytidine Selectively Increases Gamma-Globin Synthesis in a Patient with Beta+ Thalassemia," *New England Journal of Medicine* 307 (1982): 1469–1475.

267 G.J. Dover et al., "5-Azacytidine Increases Fetal Hemo-Globin Production in a Patient with Sickle Cell Disease," *Progress in Clinical and Biological Research* 134 (1983): 475–488.

268 N.L. Letvin et al., "Augmentation of Fetal-Hemo-Globin Production in Anemic Monkeys by Hydroxyurea, *New England Journal of Medicine* 310 (1984): 869–873.

269 O.S. Platt et al., "Hydroxyurea Enhances Fetal Hemoglobin Production in Sickle Cell Anemia," *Journal of Clinical Investigation* 74 (1984): 652–656.

270 S. Charache et al., "Effect of Hydroxyurea on the Frequency of Painful Crises in Sickle Cell Anemia. Investigators of the Multicenter Study of Hydroxyurea in Sickle Cell Anemia," *New England Journal of Medicine* 332 (1995): 1317–1322.

271 J.B. Clegg, M.A. Naughton, and D.J. Weatherall, "Separation of the Alpha and Beta-Chains of Human Hemoglobin," *Nature* 219 (1968): 67–70.

272 Y.W. Kan and Nathan, "Beta Thalassemia Trait: Detection at Birth. *Science* 161 (1968):589–590.

273 Y.W. Kan et al., "Detection of the Sickle Gene in the Human Fetus. Potential for Intrauterine Diagnosis of Sickle-Cell Anemia," *New England Journal of Medicine* 287 (1972): 1–5.

274 Y.W. Kan et al., "Successful Application of Prenatal Diagnosis in a Pregnancy at Risk for Homozygous Beta-Thalassemia," *New England Journal of Medicine* 292 (1975): 1096–1099.

275 B.P. Alter et al., "Prenatal Diagnosis of Sickle-Cell Anemia and Alpha G Philadelphia. Study of a Fetus Also at Risk for H b S/ Beta+-Thalassemia," *New England Journal of Medicine* 294 (1976): 1040–1041.

276 Y.W. Kan, M.S. Golbus, and R. Trecartin, "Prenatal Diagnosis of Sickle Cell Anemia," *New England Journal of Medicine* 294 (1976): 1039–1040.

277 B.P. Alter et al., "Prenatal Diagnosis of Hemoglobinopathies. A Review of 15 Cases," *New England Journal of Medicine* 295 (1976): 1437–1443.

278 S.H. Orkin et al., "Application of Endonuclease Mapping to the Analysis and Prenatal Diagnosis of Thalassemias Caused by Globin-Gene Deletion," *New England Journal of Medicine* 299 (1978): 166–172.

279 "Doctors Isolate a Human Gene, Allowing Birth-Defect Detection," *New York Times* July 27, 1978, A1.

280 P. Malone, "Major Breakthroughs in Genetic Research," *Washington Post*, August 27, 1978.

281 Nathan, "Ethical Problems in Fetal Research," *Journal of General Education* 27 (1975): 165–175.

282 Nathan, "Fetal Research: An Investigator's View," *Villanova Law Review*, Vill L Rev 384 (1976).

283 F.H. Lovejoy and Nathan, "Careers Chosen by Graduates of a Major Pediatrics Residency Program, 1974-1986," *Academic Medicine* 67 (1992): 272–274.

284 D.A. Goldmann et al., "A Service Chief Model for General Pediatric Inpatient Care and Residency Training," *Pediatrics* 89 (1992): 601–607.

285 F.H. Lovejoy et al., "The Merger of Two Pediatric Residency Programs: Lessons Learned," *Journal of Pediatrics* 153 (2008): 731–733.

286 A. Goudnough, "Suit Accuses Pediatrician of Abuse," *New York Times*, April 8, 2008.

287 T. Lewin, "Pediatrician in Abuse Case Kills Himself." *New York Times*, February 25, 2011.

288 Lewin, "Pediatrician in Abuse Case Kills Himself."

289 Aubrey J. Katz and Another [Alex F. Flores] v. The Children's Hospital Corporation, 33 Mass. App. Ct. 574, September 11, 1992.

290 J. Robinson, "The Staying Power of the Well-To-Do," *Boston Globe*, November 2, 1993, 61.

291 D. Golden, "Top Doctor Said to Be Target of Funds Probe," *Boston Globe* November 10, 1993, 1.

292 J. Ellement, "Doctor Guilty of Stealing," *Boston Globe* May 27, 1995, 13.

293 J. Rakowsky, "Accused Doctor Is Ordered to Pay $6.5m to Foundation," *Boston Globe*, December 22, 1994, 1.

294 D. Golden, "Cardiologist Says Accusations Are Part of Vendetta," *Boston Globe*, May 18, 1994, 1.

295 P. Nealon, "Pediatric Radiologist Faces Criminal Charges. Prosecutor Says $70,000 Embezzled," *Boston Globe*, March 2, 1999, 18.

296 B.P. Alter et al., "Investigations of the simian Ontogenic Switch from Fetal to adult Hemoglobin at the Progenitor Cell Level," *Journal of Clinical Investigation* 78 (1986): 1497–1503.

297 V.G. Sankaran et al., "Human fetal Hemoglobin Expression Is Regulated by the Developmental Stage-Specific Repressor BCL11A," *Science* 322 (2008): 1839–1842.

298 B.A. Miller et al, "Influence of Hydroxyurea on Fetal Hemoglobin Production in Vitro," *Blood* 70 (1987): 1824–1829.

299 B.A. Miller et al., "High Fetal Hemoglobin Production in Sickle Cell Anemia in the Eastern Province of Saudi Arabia Is Genetically Determined," *Blood* 67 (1986): 1404–1410.

300 B.A. Miller et al., "Analysis of Hemoglobin F Production in Saudi Arabian Families with Sickle Cell Anemia," *Blood* 70 (1987): 716–720.

301 B.A. Miller et al., "Molecular Analysis of the High-Hemoglobin-F Phenotype in Saudi Arabian Sickle Cell Anemia," *New England Journal of Medicine* 316 (1987): 244–250.

302 S.G. Emerson et al., "Purification of Fetal Hematopoietic Progenitors and Demonstration of Recombinant Multipotential Colony-Stimulating Activity," *Journal of Clinical Investigation* 76 (1985): 1276–1290.

303 R.E. Donahue et al., "Demonstration of Burst-Promoting Activity of Recombinant Human GM-CSF on Circulating Erythroid Progenitors Using an Assay Involving the Delayed Addition of Erythropoietin," *Blood* 66 (1985): 1479–1481.

304 C.A. Sieff et al., "Human Recombinant Granulocyte-Macrophage Colony-Stimulating Factor: A Multilineage Hematopoietin," *Science* 230 (1985): 1171–1173.

305 A.W. Nienhuis et al., "Recombinant Human Granulocyte-Macrophage Colony-Stimulating Factor (Gm-Csf) Shortens the Period of Neutropenia After Autologous Bone Marrow Transplantation in a Primate Model," *Journal of Clinical Investigation* 80 (1987): 573–577.

306 M.A. Eagle, "Cardiac Involvement in Cooley's Anemia," *Annals of the New York Academy of Sciences* 119 (1964): 694–702.

307 R.S. Smith, "Iron Excretion in Thalassemia Major After Administration of Chelating Agents," *British Medical Journal* 2 (1962): 1577–1580.

308 R.D. Propper, S.B. Shurin, and Nathan, "Reassessment of the Use of Desferrioxamine B in Iron Overload," *New England Journal of Medicine* 294 (1976): 1421–1423.

309 R.D. Propper et al., "Continuous Subcutaneous Administration of Deferoxamine in Patients with Iron Overload," *New England Journal of Medicine* 297 (1977): 418–423.

310 D.J. Weatherall, M.J Pippard, and S.T. Callendar, "Iron Loading and Thalassemia—Experimental Successes and Practical Realities," *New England Journal of Medicine* 297 (1977): 445–446.

311 L. Wolfe et al., "Prevention of Cardiac Disease by Subcutaneous Deferoxamine in Patients with Thalassemia Major," *New England Journal of Medicine* 312 (1985): 1600–1603.

312 N.F. Olivieri et al., "Survival in Medically Treated Patients with Homozygous Beta-Thalassemia," *New England Journal of Medicine* 331 (1994): 574–578.

313 G.M. Brittenham et al., "Efficacy of Deferoxamine in Preventing Complications of Iron Overload in Patients with Thalassemia Major," *New England Journal of Medicine* 331 (1994): 567–573.

314 N.F. Olivieri et al., "Iron-chelation Therapy with Oral Deferiprone in Patients with Thalassemia Major," *New England Journal of Medicine* 332 (1995): 918–922.

315 N.F. Olivieri et al., "Long-Term Safety and Effectiveness of Iron-Chelation Therapy with Deferiprone for Thalassemia Major," *New England Journal of Medicine* 339 (1998): 417–423.

316 I.R. Wanless et al., "Lack of Progressive Hepatic Fibrosis During Long-Term Therapy with Deferiprone in Subjects with Transfusion-Dependent Beta-Thalassemia," *Blood* 100 (2002): 1566–1569.

317 L.J. Anderson, "Comparison of Effects of Oral Deferiprone and Subcutaneous Desferrioxamine on Myocardial Iron Concentrations and Ventricular Function in Beta-Thalassaemia," *Lancet* 360 (2002): 516–520.

318 E. Nisbet-Brown et al., "Effectiveness and Safety of ICL670 in Iron-Loaded Patients with Thalassaemia: A Randomised, Double-Blind, Placebo-Controlled, Dose-Escalation Trial," *Lancet* 361 (2003): 1597–1602.

319 C. Bollig et al., "Deferasirox for Managing Iron Overload in People with Thalassaemia, *Cochrane Database of Systematic Reviews* 15, no. 8 (2017).

320 Nathan, "Lessons from an Unexpected Life: A Doctor, a Patient, and a Formerly Fatal Disease," *Harvard Magazine* (July-August 2009): 36–41.

321 D. Warsh," Molecular Medicine vs. Bedside Manner in the Lehman Case," *Boston Globe*, September 7, 1995, 83.

322 Knox, "New Dana-Farber Head Vows 'Never Again,'" *Boston Globe,* September 16, 1995, 1.

323 Knox, "President of Troubled Dana-Farber Steps Down," *Boston Globe*, September 13, 1995, 1.

324 Gary Countryman, personal communication.

325 Knox, "New Dana-Farber Head Vows 'Never Again.'"

326 Knox, "New Dana-Farber Head Vows 'Never Again.'"

327 Knox, "New Dana-Farber Head Vows 'Never Again.'"

328 Warsh," Molecular Medicine vs. Bedside Manner in the Lehman Case."

329 S. Allen, "With Work, Dana-Farber Learns from '94 Mistakes," *Boston Globe*, November 30, 2004, 1.

330 James Conway and Saul Weingart, "Organizational Change in the Face of Highly Public Errors—I. The Dana-Farber Cancer Institute Experience," Patient Safety Network, May 1, 2005, https://psnet.ahrq.gov/index.php/perspective/organizational-change-face-highly-public-errors-i-dana-farber-cancer-institute.

331 Knox, "Dana-Farber Wins Near-Perfect Score: Changes Follow 2 Patient Overdoses," *Boston Globe*, June 5, 1996, 44.

332 S. Allen, "With Work, Dana-Farber Learns from '94 Mistakes."

333 Knox, Dana-Farber Puts Focus on Mistakes in Overdoses."

334 Knox, "Licensing Board Reprimands 3 Dana-Farber Pharmacists," *Boston Globe*, September 26, 1996, 36.

335 B. Mohl, "Doctor Penalized for Error in Dosage," *Boston Globe*, November 10, 1998, 31.

336 Dembner, "Trial Set in MD Defamation Suit: Jurors to Hear Case in Columnist's Death," *Boston Globe*, January 8, 2002, 18.

337 Knox, "18 Nurses Face State Action in Chemotherapy Overdoses," *Boston Globe*, January 5, 1999, 1.

338 M.B. McCarthy, "A Nursing License," *Boston Globe*, March 27, 2000, 13.

339 Knox, "State Board Clears Two Nurses in 1994 Chemotherapy Overdose," *Boston Globe*, March 16, 2000, 36.

340 L.L. Leape, "Faulty Systems, Not Faulty People," *Boston Globe*, January 12, 1999, 15.

341 The settlement with Lehman's family was for $4.2 million.[341] The terms of the settlement with Bateman were never made public.

342 Dembner, "Trial Opens in Defamation Case: Dana-Farber Targeted Doctor, Lawyer Argues," *Boston Globe*, January 10, 2002, 24.

343 Knox, "Farber Will Pay Millions in Overdose: Columnist's Family to Fund Research," *Boston Globe*, August 24, 1995.

344 Knox, "Survivor's Spirit Beats a Chemotherapy Error," *Boston Globe*, December 17, 1995, 1.

345 *Ayash v. Dana-Farber Cancer Institute and Others*.

346 *Ayash v. Dana-Farber Cancer Institute and Others*.

347 Dembner, "Doctor Testifies She Was Blindsided: Ayash Takes Stand in Defamation Trial," *Boston Globe*, January 26, 2002, 18.

348 Knox, "Doctor's Orders Killed Cancer Patient."

349 Dembner, "Doctor Testifies She Was Blindsided."

350 "For the Record," *Boston Globe*, June 4, 1995, 2.

351 Knox, "Dana-Farber Probe Widens: Three Suspended from Patient Care," *Boston Globe*, April 1, 1995, 13.

352 Dembner, "Doctor Testifies She Was Blindsided."

353 Knox, "Dana-Farber Tests Signaled an Overdose, Records Show," *Boston Globe*, May 2, 1995, 1.

354 Dembner, "Doctor Testifies She Was Blindsided."

355 Knox, "Dana-Farber Studies Patterns in Overdoses," *Boston Globe*, March 26, 1995, 1.

356 Knox, "Dana-Farber Puts Focus on Mistakes in Overdoses."

357 C. Stein, "Doctor Sues Dana-Farber and Globe in Overdose Case," *Boston Globe*, February 3, 1996, 1.

358 *Ayash v. Dana-Farber Cancer Institute and Others*.

359 Nealon, "Reporter Ordered to Reveal Sources," *Boston Globe*, February 26, 1998, 30.

360 T.C. Palmer Jr, "Globe Reporter Avoids Jail in Libel Case," *Boston Globe*, July 24, 1998, 31.

361 C. Rodriguez, "Judge imposes Fines on Globe, Reported," *Boston Globe*, August 15, 1998, 19.

362 S. Pfeiffer, "Court Protects Anonymity of Globe Sources in Dana-Farber Case," *Boston Globe*, February 27, 1999, 24.

363 J. Ellement, "Judge Tells Reporter to Reveal Sources: Disclosure Aids Doctor's Suits," *Boston Globe*, October 26, 1999, 23.

364 S. Murphy, "Judge Rules Against Globe: Finds for Doctor in Overdose Case," *Boston Globe*, April 6, 2001, 43.

365 Palmer, "Globe Reporter Avoids Jail in Libel Case."

366 Dembner, "Supervisory Doctors Weren't Disciplined in Overdoses, Court Told," *Boston Globe*, January 19, 2002, 21.

367 Dembner, "Colleagues Described Doctor as Rigid, Witness Says," *Boston Globe,* January 11, 2002.

368 Dembner, "Researcher Cites 'Politics': Doctor Speaks on Suspension of Cancer Project," *Boston Globe*, January 30, 2002, 29.

369 Dembner, "Doctor Testifies on Role in Patient Death," *Boston Globe*, January 31, 2002, 25.

370 Dembner, "Defense Denies Globe Articles Harmed Doctor: Says Paper Made 'Honest Mistake,'" *Boston Globe*, February 7, 2002, 34.

371 Dembner, "Doctor Awarded $4m From Globe, Cancer Institute," *Boston Globe*, February 3, 2002, 53.

372 Dembner, "Jury Begins Deliberating in Defamation Case: Parties State Cases in Closing Argument," *Boston Globe*, February 8, 2002, 35.

373 Dembner, "Doctor Awarded $4m From Globe, Cancer Institute."

374 Allen, "SJC Upholds $2.1m Jury Award in Globe Libel Case: Appeal Possible, Newspaper Says," *Boston Globe*, February 10, 2005, 27.

375 Interestingly, during a deposition for her lawsuit, Ayash claimed that she knew the identity of the source for the March 23, 1995, article that libeled her.

376 Pfeiffer, "Court Protects Anonymity of Globe Sources in Dana-Farber Case."

377 DGN memoir, 111.

378 DGN, personal communication.

379 "Stanley J. Korsmeyer: Faculty of Medicine—Memorial Minute," *The Harvard Gazette*, May 18, 2006.

380 I.J. Wolf, *Aphorisms and Facetiae of Béla Schick* (Orange, New Jersey: Knoll Pharmaceutical Company, 1965), 25.

381 A Partial list includes David Williams, MD; Scott Armstrong, MD, PhD; Vijay Sankaran, MD, PhD; Katherine (Katie) Janeway, MD; Natasha Archer, MD; Mariella Filbin, MD, PhD; and Joanne Wolfe, MD.

382 Nathan, "Clinical Research: Perceptions, Reality, and Proposed Solutions," *JAMA* 280 (1998): 1427–1431.

383 The others are: Edwards A. Park (Howland in 1952, Kober in 1950); James L. Gamble (Howland in 1955, Kober in 1951); and Helen Taussig (Howland in 1971, Kober in 1987).

ACKNOWLEDGMENTS

In addition to David Nathan himself, I owe debts of gratitude to his wife, Jean, and his children, Linda Nathan, Deborah Charness, and Geoffrey Nathan, for their insights and generosity. I would also like to thank Ed Benz and Gary Countryman for the substantial time they spent with me talking about Nathan, and John Rosenberg of *Harvard Magazine* for his advice. I'm indebted to my sister, Joni Clemons, for encouraging me to write this book. Finally, I want to express my deep appreciation to my wife, Lynn White, for her incredibly helpful comments and her forbearance as she read drafts of this work.

ABOUT THE AUTHOR

Photo by Rick Wenner

Barrett Rollins is an oncologist and cancer researcher who has published over one hundred scholarly articles, chapters, and books including *In Sickness: A Memoir*. He is the Linde Family Professor of Medicine at Harvard Medical School and was, for sixteen years, chief scientific officer at Dana-Farber Cancer Institute. Born and raised in Cleveland, he graduated from Amherst College—which has also given him an honorary DSc—and received his MD and PhD from Case Western Reserve University where he was honored with its Distinguished Alumni Award. He is a long-time trustee of the Interlochen Center for the Arts and lives in Boston with his wife and dogs.